Women in
Western Political Thought

Women
in Western
Political Thought

Susan Moller Okin

PRINCETON UNIVERSITY PRESS

PRINCETON, NEW JERSEY

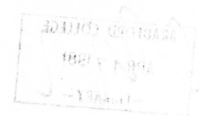

Copyright © 1979 by Princeton University Press

Published by Princeton University Press, Princeton, New Jersey
In the United Kingdom: Princeton University Press,
Guildford, Surrey

ALL RIGHTS RESERVED

Library of Congress Cataloging in Publication Data will be
found on the last printed page of this book

This book has been composed in Linotype Baskerville

Clothbound editions of Princeton University Press books
are printed on acid-free paper, and binding materials are
chosen for strength and durability.

Printed in the United States of America by
Princeton University Press, Princeton, New Jersey

FOR
Bob and Laura

Contents

Acknowledgments

I have benefited from the assistance of several institutions and many persons while writing this book. I am grateful to the American Association of University Women for supporting me and to the Dartmouth College Library for sheltering me and allowing me to use its resources. For their skill and patience in the typing of the manuscript, I thank Charlene Adams, Kirsti Gamage, Lisa Robinson and Gerilyn Spaulding. My warm thanks are due to Marlene Gerber Fried and Joan Smith, and to Judith N. Shklar and Dennis F. Thompson, for their long-standing support, criticism and intellectual inspiration. I have also benefited from the comments and criticisms of Jeffrey Abramson, Amy Gutmann, Virginia Held, Stanley Hoffmann, Victor Menza, Gordon Schochet, John Schrecker, Sanford Thatcher, and Christian and Holly Wolff.

Finally, I would like to express my deep gratitude to Michael Walzer, without whose initial encouragement and continual criticism and advice the idea from which this study grew may never have developed into a doctoral dissertation, and thence into a book.

Articles based on sections of Parts I, III and IV of this book have appeared in *Philosophy and Public Affairs* (1977), *The Journal of Politics* (1979), and *The New Zealand Journal of History* (1973).

Women in
Western Political Thought

Introduction

The current feminist movement has inspired a considerable amount of scholarship in areas previously unexplored. The recent focus on women in the fields of history, legal studies, anthropology, sociology, and literary criticism has resulted in a number of innovative and important works, such that it is no exaggeration to say that these fields will never look the same again. No one, however, has yet examined systematically the treatment of women in the classic works of political philosophy—those works in which great thinkers throughout history have revealed to us their thoughts about the political and social life of the human race. This book is an attempt to reduce the consequent gap in our knowledge.

It is important to realize from the outset that the analysis and criticism of the thoughts of political theorists of the past is not an arcane academic pursuit, but an important means of comprehending and laying bare the assumptions behind deeply rooted modes of thought that continue to affect people's lives in major ways. Women, in the course of the present century, have officially become citizens in virtually every country of the Western world and in much of the rest of the world as well. From being totally relegated to the private sphere of the household, they have become enfranchised members of the political realm. However, women are increasingly recognizing that the limited, formal, political gains of the earlier feminist movement have in no way ensured the attainment of real equalities in the economic and social aspects of their lives. Though women are now citizens, it is undeniable that they have remained second-class citizens. Measured in terms of characteristics traditionally valued in citizens, such as education, economic independence, or occupational status, they are still far behind men. Likewise, measured in terms of political par-

ticipation—especially at higher levels—and political power, they are nowhere near the equals of men. In the past
decade, moreover, women have been demanding these more
substantial equalities, and an end to their relegation to
second-class citizenship. They have been claiming the right
to be members of society and citizens of the state on an
equal level with men, and, in principle at least, their claims
have been gaining recognition.

The fact that women have gained formal citizenship, but
have in no other respect achieved equality with men, has
impelled me to turn to the great works of political philosophy, with two major questions in mind. I have asked, first,
whether the existing tradition of political philosophy can
sustain the inclusion of women in its subject matter, and if
not, why not? For if the works which form the basis of our
political and philosophical heritage are to continue to be
relevant in a world in which the unequal position of wom-
en is being radically challenged, we must be able to recognize which of their assumptions and conclusions are inherently connected with the idea that the sexes are, and
should be, fundamentally unequal.

Second, and clearly related to the first inquiry, I have
aimed to discover whether the philosophers' arguments
about the nature of women and their proper place in the
social and political order, viewed in the context of the complete political theories of the philosophers, will help us to
understand why the formal, political enfranchisement of
women has not led to substantial equality between the
sexes. It is not my purpose to argue any causal connection
between the arguments and ideas of the great philosophers,
on the one hand, and modern ideas or practices, on the
other. However, I do argue that modes of thought about
women that closely parallel those of some of the philosophers discussed here are still prevalent, in the writings of
modern thinkers, and in the ideologies of modern political
actors and institutions. This claim is substantiated in Part
v, where we turn to analysis of some crucial contemporary

views on women—those of influential social scientists and of the highest courts in the U.S.—and discover striking similarities between them and the ideas of the political theorists analyzed in the preceding chapters. By critical study of the arguments about women conceived by some of the finest minds in the history of Western thought, I hope to add to our comprehension of modern arguments which parallel them in important ways, and which constitute a continuing attempt to justify the unequal treatment of women.

It must be recognized at once that the great tradition of political philosophy consists, generally speaking, of writings by men, for men, and about men. While the use of supposedly generic terms like "man" and "mankind," and of the allegedly inclusive pronoun, "he," might lead one to think that philosophers have intended to refer to the human race as a whole, we do not need to look far into their writings to realize that such an assumption is unfounded. Rousseau, for example, tells his reader at the beginning of the *Discourse on the Origins and Foundation of Inequality among Men* that "It is of man that I am to speak." It subsequently becomes very clear that it is only the inequality between males that is the subject of his investigation, and the inequality between the sexes is assumed in passing.[1] Past and present feminists, only too aware of such practices, have pointed out the dangerous ambiguity of such linguistic usage in a patriarchal culture.[2] For it enables philosophers to enunciate principles as if they were universally applicable, and then to proceed to exclude all women from their scope.

Even when philosophers have used words which in their respective languages refer unambiguously to any human being, they have felt in no way deterred from excluding women from the conclusions reached. Aristotle, for example, discusses at length what is the highest good for a human being (*anthropos*). He then proceeds to characterize all women as not only conventionally deprived of, but constitutionally unfitted for, this highest good. Again, Kant uses the most inclusive terms of all for the subjects of his ethical and political theory; he even says that he is not confining his discussion to humans, but that it is applicable to "all rational beings." Subsequently, however, he proceeds to justify a double standard of sexual morality, to the extent that a woman is to be condoned for killing her illegitimate child because of her "duty" to uphold, at all costs, her "sexual honor." He also reaches the conclusion that the only characteristic that permanently disqualifies any person from citizenship in the state, and therefore from the obligation to obey only those laws to which consent has been given, is that of being born female.[3] Thus, even words such as "person," "human," and "rational being," apparently, do not necessarily include women.

This phenomenon, made possible by the ambiguity of our language, is not confined to political philosophy. The grand statements of our political culture, too, such as the Declaration of Independence and the Constitution, are phrased in universal terms, but, as the chapter on women and the law will make clear, they have frequently been interpreted in such a way as to exclude women. Thus when the Founding Fathers declared it to be a self-evident truth that "all men are created equal," not only did they intend the substantial slave population to be excluded from the scope of their statement, but they would have been amused and skeptical (as indeed John Adams was to his wife's appeal that they not forget the ladies) at the suggestion that women were, and should be considered, equal too.[4] Similarly, though the Constitution is phrased in terms of "persons," there was clearly no idea in its framers' minds that this word might be interpreted so as to include women on the same terms as men.[5]

"Human nature," we realize, as described and discovered by philosophers such as Aristotle, Aquinas, Machiavelli, Locke, Rousseau, Hegel, and many others, is intended to refer only to male human nature. Consequently, all the rights and needs that they have considered humanness to entail have not been perceived as applicable to the female half of the human race. Thus there has been, and continues to be, within the traditions of political philosophy and political culture, a pervasive tendency to make allegedly general statements as if the human race were not divided into two sexes, and then either to ignore the female sex altogether, or to proceed to discuss it in terms not at all consistent with the assertions that have been made about "man" and "humanity."

In spite of this general neglect of women, however, several of the most important and most interesting of political philosophers have had a considerable amount to say about them. The first four parts of this book comprise an analysis of the arguments of Plato, Aristotle, Rousseau and Mill, on the subject of women, their nature, their socialization and education, and their proper role and station in society. It would be fruitless, if not impossible, to treat such a subject in a vacuum. What I have done, therefore, is to analyze these philosophers' ideas about women in the context of their entire theories of politics and society, and with particular reference to each philosopher's conception of the role of the family. Throughout the study, I have examined the various ideas about women and the arguments which sustain them, with a concern both for their internal logic and for their consistency with each philosopher's argument and conclusions about men, and about politics and society as a whole.

Clearly, in choosing four philosophers, I do not pretend to have covered the treatment of women within the entire tradition of political philosophy. Apart from the omission of the socialists which requires explanation, however, I have chosen those four who of all political theorists have made the most substantial, most interesting, and most thought-provoking contributions on the subject.

The problem regarding Marx, the Marxists, and other

socialists, is that, taken together, they had so much to say, and such insight to offer, on the subject of women in society, that their ideas warrant a separate study. It was the utopian, Charles Fourier, who first both used the status of women in a society as the fundamental measuring stick of its advancement, and considered the progress of women toward liberty to be a fundamental cause of general social progress. "Other events influence these political changes"; he asserts, "but there is no cause which produces social progress or decline as rapidly as a change in the condition of women. . . . The extension of the privileges of women is the fundamental cause of all social progress."[6] Fourier's initiatives were not ignored by subsequent feminists and/or socialists, including Flora Tristan, Marx and John Stuart Mill. Marx developed the idea of the relationship between the equality of women and general social progress, in the *1844 Manuscripts*:

> The relation of man to woman is the *most natural* relation of human being to human being. It indicates, therefore, how far man's *natural* behaviour has become *human*, and how far his *human* essence has become a *natural* essence for him, how far his *human nature* has become *nature* for him. . . . From this relationship man's whole level of development can be assessed.[7]

Though Marx himself did not develop this as a major theme in his works, Engels, Bebel, and the critical theorists of the Frankfurt School have developed further the socialist criticism of woman's position in society, and of the traditional family.

Socialist writings on women require separate study because of two features which are characteristic of, though not unique to, socialist modes of thought. First, socialist theorists have been far less inclined than most other political theorists to regard the family as a necessary and fixed human institution, and have been very much aware of the relationship between various forms of family organization and different forms of economic structure, particularly property relations. This has meant that most, though not all, socialists who have written about women have taken a critical and questioning view of woman's role within the family, rather than accepting it as a given. Second, socialist thought is noticeably lacking in the tendency to idealize "nature" and the "natural," and is inclined to replace these criteria for social excellence by the specifically "human" and "cultural." It is largely because of the importance of both these modes of thought for the subject of women, that the contribution of the socialists to the subject is so considerable. The study of that contribution is a task I hope to undertake, and for which the present work constitutes an essential foundation.

From my analysis of the arguments and conclusions of Plato, Aristotle, Rousseau and Mill, concerning women and their proper social and political role, two interconnected themes emerge. First, the most important factor influencing the philosophers' conceptions of, and arguments about, women has been the view that each of them held concerning the family. Those who have regarded the family as a natural and necessary institution have defined women by their sexual, procreative, and child-rearing functions within it. This has lead to the prescription of a code of morality and conception of rights for women distinctly different from those that have been prescribed for men. The assumption of the necessity of the family leads the theorists to then regard the biological differences between the sexes as entailing all the other, conventional and institutional differences in sex role which the family, especially in its most patriarchal forms, has required.

Second, as a consequence of the above, the constricted role in which woman has been placed has been regarded as dictated by her very nature. Thus, where philosophers have explicitly discussed women, they have frequently not extended to them their various conceptions of "human nature." They have not only assigned women a distinct role, but have defined them separately, and often contrastingly, to men. They have sought for the nature of women not, as for the nature of men, by attempting to separate out nature from the effects of nurture, and to discover what innate potential exists beneath the overlay which results from socialization and other environmental factors. The nature of women, instead, has been seen to be dictated by whatever social and economic structure the philosophers favor and to be defined as whatever best suits her prescribed functions in that society. Philosophers who, in laying the foundation for their political theories, have asked "What are men like?" "What is man's potential?" have frequently, in turning to the female sex, asked "What are women *for*?" There is, then, an undeniable connection between assigned "female nature" and social structure, and a functionalist attitude to women pervades the history of political thought.

The conclusions drawn here are, first, that women cannot simply be added to the subject matter of existing political theory, for the works of our philosophical heritage are to a very great extent built on the assumption of the inequality of the sexes. In the case of theorists for whom equality, in some form or other, is an important value, the unequal treatment of women tends to be concealed by the adoption of the male-headed family, rather than the individual adult, as the primary unit of political analysis. Indeed, the thoroughly equal treatment of women, involving far more than the right to vote, requires the rethinking of some of the most basic assumptions of political philosophy—having to do with the family and woman's traditionally dependent and subordinate role within it.

Second, as we examine some twentieth-century perceptions of women and analyze legal discrimination against women, it becomes clear that these findings should be of interest not only to historians or students of political theory. The functionalist treatment of women—the prescriptive view of woman's nature and proper mode of life based on her role and functions in a patriarchal family structure—is still alive and influential today. Giant figures in modern sociology and psychology present arguments about women that parallel those of Aristotle and Rousseau. Moreover, when we examine the opinions handed down by the highest courts of the land in cases involving sex discrimination, we find, here too, that judges have used functionalist reasoning of a strikingly Aristotelian character in order to justify their treatment of women as a class apart. Thus, there is no doubt that a thorough understanding of this mode of argument can help us to see why women, in spite of their political enfranchisement, are still second-class citizens.

The chapters that follow require one more word of explanation. Obviously, there are many types of inequality both in the real world and in political theory. Only one type of inequality is dealt with here—the unequal treatment of women. As will become evident, the positions taken by political theorists about other types of equality and inequality are by no means necessarily parallel to, or even consistent with, their views about the equal or unequal treatment of the sexes. Those who have argued that there should be complete or virtual equality between the sexes have sometimes been distinctly inegalitarian in other respects; on the other hand, some philosophers who have made strong arguments for equality amongst men have been just as strongly opposed to equality for women. I have not undertaken to discuss this except insofar as a philosopher's more general egalitarianism or inegalitarianism affects his arguments about distinctions between the sexes, or clarifies the presentation of these arguments. This is not because I consider other types of inequality unimportant. It is, rather, because the unequal treatment of women has remained for too long shamefully neglected by students of political thought. Other types of inequality—class inequality in particular, but also inequalities based on race, religion, caste, or ethnicity, have not been so consistently ignored.

In one sense, this book might be compared with the play *Rosencrantz and Guildenstern are Dead*. In that play, building on the foundation of *Hamlet*, Tom Stoppard emphasizes this originally elusive pair, and makes them, instead of the traditional hero, into the principal focus of the drama. As a result, the play, all its characters, and their relations to each other take on an entirely new perspective. Similarly, when women, who have always been minor characters in the social and political theory of a patriarchal world, are transformed into major ones, the entire cast and the play in which it is acting look very different.

PART I

PLATO

1

Plato and
the Greek Tradition
of Misogyny

Plato's ideas on the subject of women appear at first to present an unresolvable enigma. One might well ask how the same, generally consistent philosopher can on the one hand assert that the female sex was created from the souls of the most wicked and irrational men, and on the other hand make a far more radical proposal for the equal education and social role of the two sexes than was to be made by a major philosopher for more than two thousand years? How can the claim that women are "by nature" twice as bad as men be reconciled with the revolutionary idea that they should be included among the exalted philosophic rulers of the ideal state? Before we attempt to answer these questions, it is essential to look at the Greek tradition concerning women, and the education, status and treatment of the Athenian women of the time.

From the very beginnings of Greek literature, in Hesiod's *Works and Days* and *Theogony*, a strong misogynic strain is obvious. According to Hesiod, after a period in which men alone dwelt on earth, free from disease and toil, it was Pandora, the first woman, who brought evil and misfortune to the world. And "from her is a pernicious race; and tribes of women, a great source of hurt, dwell along with mortal men."[1] Thus the fateful degeneration of the human race began with the appearance of woman, man's eternal punishment. Though she is, unfortunately, necessary for reproduction and can be useful in the household—so that Hesiod advises the aspiring farmer to "First of all get a house, and a woman, and a ploughing ox"[2]—he warns his readers that never, on any account, is she to be trusted.

From the Homeric epics we derive a similar picture, though one which is less overwhelmingly hostile to the female sex. In *The World of Odysseus*, M. I. Finley says:

> There is no mistaking the fact that Homer fully reveals what remained true for the whole of antiquity, that women were held to be naturally inferior and therefore limited in their function to the production of offspring and the performance of household duties, and that the meaningful social relationships and strong personal attachments were sought and found among men.[3]

There are depicted, in both epics, goddesses of considerable strength, dignity and prestige, but we must remember that, for the Greeks, the title "goddess" did not necessarily connote all the characteristics that were associated with human femaleness. The most powerful of goddesses, especially Athena, were praised for their "manliness."[4] In the *Iliad*, mortal women are seldom depicted as anything but causes of jealousy and war, or as part of the booty, along with animals and slaves. In the *Odyssey*, women play a more conspicuous part. With the partial and strange exception of Arete, Queen of the Phaeceans,[5] however, they are consistently relegated to second-class status. In spite of the fact that Penelope is described as "wise" and as having an "excellent brain," spinning and weaving are clearly her proper functions, and on several occasions she is ordered by her son Telemachus to return to the tasks that befit her, much as if she were a slave. Aristocratic women and even goddesses are shown engaged in domestic tasks such as washing clothes, bathing and making up beds for guests, preparing food, and, almost ceaselessly, working with wool. As Finley says, "Denied the right to a heroic way of life, to feats of prowess, competitive games, and leadership in organized activity of any kind, women worked, regardless of class."[6] They lived in separate quarters from the men, very rarely participated in feasts and festivities, and were sent off or sold as brides to the men their fathers chose for them.

The Homeric epics describe a world in which the standards of excellence applied to persons depend on their respective positions and functions in society. A thorough grasp of this conception of ethics is essential for understanding the classical writings at least up to and including Aristotle. The highest words of praise, *agathos* (good) and *arete* (excellence or virtue), were originally applied only to those who fulfilled the role of a Homeric aristocratic man.[7] The words *meant* that the individual to whom they were applied possessed both the internal skills and external resources necessary for the performance of this role. As A. W. H. Adkins says, "To be *agathos*, one must be brave, skillful, and successful in war and in peace, and one must possess the wealth and (in peace) the leisure which are at once the necessary conditions for the development of these skills and the natural reward of their successful employment."[8] Most of society, and notably women, were ineligible for such an aristocratic and male standard of excellence. Thus, "woman's *arete*" was a qualitatively different concept. The virtues required in women, in order for them to best perform their assigned functions, were the quiet virtues of beauty and stature, skill in weaving and other household accomplishments, and, above all, marital fidelity. The obvious reason for this different standard of excellence in women is, as Adkins points out, that it was men who determined the standards, in this strictly patriarchal culture, so that it was women's performance of their functions in relation to men that was considered important. Thus, being confined within the household, women did not need the competitive and aggressive virtues required by the warrior men.[9]

While the behavior of the Homeric heroes shows clearly that monogamous sexuality was not imposed on men, the worst possible crime a woman could commit was unfaithfulness to her husband.[10] Helen, and even worse, Clytemnaestra, traitor as well as adulteress, are the real villains of the Homeric epics, and the latter is constantly held up as a foil to the virtuous Penelope. Woman's susceptibility to seduction is accentuated as her weakest point and her characteristic evil. Even the virtuous Penelope is afraid she will be "bewitched" as Helen was, and in spite of her long-lasting fidelity, the suspicion that she may at length betray or forget Odysseus permeates the poem. Thus the theme of the evil and treacherous female is found in Homer as in Hesiod; Clytemnaestra, we are told, has "branded not herself alone but the whole of her sex and every honest woman for all time to come."[11]

From the heroic to the classical age, the status of women was generally thought not to have improved, and this was especially true of classical Athens.[12] The narrowly defined function of women as childbearers and housekeepers is well documented in classical Greek literature. Xenophon's *Oeconomicus*, for example, presents a picture of the exemplary wife for an Athenian landowner. Reared "under diligent supervision in order that she might see and hear as little as possible and ask the fewest possible questions," she is given by her parents to a husband at the age of fifteen, and trained by him just to the extent that she can manage his domestic affairs.[13] The traditional male-female division of labor is presented to her as foreordained by the gods and deeply rooted in the natural qualities of the two sexes. Victor Ehrenberg, in his studies of Greek society, confirms that this is a description of the typical life such a woman would have led. "Marriage was a matter of paternal wishes and economic considerations," he says. "Girls were not educated: they only learned the arts of housekeeping." Even Iphigenia is presented as unable to write, and Ehrenberg makes the interesting observation that the few outstanding female characters of Aristophanes' comedies do not cast doubt on this general impression; rather they acquire their "full brilliance only by their complete contrast with the background of women's everyday life."[14]

The seclusion of respectable women was rigidly enforced throughout their lives. Generally confined to separate quarters within the house, closed off from the men's apartments by a locked door, wives and daughters were not regarded as fit to participate in serious discussion, with the consequence that the denial to them of intellectual experience continued through adulthood. They were treated as minors, the same things being forbidden to them as to boys under the age of eighteen. Even if unmarried, a woman was not allowed to bring suit under Attic law, except via her legal guardian, or to dispose of more than the worth of a bushel of barley. Women were denied access to all those places where the boys and men discussed and learned about civic and intellectual affairs—the *gymnasia*, the market place, the law courts and *symposia*. As John Addington Symonds has summarized the situation, in his account of the homosexual culture of the Greek aristocracy: "all the higher elements of spiritual and mental activity, and the conditions under which a generous passion was conceivable, had become the exclusive privileges of men. . . . The exaltation of the emotions was reserved for the male sex."[15]

It was not only the activities and movement of Athenian women that were harshly limited; as in the Homeric age, this repression was extended with equal force to their personalities, too. There is much evidence in Greek drama of the application of that "ancient saw" that Aristotle quotes from Sophocles' *Ajax*—"a modest silence is a woman's crown."[16] Pericles' funeral oration, too, displays clearly the disparity between the contemporary standards of excellence that were applied to men and to women. For in the course of this panegyric, which is a classic example of the importance that the Greeks placed on fame and "being talked about," Pericles advises the widowed women to display that "female excellence" which accords with their "natural character." The greatest glory, he says, will be "hers who is least talked of among the men whether for good or for bad."[17]

Ironically, the claims of respectability meant that the women whom an upper-class Athenian might marry were significantly less likely to have acquired any knowledge of their society and its culture than were those he was free to turn to as courtesans or prostitutes. The rigid distinction between the two types of women, which has of course persisted until modern times, and also the Greeks' basically proprietary attitude toward women, are both well illustrated by the following statement from Demosthenes' account of the lawsuit, *Against Naera*:

> For this is what living with a woman as one's wife means—to have children by her and to introduce the sons to the members of the clan and of the deme, and to betroth the daughters to husbands as one's own. Mistresses we keep for the sake of pleasure, concubines for the daily care of our persons, but wives to bear us legitimate children and to be faithful guardians of our households.[18]

Thus those women who were eligible to become the wives of Plato's contemporaries were valued for their chastity, their frugality and their silence—not for their personalities in any positive sense. The extent to which this objectification could be taken is indicated by Creon's answer when asked if he intends to kill his own son's bride: "Well, there are other fields for him to plough."[19] There is, then, much evidence to show that the women of the higher classes in classical Athens were reduced to one primary function. Lacking any role in those areas of life which were regarded as important by the men, lacking even that aura of mystery that their sex was later to acquire under Christianity and as the love objects of the romantic tradition, they were valued only as the instruments of reproduction of legitimate heirs.

It may seem strange that in such a climate the emancipation of women should have become a subject of discussion.
However, just as in Victorian Britain, where the repression
of women had again reached a peak, at the beginning of the
fourth century, the status of women appears to have become
a live issue in Athens. Aristophanes' comedies, *Ecclesiazusae*
and *Lysistrata*, are good evidence that it was one of those
current talking points ripe for satire. In addition, there
seems to be little doubt that the historical Socrates put
forward ideas about women that were far from typical at the
time. In Xenophon's *Symposium*, he is depicted asserting
that "woman's nature is nowise inferior to man's," albeit
with the rather paradoxical corollary that "all she wants is
strength and judgment."[20] Within Platonic dialogues other
than the *Republic*, too, there are several passages in which
Socrates proposes a far more androgynous view of human
nature, and specifically of human virtue, than was at all
usual in the cultural context. In the *Meno*, for example, in
the course of an attempt to discover the nature of virtue,
he makes the radical assertion that virtue is the same quality
in a woman as in a man, not different, as Meno has tried to
claim by referring to the traditionally different duties and
life styles of the two sexes. Both, says Socrates, need temperance and justice, if they are to be good at their respective
tasks, whether the management of the household or of the
city. Virtue is therefore a human quality, and is not to be
defined differently according to the sex of the individual
concerned.[21] In the *Protagoras*, moreover, Socrates displays
his rejection of the prevalent norms about women by praising Sparta and Crete, not only for their ancient philosophical traditions, but for presenting examples of women as well
as men "who are proud of their intellectual culture."[22]

Nevertheless, there are in the dialogues numerous other
examples of extremely misogynic assertions voiced by Socrates, and since it is impossible to separate the ideas of the
historical Socrates from those of Plato, it is pointless to try.
The important point to note is that, whether originating

from Socrates or not, there was in Plato's youthful environment a trace of radical thought about women, overlying a strong tradition of misogynic prejudice.

The prevailing depiction of women in the Platonic dialogues is extremely deprecating. To a large extent, this representation of the female sex simply reflects either the contemporary degradation of women or the fact that Plato and his companions (and consequently their theory of love) were predominantly homosexual. However, there are also passages in the dialogues that imply more than an adverse judgment against the women of Athenian society, and indicate a general belief on the author's part that the female sex is inevitably and innately inferior to the male. I will examine passages of both these types in turn.

The fact that no woman participates in any of the dialogues in person merely constitutes evidence of the prevailing attitudes of the time and the characteristics of Athenian life they produced. It cannot reasonably be said to tell us anything about Plato's own views about women's capacities for intellectual discourse. That the women of the household in which the *Symposium* takes place are not present at the dinner party, but are "inside there," says nothing about Plato except that he chose to set his dialogues realistically in the context of contemporary society. In fact, the high point of the discourse is supposed to have come from the mouth of a woman, the priestess Diotima. Similarly, Plato's characterization of woman as one who spins and works with wool is merely an accurate description of her role in his culture. Moreover, even much of his language that is deprecating to the female sex—such as the use of "womanish" to mean "cowardly"—should be read not as peculiar to Plato, but as current usage.[23]

However, Plato certainly shared his fellow Athenians' contempt for the women of his day. He categorizes them together with children and animals, with the immature, the sick and the weak.[24] Even the *Republic* is by no means free of such representation of women. Before the revolutionary idea of including women among the ranks of the guardians is introduced, it is stressed that the impressionable young guardians are at all costs to be prevented from imitating the female sex in what are regarded as its characteristic activities—bickering, boasting, uncooperative self-abandonment, blasphemy, and the frailties of sickness, love and labor. Women, easily deceived by worthless gaudiness, superstitious, prone to excessive grief, lacking in knowledge of what is good for them, and inferior in intellect and in general to men, are no more fit to serve as role models for the chosen youth than are madmen, craftsmen or slaves.[25] In the *Laws*, moreover, a significant part of Plato's reason for forbidding homosexual intercourse is that, in addition to rendering the lover unmanly on account of his surrender to his lusts, it obliges the loved one to play the role of the much despised female.[26]

Although Plato disapproved of the physical practice of sodomy, the entire Platonic philosophy of love, as presented in the *Phaedrus* and the *Symposium*, reflects the pervasive homosexual culture of the Athenian upper classes. As Gregory Vlastos has said of the theory of love, "A proper study of it would have to take account of at least three things about its creator: He was a homosexual, a mystic, and a moralist."[27] As Vlastos has well demonstrated, Plato's own homosexuality, taken together with his conflicting belief that anal intercourse was "contrary to nature"—a degradation not only of man's humanity but of his animality—explain much of the origin of the idea that the physical aspect of love ought to be conquered and transcended so that the real object of love, which is the idea of beauty itself, can be attained. The Platonic theory of love can thus be understood, in large part, in terms of the need to sublimate unacceptable impulses.

Throughout the two dialogues on love, the love of women is consistently deprecated. It is notable that nobody, including Socrates, makes any objection to the accounts of love of either Pausanius or Aristophanes, and both are biased heavily against heterosexuality. Pausanius divides love into two kinds—that patronized by the elder, heavenly Aphrodite, "whose attributes have nothing of the female, but are altogether male," and that of the younger, earthly Aphrodite, "whose nature partakes of both male and female." The latter controls the passions of the vulgar, who are as much attracted by shallow people as profound, as much by women as boys, and who regard copulation as the most important aspect of the relationship. The former, by contrast, "innocent of any hint of lewdness," inspires its followers toward male lovers only, "preferring the more vigorous and intellectual bent."[28] According to Aristophanes, whose myth of the originally double inhabitants of the earth underlies his rather comical account of love, the really fortunate men are not those who seek out their lost female half, but those who are halves of what was once a double male, and whose sexual impulses therefore impel them to members of their own sex. Those men who have "the most virile constitution," the only ones who "show any real manliness in public life," are those who love boys rather than women, prefer to spend all their lives with men, and marry and beget children only in deference to social custom.[29]

In Socrates' own speech, attributed though it is to the wisdom of a woman, the same bias continues to prevail. Although it is a characteristic of heterosexual love, procreation, which is taken as the symbol around which the theory of love is built, Socrates consistently denigrates mere physical procreation—the production of "offspring of the flesh," in favor of that superior procreancy which is of the mind, and whose adherents "conceive and bear the things of the spirit." In contrast to love which chooses a woman for its object and raises a family, it is only through love of a male that the lover, through the procreation of thoughts, poetry or law, can transcend the love of a particular individual and come eventually to knowledge of the very soul of beauty.[30] Gregory Vlastos implies that the use of the heterosexual image of procreation somehow tempers the hostility to heterosexuality and to women that seems to be inherent in the theory. He concludes that at the climax of the whole philosophy of love, where the idea of beauty is at last encountered face to face, "the homosexual imagery is dropped" and "what started as a pederastic idyl ends up in transcendental marriage."[31] It is not made clear exactly what Vlastos means by this. However, if he is implying, as he seems to be, that there is any inclusion of heterosexuality in the theory of the higher type of love, his conclusion is unfounded. In spite of Plato's use of an image that, as Vlastos says, has "a heterosexual paradigm," it is clearly only the symbolic version of procreation—that of the spirit, which is only achieved in homosexual love—that is thought worthy of philosophical treatment. As Socrates asks, "who would not prefer such fatherhood to merely human propagation?"[32] Just as Plato uses an image with an originally heterosexual application here, so he uses the image of the craftsman weaver throughout the *Statesman*. In neither case, however, is the reader justified in transferring to the real subject of discussion any of the qualities of the metaphorical subject except those that are explicitly intended to be so transferred. The heterosexual aspect of the one image, therefore, is no more legitimately transferred to Plato's real sphere of concern, than is the manual labor aspect of the other. It is quite clear, despite Vlastos' suggestion, that Plato's vision of love as a pathway to philosophic joy entirely excludes women. Given the Athenian social structure and the position of women within it, however, this can hardly strike us as surprising. Since, in a culture as intellectual and civically conscious as that of the Greek aristocratic man, it was virtually impossible for any real intimacy to develop between him and a woman such as the women were forced to become, Plato's belief that only love between men could be of the most elevated type is quite understandable. Given the contemporary context, then, it is no wonder that the *Phaedrus* and the *Symposium* demonstrate such a preference for homosexual over heterosexual love, and so strong an affirmation of the ethical superiority of the former.[33]

It can reasonably be argued that in all the above instances, the contempt expressed or implied toward women is not by way of judgment on the entire female sex, past, present and future, but is rather aimed at the Athenian women of Plato's time. There are, however, several significant passages in the dialogues which indicate belief in the general inferiority of any female human being at any time. The most outstanding passages of this sort are, ironically, contained in the *Timaeus*, the dialogue whose dramatic date is the very day after the *Republic*.[34] Here, the origins of the human race are recounted, in a manner very reminiscent of Hesiod. "Human nature," we are told, "was of two kinds, the superior race would hereafter be called man." The original creation consisted only of men,[35] and those who conquered their passions and lived virtuously during their stay on earth were allowed to return to the happiness of the stars from which they came. For any who failed on earth, however, by being cowardly and unrighteous, the punishment was to be reborn as a woman. Thus, according to Plato's myth, was woman created. Not only was she derivative from man, as in the Genesis myth, but she was derivative from those men who were wicked failures. If no improvement ensued after this punishment, it was followed by the penalty of rebirth as one of the lower animals, "some brute who resembled him in the evil nature which he had acquired." The only way for a soul so debased to reattain "the form of his first and better state" was through demonstrating the victory of his rational over his irrational part. Thus we are presented with a hierarchy of goodness and rationality, in which woman is placed midway between man and the beasts.[36] In the *Laws*, too, women are asserted to be twice as much disposed toward evil as men, and therefore in need of special discipline.[37] Moreover, the wish to reenact the creation myth of the *Timaeus* is expressed in the *Laws*, in the form of the proposal that, were such a process possible, the most suitable penalty for a man who has displayed his cowardice by flinging away his shield is for him to be transformed into a woman.[38]

Such passages as these, in which the assertions are not restricted to any time or place, certainly imply that Plato believed women to be, inevitably and regardless of circumstances, inferior in reason and virtue to men. Some scholars have explained such statements as "lapses." Cornford, for example, says that sometimes "Plato slips into a popular way of speaking about women," and Levinson says it is "as if for the moment he had forgotten his more advanced beliefs."[39] But Plato was not the kind of thinker we can readily believe forgot his beliefs, especially on a subject to which he devoted a considerable amount of attention in some of his major dialogues. Nevertheless, there is a distinct gulf between Plato's general attitude to and beliefs about women, which reflect much of the highly misogynic Greek tradition, and the radical proposals for the equality of the female guardians, which are set out in Book v of the *Republic*. It is only by examining these latter proposals in the context of the overall aims and structure of the ideal society that we will be able to find them intelligible.

2

Philosopher Queens
and Private Wives

The aim of the true art of
ruling, as Plato conceives of it, is not the welfare of any
single class or group, but the greatest possible happiness of
the entire community.[1] "Happiness," however, can be a
misleading word, for if it leads us to thoughts of freedom,
individual rights, or equality of opportunity, we are far
from Plato's idea of happiness (*eudaimonia*). Neither
equality nor liberty nor justice in the sense of fairness were
values for Plato. The three values on which both his ideal
and his second-best cities are based are, rather, harmony,
efficiency and moral goodness: the last is the principal key
to his entire political philosophy. Because of his belief in
the intrinsic value of the soul, and the consequent importance of its health, Plato does not think that happiness
results from the freedom to behave just as one wants; it is
regarded as in no way attainable independently of virtue.
Statesmen, therefore, should "not only preserve the lives of
their subjects but reform their characters too, so far as
human nature permits of this."[2] Though the ultimate aim
of the true ruler is the happiness of all his subjects, the
only way he can attain this is by raising them all, by means
of education and law, to the highest possible level of
wisdom and virtue.

The gravest of all human faults, however, is considered
by Plato to be one that is inborn in most people—that
"excessive love of self" which is "the cause of all sins in
every case."[3] Worse still, whereas the soul, and next the
body, should take priority, the all too prevalent tendency is

to give one's property—in truth the least valuable of possessions—one's greatest attention.[4] Thus the ruler's task in promoting his subjects' virtue is two-fold. He must aim to overcome both their extremes of self-love and also their fatal preference for material possessions over the welfare of their souls. A person who is to be virtuous and great must be able to transcend his own interests, but above all to detach himself from the passion to acquire. As Glenn Morrow has noted, there is abundant evidence in both the *Republic* and the *Laws* that Plato regarded the maintenance of a temperate attitude toward property as essential for the security and well-being of a state.[5] It was acquisitiveness, after all, that had led the first city Socrates depicted—the simple, "true" and "healthy" city—into war with its neighbors and all the complications which this entailed. Again, the recurrent theme of Book VIII of the *Republic*, in which the process of political degeneration is analyzed, is the corruption that results from increasing possessiveness.[6]

The *Republic* is an extremely radical dialogue. In his formulation of the ideal state, Plato is prepared to question and challenge the most sacred contemporary conventions. The solution he proposes for the problem of selfishness and divisive interests is for private property and hence private interests to be abolished, to the greatest possible extent. For in this city, not just the harmony but the unity of interest is the objective. "Have we any greater evil for a city," asks Socrates, "than what splits it and makes it many instead of one? Or a greater good than what binds it together and makes it one?" He concludes that the best-governed city is that "which is most like a single human being."[7] Nothing can dissolve the unity of a city more readily than for some of its citizens to be glad and others to grieve because of the same happening, so that all do not work or even wish in concert. The way to achieve the highest possible degree of unity is for all the citizens to feel pleasure and pain on the same occasions, and this "community of pleasure and pain" will occur only if all goods are possessed in common.

The best-governed city will be that "in which most say 'my own' and 'not my own' about the same thing, and in the same way."[8]

We need have no doubt that, if he had thought it possible, Plato would have extended the communal ownership of property to all the classes of his ideal city. The first of the "noble lies," according to which all the citizens are to be told that they are one big family, can be read as the complete expression of an ideal which can unfortunately be met only in part. It is because of his belief in the tendency of most human beings to selfishness that Plato considers the renunciation of private property to be something that can be attained only by the best of persons. This is made clear in the *Laws*, where he rejects the possibility of eliminating ownership for the citizens of his projected "second-best" city, since tilling the soil in common is "beyond the capacity of people with the birth, rearing and training we assume."[9] What is impossible for the citizens of the second-best city, with all their carefully planned education, must regretfully be regarded as beyond the capacity of the inferior classes in the ideal city. Thus it is the guardian class alone which is to live up to the ideal of community of property and unity of interests.[10]

The overcoming of selfish interests is regarded as most necessary for those who are to have charge of the welfare and governance of all the other citizens, quite apart from the fact that they are the best equipped to overcome them. Since a person will always take care of what he loves, the guardians, especially, must love the whole community, and have no interests other than its welfare. For them above all, then, the permitted property arrangements must be "such as not to prevent them from being the best possible guardians and not to rouse them up to do harm to the other citizens."[11] The possession by the rulers of private lands and wealth would, Plato argues, inevitably lead to the formation of factions, and make of the rulers "masters and enemies instead of allies of the other citizens."[12] The combination of wealth and private interests with political power is intolerable and can lead only to the destruction of the city.

Plato's ideal for the guardians is expressed by the proverb, "friends have all things in common."[13] But if communal ownership of inanimate property is a great aid to the required unity of the city, it appears to follow that communal ownership of women and children will conduce to even greater unity. It is quite clear from the way Plato argues that he regards the communalization of property as implying the simultaneous abolition of the family. He does not regard the two as distinct innovations requiring independent justifications. In fact, the first mention of the abolition of the family is slid over, almost as a parenthesis,[14] and both in the *Republic* and the brief summary that is presented in the *Laws*, the two proposals are justified by the same arguments and frequently at the same time. In the *Laws*, especially, in the passages where Plato looks back to the institutions of the ideal city, the classification of women and children together with other possessions occurs frequently. Thus he talks of "community of wives, children, and all chattels," and later, by contrast, of that less desirable state of affairs in which "women and children and houses remain private, and all these things are established as the private property of individuals."[15]

Thus women are classified by Plato, as they were by the culture in which he lived, as an important subsection of property. The very expression, "community (or common having) of women and children," which he uses to denote his proposed system of temporary matings, is a further indication of this, since the phenomenon could just as accurately be described as "the community of men," were it not for its inventor's customary way of thinking about such matters.[16]

Just as other forms of private property were seen as destructive of society's unity, so the concept of "private wives" is viewed by Plato as divisive and subversive in the

same way. Thus, in contrast to the unified city he is proposing, he points to those institutional arrangements which
foster the ascendance of particularism and factionalism,
with "one man dragging off to his own house whatever he
can get his hands on apart from the others, another being
separate in his own house with separate women and children, introducing private pleasures and griefs of things that
are private."[17] Again, in the *Laws*, he strikes out at the same
time against Athenian practices with regard both to private
property and to women: "we huddle all our goods together,
as the saying goes, within four walls, and then hand over
the dispensing of them to the women."[18] It is clear that
conventional marriage and woman in her traditional role
as guardian of the private household were seen by Plato as
intimately bound up with that whole system of private
possessions which separated citizens from each other, made
them hostile and envious, and was the greatest impediment
to the unity and well-being of the city.

It is in Book VIII of the *Republic*, however, as Plato re-
views the successively degenerate forms of the political order, that we can see his association of the private possession
of women with corruption at its most graphic. Just as
women were communalized at the same time as other
property, so are they now, without separate explanation,
made private at the same time as other property, as the
course of the city's degeneration is described. Once private,
moreover, women are depicted as hastening the course of
the decline, due to their exclusive concern with the particular interests of their families. First, when the rulers
begin to want to own land, houses and money, and to set up
domestic treasuries and private lovenests, they will fail as
guardians of the people, and the city will start to degenerate.[19] Thereafter, the private possession of women is depicted as a major cause of further corruption. The mother's
complaints that her husband's lack of concern for wealth
and public prestige disadvantages her among the other
women make the timocratic youth begin to despise his

worthy father and to feel challenged into showing that he is more of a man. The wife, then, with her selfish concerns, who "chants all the other refrains such as women are likely to do in cases of this sort," is, like Pandora, the real originator of the evils that follow.[20]

The fact that Plato identifies the abolition of the family so closely with the communalization of property, and does not appear to regard the former as an emotional deprivation of any more severity than the latter, must be understood in the context of the functions and status of the family in contemporary upper-class Athenian life. In view of the chattel status of Athenian women, and the "peculiarly close relation thought to hold between a family and its landed property," Plato's intertwining of two issues which appear to us to be much more distinct is not hard to explain.[21] As we have seen, it was almost impossible for husbands and wives to be either day-to-day companions or emotional and intellectual intimates. Consequently, as recent scholars of Greek life agree, "the family does not bulk large in most Greek writing, its affective and psychological sides hardly at all," and "family life, as we understand it, hardly existed" in late fifth-century Athens.[22] The prevailing bisexuality meant that "two complementary institutions coexisted, the family taking care of what we may call the material side, pederasty (and the courtesan) the affective, and to a degree the intellectual, side of a man's intimate life."[23]

On the other hand, while the family was certainly no center of the upper-class Greek's emotional life, it did function in ways that the modern family does not—ways which rendered it potentially far more socially divisive. The single-family household had emerged from the clan in comparatively recent times, and it was only gradually that the *polis* was gaining the loyalty that had previously belonged to the once autonomous clan. Antigone represents the paradigm of this conflict of loyalties, and there were in fact various areas of life where it had not yet become clear whether family or civic obligations should prevail. The extent to which the victim's kin, rather than the rulers, were responsible for ensuring that crime was properly avenged is well documented in the *Laws*.[24] Again, the predominance of duties to parents over any notion of legal justice is clearly indicated in the *Euthyphro*, where Socrates is incredulous that a man could even think of prosecuting his own father for the murder of anyone who was not a relative.[25] Despite its minimal functioning as an emotional base, then, the Athenian family of the early fourth century, as a firm economic entity and the focus of important duties, constituted an obviously divisive force and potential threat to civic loyalty.

Those Plato scholars who have expressed profound horror at the idea that the family be abolished and replaced by those mating arrangements designed to produce the best offspring seem to have treated the issue anachronistically, by neglecting to consider the function of the family in Athenian life. When Grube, for example, objects to the system of temporary matings advocated for the guardians as "undesirable because it does violence to the deepest human emotions" and "entirely ignores the love element between the 'married' pair,"[26] he seems to forget that at the time the family was simply not the locus for the expression of the deepest human emotions. Even a cursory knowledge of the *Symposium*, with its deprecating comparison of those who turn their love toward women and raise families with those whose superior spiritual love is turned toward boys and philosophical searching, reveals that Plato and his audience would not have regarded the abolition of the family as a severe limitation of their intimate lives. Stranger still is the attitude taken by Leo Strauss, who not only assumes that the family is "natural" and any move to abolish it "convention," but makes the issue of whether the abolition of the family is possible or not into an acid test for determining the feasibility of the entire ideal state.[27] Those passages of the *Republic* to which he refers in order to demonstrate the supposed "fact that men seem to desire naturally to have children of their own" are quite remarkably inadequate to prove his point. Moreover, his objection that Plato's controls on heterosexual behavior means that "the claims of *eros* are simply silenced" implies a complete denial of the prevailing homosexual *eros* of the time. It is in fact very probable that Plato's audience would have regarded the ideal state's restrictions on their homosexual behavior as far more repressive of their sexual feelings than the abolition of the family and the controls placed on heterosexual intercourse.

The same scholars—Grube, Taylor and Strauss—who reject the abolition of the family as impossible, are those most intolerant of the proposed alternative, in which partners are chosen for each other supposedly by lot but, in fact, for eugenic purposes. Those who reject such proposals as quite impracticable, given human nature, because of their "intolerable severity"[28] would do well to consider the position of respectable Greek women. For they were just as controlled and deprived with respect to their sexual lives as both sexes of guardians were to be in the ideal city, and without having available to them the compensations of any participation in life outside the domestic sphere. The Greek woman was not permitted to choose her sexual partner, any more than Plato's guardians were. Moreover, in her case the partner had not only the absolute right to copulate with and reproduce via her for the rest of her life, but also all the powers which her father had previously wielded over her. Once married, a woman had no condoned alternative sexual outlets, but was entirely dependent on a husband who might have any number of approved hetero- or homosexual alternatives, for any satisfaction that he might choose to give her. The extent of the double standard is clearly brought into relief by the fact that the Greek word for adultery *meant* nothing but sexual intercourse between a married woman and a man who was not her husband. Needless to say, the punishments were very severe.

Even if her husband died, a woman had no control over her life or her body, since she was returned to the custody of her father or guardian, who could remarry her at his pleasure. Alternatively to marriage, a citizen could give his sister or daughter into concubinage, whence she could be sent to a brothel, without any reproach to her owner.[29]

If Athenian women of the highest class, living in one of the most highly cultured societies the world has known, could be controlled and deprived to this extent, it is hardly arguable that the exigencies of human nature render the Platonic mating system, with its requirement of supposedly "unnatural continence,"[30] impossible to enact. Women's sexual lives have been restricted throughout the greater part of world history, just as rigidly as Plato proposes to control the intimate lives of his guardians. "The claims of *eros*" have been "simply silenced" in women with considerable success. It is apparent from much of the history of the female sex that, with a suitable indoctrination and the backing of strong sanctions, human beings can be conditioned to accept virtually any extent of control on their sexual and emotional lives. The point is, of course, that the scholars concerned have used the terms "human emotions" and "human nature" to refer only to men. What seems really horrific to Grube, Taylor and Strauss is that whereas the Greeks, like many other peoples, merely reserved women for the production of legitimate issue and controlled their lives accordingly, Plato has dared to suggest that the sexual lives of both male and female guardians should be controlled for the purpose of producing the best possible offspring for the community.

The significance of Plato's abolition of the family is profound, and, as we shall discuss below,[31] the proposal has been echoed by a number of subsequent theorists or rulers of utopian societies that depend to a very high degree on cohesion and unity. As Stanley Diamond has asserted, in an illuminating essay which analyzes the significance of Plato's treatment of the family: "The obvious aim is to disengage (the guardians) from all connections and motives which might diminish their dedication to the state. . . . Plato clearly sensed the antagonism between state and family, and in order to guarantee total loyalty to the former, he simply abolished the latter."[32] Moreover, it is important to notice that Plato's revolutionary solution to the conflict was not simply to obliterate the primary ties of kinship, but to extend them throughout the entire ruling class. The guardians were in fact "to imagine that they were all one family,"[33] and it is stressed in many ways that the formation of the rulers into one family is to be no mere formality. Not only are they all to address each other as brother, parent, and so on, but "it would be ridiculous," Glaucon agrees, "if they only mouthed, without deeds, the names of kinship."[34] Thus, the fear and shame associated with violence toward a parent will operate as an unusually strong sanction against attack on anyone at all of the older generation. Likewise, lawsuits and factional disputes will be no more common than they would be within a family, and the city's success in war will be in large part due to the fact that soldiers will be no more likely to desert their comrades than to abandon members of their own families.[35] Indeed, as Gregory Vlastos has concisely stated, "The ideal society of the *Republic* is a political community held together by bonds of fraternal love."[36]

For the purposes of this study, the most important consequence of Plato's transformation of the guardian class into a single family is the radical implication it has for the role of women. Jean-Jacques Rousseau, in the course of bitterly attacking Plato both for doing away with the family and for giving equal opportunities to women, reveals in spite of his hostility a very perceptive understanding of the connection between the two innovations. "I am well aware that in the *Republic* Plato prescribes the same exercises for women as for men," he says. "Having dispensed with the individual family in his system of government, and not knowing any longer what to do with women, he finds him-

self forced to turn them into men."[37] If we substitute the
word "people" for "men," since for Rousseau, as we shall
see, in many important ways only men were people, Rousseau appears to be right. Scholars who have considered the
connection between the first two "waves of paradox" of
Book v—the granting of equal opportunities to women
and the abolition of the family—do not, however, agree.
Some have stressed the independence of the two proposals,
some have maintained that there is probably a causal link
between them but have been unwilling to commit themselves on its direction, and at least one has rather dogmatically asserted, without giving any reasons, that it is the
emancipation of women which leads to the abolition of the
family.[38] For a number of reasons, however, it seems that
to the extent that a causal relationship exists between the
two paradoxes, its direction is as Rousseau states it.

In the ideal city, since there is no private wealth or marriage for those in the guardian class and living arrangements
are communal, there is no domestic role such as that of the
traditional housewife. Since planned breeding and communal child-rearing minimize the unpredictability of pregnancy and the time demands made on mothers, maternity
is no longer anything approaching a full-time occupation.
Thus, women can no longer be defined by their traditional
roles. However, every person in the ideal city is defined by
his or her function; the education and working life of each
citizen is dedicated totally to the optimal performance of a
single craft.[39] If for the female guardians the relationship
to particular men, children and households has ceased to
be crucial, there seems to be no alternative for Plato but to
consider women as persons in their own right. If they are
to take their place as members of the guardian class, each
must necessarily share in the functions of that class. Thus
Plato had to convince his disbelieving audience that women
were indeed able to perform tasks very different from those
that society had customarily assigned to them. Since the
general climate of opinion was so hostile to this way of

thinking, the Socratic assertions that woman's nature is not inferior to man's, and that male and female virtue are the same, must undoubtedly have paved the way for the arguments Plato proceeds to put forward.

The arguments of *Republic* v about the nature of women will be analyzed in more detail in Chapter 3, but the main points need to be summarized here. Socrates first reminds his audience that they have all firmly agreed that each individual should be assigned work that is suited to his or her nature. But, he says, since no one will claim that there is no difference of nature between the male and the female, they are now in danger of contradicting themselves, if they argue that the female guardians should do the same work as the male. There are, however, we are reminded, many ways in which human beings can differ in their natures, and we by no means regard all of them as relevant in assigning different functions to different persons. Up to this point, Socrates asserts, we have not considered "what form of different and same nature, and applying to what, we were distinguishing when we assigned different practices to a different nature and the same ones to the same."[40] But, he continues, is it not reasonable to consider only those differences and similarities that have some bearing on the activity in question? We do not, for example, worry about whether a man is bald or long-haired when assessing his capability to be a good shoemaker. There seems, therefore, to be no reason to consider the difference between the sexes with regard to their procreative function—"that the female bears and the male mounts"—as relevant in deciding whether they should play equal roles in the ruling class. Socrates lays the burden of proof firmly on whoever should claim that it is. He argues, rather, that since it is the characteristics of the soul that determine whether a person has the requisite nature for a certain pursuit, and since sex is no more related to the soul than the presence or absence of hair, members of both sexes will be skilled in all the various arts, depending on the nature of their individual souls. Thus, though he asserts that women in general are not as capable as men in general, especially in physical strength, individual members of both sexes will be capable of performing all the functions needed by the city, including guardianship and philosophy. The only way to ensure that persons are assigned the jobs for which they are best suited is to assess the merits of each, independently of sex.

This argument, simple as it seems, is unique among political philosophers in their assessments of the role of women. It has revolutionary implications. Plato's bold suggestion that perhaps there is no difference between the sexes apart from their roles in procreation is possible only because the requirement of unity within the ruling class, and the consequent abolition of private property and the family, entail the abolition of wifehood and the minimization of the role of motherhood. Once the door is open, moreover, the possibilities for women are acknowledged to be boundless. The abandonment of traditional sex roles among the guardians is total—even caring for the youngest children is prescribed as work for men as well as women.[41] Plato concludes that, though females as a group are less able, the best of women can share with the best of men in the most elevated of functions involved in ruling the city. The "philosopher monarchs," as they should always have been called, were to include both sexes.[42]

The overwhelming hostility from male scholars to Plato's first wave of paradox is discussed in an Appendix. However, one charge that has been laid against him must be dealt with here. Leo Strauss and Allan Bloom have claimed that Plato's arguments for the equality of women depend on his "abstracting from" or "forgetting" the body, and particularly his "abstracting from the difference between the sexes with regard to procreation."[43] Clearly they do not. Plato is very careful to take into account those differences between the sexes that are palpably biological and therefore inevitable—pregnancy, lactation and a degree of difference in physical strength. The mistake these scholars, in the company of millions of other people, make is that of assuming, as Plato very rationally does not, that the entire conventional female sex role follows logically from the single fact that women bear children. The real significance of the treatment of the subject of women in Book v of the *Republic* is that it is one of the very few instances in the history of thought when the biological implications of femaleness have been clearly separated out from all the conventional, institutional, and emotional baggage that has usually been identified with them. Plato's abolition of the private sphere of the guardians' lives entailed as a corollary the radical questioning of all the institutionalized differences between the sexes.

During the course of the argument about the proper education and role of women, Socrates twice indicates that these and the abolition of the family are really parts of the same issue. He talks, first, of the "right acquisition and use of children and women" and later of "the law concerning the possession and rearing of the women and children."[44] In addition, the way the question of the emancipation of the female guardians is raised is in itself significant. Having introduced in an aside the proposal that the guardians will have women and children in common as well as their other possessions, Socrates is challenged, at the beginning of Book v, to justify this important decision. In answer, he embarks on his discussion, first, of the equal education and treatment of women, and second, of the communal breeding and rearing arrangements. It seems, then, that having decided to do away with the conventional role of women by doing away with the family, he feels impelled to make the proposal seem more feasible by demonstrating that, indeed, women are capable of filling many other roles and can be well utilized outside of their traditional sphere. A brief passage from the *Laws* suffices to indicate how aware Plato was of the danger of freeing women from their confined, domestic role without giving them any alternative function. The example of the Spartans ought, he thought, to be enough to discourage any legislator from "letting the female sex indulge in luxury and expense and disorderly ways of life, while supervising the male sex."[45] Thus it was his dismantling of the family which not only enabled Plato to rethink the question of woman's role and her potential abilities but, more accurately, forced him to do so.

Two additional arguments strengthen the case that it is the abolition of the family which leads Plato into emancipating the female guardians rather than vice versa. First, no mention is made of the women of the inferior classes. We are told that among these householders and farmers, private land, houses and other property are to be preserved. The close connection between these things and the private ownership of women and children implies, though we are not specifically told this, that the family, too, is preserved for the lower classes.[46] Moreover, we can have no doubt that one of Plato's primary aims in the organization of the artisans is maximum efficiency, which presumably implies the best possible use of all members of these classes. In spite of this objective, however, and although the argument in Book v concerning women's talents is applicable just as much to the other crafts as to that of governing the city, there is no suggestion of applying it to any class of women but the guardians. The only possible explanation of this seems to be that, where the family is retained, and women are private wives and functional mothers, their equality with men in other roles is not considered to be an open issue.

Second, as we shall now see, what happens to women in Plato's second-best city—as described in the *Laws*—overwhelmingly confirms our hypothesis. On the subject of women, Plato in the *Laws* shows a marked ambivalence. His dilemma results from his inability to reconcile his increasingly firm beliefs about the potential capabilities of the female sex with the reintroduction of private property and the family into the social structure of his city. On the one hand, having once thought about women as individuals, and as half of society with vast unused talents, Plato seems to have become more convinced than ever, by the time he wrote the *Laws*, that existing practice with regard to women was foolish, and that they should be educated and used, like men, to their greatest capacity. In theory, the radical statements about women from *Republic* v are carried in the *Laws* to new extremes. On the other hand, the *Laws* is a considerably less revolutionary document than the *Republic*; far from being "a pattern laid up in heaven," whose realization on earth is so remote a possibility that it is immaterial whether it could exist or not, the second-best city is presented as a much less utopian construct.[47] The very title of the dialogue, usually translated "Laws," is in fact more accurately rendered as "Tradition." A significant casualty of this "realism" is Plato's conception of the role of women. What is proposed for them in general terms is simply not carried out in the detailed institutions of the society, in which they are again private wives and the functioning mothers of particular children.

As we shall presently see, Plato's arguments and conclusions in the *Laws* about the natural potential of women are far more radical than those put forward in the *Republic*. He appears, in fact, to attribute to the different rearing and education afforded the two sexes practically all of the differences in their subsequent abilities and achievements. Pointing to the example of the Sarmatian women, who participate in warfare equally with the men, as proof of the potential of the female sex, he argues that the Athenian practice of maintaining rigid sex roles is absurd. Only a "surprising blunder" of a legislator could allow the waste of half the state's available resources, by prescribing that "most irrational" practice—"that men and women should not all follow the same pursuits with one accord and with all their might."[48]

However, having made the general proclamation that the law should prescribe the same education and training for girls as for boys, and that "the female sex must share with the male, to the greatest extent possible, both in education and in all else"—should "share with men in the whole of their mode of life,"[49] Plato's Athenian legislator fails to apply these precepts in many of the most crucial instances. In order to understand the inconsistency between the general statements about women and the very different detailed specifications that are set out with regard to the most important of civic duties, we must consider the effects on women of the reinstatement of the family.

Though it is clearly a source of regret to Plato, he reconciles himself to the fact that the citizens of the second-best city, not being gods or sons of gods, are not capable of holding their property in common. Moreover, the reinstatement of private property, one of the most far-reaching differences between the *Laws* and the *Republic*, brings with it in the same paragraph the reintroduction of marriage and the family.[50] It is clear from the context that it is primarily the need for a property-holding man to have an heir that necessitates the disappearance of the communal ownership of women and children simultaneously with that of other property. However, the identification of women and children together with other possessions was so natural to the Greek mind that no special justification is felt to be necessary. The failure to achieve communism of property means, it seems, that women, too, become private possessions.

The family, moreover, is the very basis of the polity planned in the *Laws*. As Glenn Morrow has noted, "The state is a union of households or families, not a collection of detached citizens," and "The vitality of the family in Plato's state is evident at many points in his legislation."[51] The existence of family shrines, the complex and detailed marriage and inheritance laws, the family's crucial role in the prosecution of criminal justice, and the denial to sons of the right to defend themselves against their fathers—all these provisions indicate the central and authoritative position of the family.[52] The marriage laws are the first to be drawn up, and their implications for the position of women are immediate and extensive. In contrast to the temporary mating system of the *Republic*, in which neither sex had any more freedom to choose or right to refuse a mate than the other, with the reintroduction of permanent marriage, the matter of choosing a spouse is, without any explanation, quite different for women than for men. Marriage is indeed compulsory for all, since procreation is regarded as a universal duty. But whereas a man decides whom he will marry, provided he seeks a partnership that will result in the best offspring for his society, a woman is "given" in marriage.[53] The "right of valid betrothal" of a woman belongs in turn to a long succession of male kindred, and only if she has no close male relatives at all is she to have any say in choosing her husband. Ironically, considering this preemption of women's choice, Plato refuses to enforce legally the prohibition of unsuitable marriages, since he considers that to do so "besides being ridiculous, would cause widespread resentment."[54] Apparently what was customary for women was considered intolerable control if applied to the choices made by men.

The status of women as determined by the marriage laws is closely related to the fact that women are also virtually excluded from the ownership of property. Even if she has no brothers, a daughter may participate in the inheritance of the family estate only by serving as the instrument through which the husband chosen for her by her father can become her father's heir.[55] The *Laws*, in fact, provides very clear documentation of the essential linkage of property and inheritance to the marriage system and position of women. When a man owns inheritable property, he must own a wife too, in order to ensure a legitimate heir. The fact that women thereby become private wives means that in many ways they are treated as property rather than as persons. They themselves cannot inherit real property, which to a large extent defines personhood within the society (a disinherited son must leave the city unless another citizen adopts him as his heir);[56] and they are treated as commodities to be given away by their male relatives. Given these basic features of the social structure of the city, it is not surprising that Plato, in spite of general pronouncements to the contrary, is not able to treat or use women as the equals of his male citizens. Their status as property seems to preempt the execution of his declared intentions.

Although the legal status of women in Plato's second-best city is an improvement on that in contemporary Athens, it is not at all one of equality with men. Glenn Morrow has said that "it is certainly Plato's expressed intention (though not fully carried out) to give women a more equal status under the law."[57] The proposed divorce laws, unlike the marriage laws, treat women considerably more equally than did those of contemporary Athens. The criminal statutes enforce the same punishments for the wounding or murder of wives as of husbands, and are generally applied without discrimination according to the sex of either plaintiff or defendant.[58] The most striking instance of equal treatment before the law is in the case of extra-marital intercourse, where the same penalties are extended to offenders of both sexes.[59] This unusual departure from the double moral standard that one might expect to find in a society so firmly based on monogamy and inheritance can probably be explained by Plato's aim to make all the members of his city as virtuous and temperate as possible. It is not that the standards are relaxed for women, after all, but that they are considerably tightened up for men. However, the Athenian concept of women as legal minors is still present in significant ways in the *Laws*. Besides not being eligible to own property, they are not allowed until the age of forty to give evidence in a court of law or to support a plea, and only if unmarried are they ever allowed to bring an action.[60] Women, then, especially if married, are still to a large extent *femmes couvertes*.

What begins to be revealed through the denial to women of certain important civil and legal rights is strongly confirmed by the roles they are allotted within the official governmental sphere. In the *Republic*, once we have been told that the women of the guardian class are to share with the men in every aspect of ruling and guarding, they are not specifically mentioned as eligible for certain offices, with the implication that they are ineligible for others. The only case where women are specifically mentioned as being eligible for office is at the end of Socrates' account of the philosophers' education. Here, presumably because the very idea must have seemed so outrageous, Plato finds it necessary to remind his audience that everything he has been saying applies equally to all those women who have the necessary abilities.[61] It is most unlikely that the guardian women, if allowed to compete for the highest rank of all, would be excluded from any other office.

In the *Laws*, by contrast, in spite of the general pronouncements cited above, Plato both specifies when a certain function, such as the priesthood, is to be performed by persons of both sexes, and makes particular mention of certain offices being filled by women, frequently with the strong implication that only women are eligible for them.[62] Thus, it is women who supervise married couples, who look after infants, whose role in the educational system is to provide the children's meals and oversee their games—in short, who perform, in positions not of the highest rank, all those domestic, nurturing, child-oriented tasks to which women have traditionally been assigned. On the other hand, there is no suggestion of any women participating in the ranks of the magistracy, or the "divine nocturnal synod," whose role parallels that of the philosophers in the *Republic*.[63] The children are given their lessons by male educational officers; as for the post of supervisor of education, which is "by far the most important . . . of the highest offices of State" and must be filled by "that one of the citizens who is in every way the most excellent," it is explicitly laid down that its occupant be male, for he must be "the father of legitimate children."[64] This specification adds weight to what is implied throughout the work—that in the second-best city, unless the eligibility of women is plainly mentioned, most offices, and especially high ones, are reserved for men.[65] Moreover, even for those positions for which a woman is eventually eligible, she does not become so until aged forty, whereas a man is eligible from the age of thirty.[66]

In spite of the controversial proposal in the *Laws* that, in the interests of order and discipline, even married women should take their meals communally, though segregated from the men, it is clear that Plato was ambivalent about the wisdom, or perhaps the feasibility, of bringing wives out of their domestic seclusion. Thus, for example, when he describes the funeral processions that are to be held for distinguished citizens, women of childbearing age are noticeably omitted from a list in which every other class of citizen has its place. They are similarly omitted from the choral competitions.[67] Most remarkable, however, given Plato's previous insistence that neither gymnastics nor riding are improper for women, and that trained women can perform in the military sphere equally as well as men,[68] is the fact that, in detailing the regulations, he proceeds to exempt women almost entirely from military service. From the very beginning, girls are to learn the military arts only "if they agree to it," whereas such instruction is obligatory for boys.[69] Then, although Plato makes the general provision that men, women and children are all to participate in military training at least one day a month, when the details are spelled out, women after the age of marriage (twenty at the latest) are again noticeably absent. They are not included either in races or in wrestling, both of which sports are presented as integral parts of the training. As for horsemanship, it is decreed that "it is not worthwhile to make compulsory laws and rules about their taking part in such sports," but that women may do so "without blame," if they like.[70] It should be noted that Plato was certainly not in the habit of making aspects of his educational systems optional—particularly those relating to the defense of the state.

Finally, the term of military service for men is from the age of twenty to sixty; "for women they shall obtain what is possible and fitting in each case, after they have finished bearing children, and up to the age of fifty, in whatever kind of military work it may be thought right to employ their services."[71] This means that for all the grand assertions about the necessity and rationality of training women equally with men to share in the defense of the state, women are in fact allowed, not compelled, to train up to the age of, at latest, twenty, are then excluded from most military activity until they are past childbearing, and are subsequently exempted again at fifty. Since in Plato's proposed society men were to have no other condoned sexual outlet than their wives, and since contraception was hardly in an advanced state, this could well mean an expectation of five years of military service from adult women. Surely this was no way to produce Amazons.

Despite Plato's professed intention to have the women of the second-best city share equally with the men in carrying out all the duties of citizenship, the fact that they are private wives curtails their participation in public life for three major reasons. The first is the practical matter of pregnancy and lactation, which is not controlled and predictable as in the *Republic*, where the guardians mate only at the behest of the rulers. The women in the *Laws*, since as permanent wives they are far less able to time or limit their pregnancies, cannot be held liable on a continuous basis for public and especially, military duties. Secondly, the reinstitution of the private household makes each wife into the mistress responsible for its welfare, and it is clear that in the *Laws* a mother is to participate far more in early child care than does the female guardian, who is not even to know which child is hers.[72]

The third reason is that it is clearly inconceivable to

Plato that women who are "private wives"—the private
property of the male citizens—should play the same kind
of public, and especially military, roles, as the female guardians, who are not defined in terms of a traditional relationship to a man. Whereas the female guardians can, like the
male, exercise naked, the young girls in the *Laws*, must
be "clad in decent apparel," as a maiden who was shortly
to become the respectable wife and private property of a
citizen could hardly be allowed to be seen naked by the
world at large.[73] In fact, Plato expresses at least as much
expectation of ridicule for his suggestion in the *Laws* that
wives should dine in public, though at segregated tables,
as he had expressed in the *Republic* for his proposal that
all the guardians of both sexes should exercise together
naked.[74] Although he regarded it as even more dangerous
to leave women undisciplined than to neglect men, and in-
sisted that women, too, should dine in public, he was
well aware that in the kind of society he was planning, there
would be enormous resistance to such an idea. Consequently, although he deplored the fact that even the supposedly
trained women of Sparta had panicked and run when an
enemy invaded their city, and thought it folly that so important a potential for defense as the entire female sex
should be neglected, he seems to have found it impossible
to hold consistently to his original proposal that women
should participate in military activities equally with men.
If merely the segregated public dining of private wives
could cause a general outcry, there was no knowing what
revolutions might be provoked by the proposal that men
should mingle with other men's private wives on the battle
field. Despite all his professed intentions in the *Laws* to
emancipate women and make full use of the talents that he
was now convinced they had, Plato's reintroduction of the
family has the direct effect of putting them firmly back into
their traditional place.

3

Female Nature and Social Structure

We have so far concentrated on the issue of the relationship between Plato's treatment of women in his ideal and second-best cities, and some of the other important characteristics of the two societies—most notably property and the family system. Now we turn, rather, to an analysis of *how* Plato argues about women. Does he apply to the case of women the same arguments and logical standards that he applies when discussing the nature of men? More significantly still, does he allow his conclusions about the nature and potential of women to be carried through to their full implications? Finally, what bearing do the answers to these questions have on the very different roles that are prescribed for women in the *Republic* and the *Laws*?

The concept of "nature" in Plato is very important and by no means simple. *Physis* is a much used word in the dialogues, together with the many adjective and verb forms of the root, and an understanding of the complexity of its meaning is crucial for a proper appreciation of Plato's thought about the relative importance of innate characteristics and environmental factors in the formation of human personality and abilities.

Plato says in the *Phaedrus* that the determination of the nature of anything is no simple matter. He stresses that we cannot "reflect about the nature of anything" without considering carefully how it acts and can act on other things and they in turn on it. To pursue the inquiry without doing so, he says, would be like the progress of a blind man.[1] This means that superficial appearances are most unlikely to indicate accurately the true nature of things; we must look closely at the environment in which they act and are acted upon, before we can presume to know anything about their natures. As we shall see, however, Plato himself, in talking about the nature of women, does not always follow his own advice.

The question of whether innate characteristics or environmental factors were of predominant importance in forming the mature human being was one that concerned the classical Greeks, and the tradition that formed the context of Plato's thought seems to have laid great stress on the innate, as opposed to the effects of nurture, in explaining how persons become what they become. It is fairly evident, for example, that the great stress of the influential poet, Theognis, was on the immutability of the innate, and the consequent impotence of education to produce intellectual achievement and good character.[2] It appears, however, that, more than most commentators have acknowledged, Plato strongly opposed this prevailing emphasis. The *Republic* and the *Laws*, at least as much as they are about politics, are about education in the very broadest possible sense of the word.[3]

One of the problems involved in discovering where Plato stands with regard to the relative weights of innate characteristics and environmental influence is that he does not always use the word *physis* and its derivatives to mean what is innate. This usage is by no means peculiar to Plato. The Greek word referred both to the "constitution, structure, essence" of a thing, and also to its development, or, as we may say, the way it grows. It had both a static and a dynamic sense.[4] Since our tendency, however, is to phrase the question as that of "nature" versus "nurture," which we regard as mutually exclusive words, Plato's different use of "nature" can be misleading. Sometimes, very clearly, Plato's "nature" or "natural" does imply innateness, as, for example, when he argues that "in natural ability the two limbs are almost equally balanced; but we ourselves by habitually using them in a wrong way have made them different."[5] However, in some passages, it is clear that what Plato calls "nature" includes elements that are by no means innate, but have been developed by training and habit. In the *Laws*, for example, while not making horsemanship compulsory for girls, he says, "But if, as a result of earlier training which has grown into a habit, their nature allows, and does not forbid, girls or maidens to take part, let them do so without blame."[6] Again, in a significant passage in the *Republic* about how the institutions of the ideal state will make it "roll on like a circle in its growth," Socrates says, "For sound rearing and education, when they are preserved, produce good natures; and sound natures, in their turn receiving such an education, grow up still better than those before them. . . ."[7] If, as these passages clearly imply, the "nature" of a person is "produced" at least in part by his or her environment, we cannot assume that everything Plato says about the natural, or the nature of an individual, is intended to refer to innate qualities. Thus when, for example, he bases his extreme division of labor on the premise that "each of us is naturally not quite like anyone else, but rather differs in his nature,"[8] there is nothing in the context—indeed nothing but the presumption that, for Plato, a person's nature was completely innate—to suggest that he considered the difference between a physician and a carpenter to be wholly, or even predominantly innate. It is clearly a case of overinterpretation for *physis* to be translated as "nature . . . from birth," as Shorey does at *Republic* 485a.

Certainly, Plato did not ignore the existence of inherited, innate characteristics, or deny their importance. In discussing the involuntariness of moral failure, he says that "all of us who are bad become bad from two causes which are entirely beyond our control," i.e. "an ill disposition of the body and bad education."[9] Again in the *Phaedrus*, the juxtaposition of innate qualities with education is clear.

Discussing how one becomes a good rhetorician, Socrates says, "Undoubtedly—it is the same as with anything else. If you have an innate capacity for rhetoric, you will become a famous rhetorician, provided you also acquire knowledge and practice, but if you lack any of these three you will be correspondingly unfinished."[10] The inborn capacity is necessary, therefore, but by no means sufficient, to produce a person competent in any art or skill. The inborn germ must be cultivated if it is to flourish. Finally, in the *Laws*, it is, we are told, because of inadequacies in their "birth, rearing and training"[11] that the citizens are adjudged incapable of holding property in common.

But this so far is fairly trivial. Few thinkers have denied totally the importance of either innate or environmental factors. The important thing is to assess where the greater emphasis lies, and there is much evidence in the dialogues that Plato attributed the greater weight to the influence of education and environment. It is undeniable that he places very strong emphasis on the importance of early childhood experience. "Don't you know," Socrates asks,

> that the beginning is the most important part of every work and that this is especially so with anything young and tender? For at that age it's most plastic, and each thing assimilates itself to the model whose stamp anyone wishes to give to it.[12]

This is why the utmost care must be taken over the stories told to the young guardians and, in the *Laws*, to all the young citizens, and the games they are to play, for it is these very things which "shape their souls." What a young child "takes into his opinions at that age has a tendency to become hard to eradicate and unchangeable."[13] Since "the starting point of a man's education sets the course of what follows too," the young guardians are not permitted to do anything, even in play, that is inappropriate to their status and future function, and the craftsmen, likewise, are to concentrate on learning their crafts from the earliest possible age.[14] Later, Socrates warns of the strong effects on personality of excessive concentration on the physical side of education and insufficient on the aesthetic, or the reverse. The former imbalance will overdevelop the spirited part of the individual's nature, to the point of savagery, whereas the latter will overdevelop the tame and orderly part of the natural disposition, with the result that the personality will be excessively soft. Clearly the message is that environment and training can make some parts of the original potential wither away, at the expense of others which become unhealthily predominant.[15]

The guardians are originally chosen, we are told, for that rare combination of abilities—the capacity to be gentle to their own but fierce toward enemies.[16] However, the detailed and extensive education they are given testifies to the fact that Plato does not consider that even individuals with such special qualities can be expected to develop in the right way without meticulous attention being paid to them. Moreover, when Socrates considers, later, the great difficulty of the tasks and requirements he is imposing on his ruling class, he asserts that they will in fact find them slight, so long as "the one great—or, rather than great, sufficient—thing" is preserved. This great, sufficient thing, however, is not, as some Plato scholars' emphases would tend to make us believe, the innate qualities of this elite band, but instead, "their education and rearing." It is "if by being well-educated they become sensible men" that they will recognize the rationality of all the social arrangements that are proposed for them.[17]

The allegory of the cave confirms the hypothesis that Plato believed nurture to be the far more weighty factor determining the level of human achievement. The whole allegory, after all, is put forward to show the vast gulf between the abilities of the educated and the uneducated to perceive reality. It is not the contrasting picture of two different types of person, distinct from birth, but rather "an image of our nature in its education and want of education."[18] Compared with what they might learn to perceive, men in their present, uneducated condition are as if hidden underground, with nothing but shadows to give them impressions of the world outside.

In the *Laws*, the predominant stress on education, which includes anything from drinking parties to legislation on all sorts of matters, seems to be even greater than before, in proportion as Plato's faith in human innate capacities seems to have declined. The citizens of the second-best city are, we are told, but "puppets for the most part," and as Glenn Morrow has said, "Plato's legislator eventually stakes all his chances upon his educational program."[19] The Athenian asserts in Book I that "well-educated men will prove good men"; the post of director of education is said to be the highest and most important in the state; even foetal environment is added to the periods of early childhood that had been held in the *Republic* to have such crucial repercussions for subsequent development; and it is stressed that *never*, even if the population should decline severely, should people whose education has been bad be introduced into the city.[20] It is in the *Laws*, above all, that Plato reveals that the entire social and legal structure of his proposed society is designed to be educative. For despite the fact that man is considered "a tame creature," Plato warns that "if his training be deficient or bad, he turns out the wildest of all earth's creatures."[21]

The myth of metals has not infrequently been looked to by those who have sought to demonstrate Plato's primary emphasis on innate factors as determinative of human character and abilities.[22] What does not seem to have been recognized by such scholars, however, is that the myth of metals is explicitly said to be a *lie*. Granted, it is not an ordinary lie, a "true" or "real" lie of the type hated by all gods and men, which leads to "ignorance in the soul of the man who has been lied to." It is, rather, an example of the lie "in speeches," which is "not quite an unadulterated lie" and which is not reprehensible, since it can be "useful to hu-

man beings as a form of remedy."[23] It is, we are told, quite
appropriate for the rulers alone to tell this kind of lie, for
the benefit of the city as a whole. Given this, the tendency
to treat the two "noble lies" that appear at the end of Book
III merely as metaphors, used to simplify the truth and
make it more graphic, seems to be quite unjustified. Moreover, the basic falsehood involved in both the myths that
are told the citizens about their origins is that the differences among the members of the different social classes are
wholly innate. So as to rationalize and preserve the hierarchy that is so important for the stability and welfare of
his ideal city, Plato proposes that his citizens should forget
their rearing and education—which have been so patently
discriminatory—should consider them as mere dreams, and
believe instead that they were fashioned by a god who made
them out of distinctly different quality materials—some of
gold, some of silver, and some of iron and bronze. Thus
the vast differences among the adult citizens, which are in
truth the result both of their innate temperaments and of
the vastly different educations they have undergone, are
all to be attributed to the former. Thus false propaganda
is used to suppress the undesirable urge for advancement.
It is the same "noble lie" that has been told to women
throughout world history.

Given Plato's predominant stress on nurture, the argument he employs in Book V of the *Republic* to demonstrate
that the male and female guardians have the same natures,
and should therefore be assigned the same tasks, is extremely strange. Up to this point, he has very strongly emphasized
the importance of both total environment and specific training for the development of abilities of all kinds. It would
seem, then, that the obvious line for him to take would be
to assert that, because of the great differences between the
contemporary rearing and education of the two sexes, one
could make no good estimate of what women's capacities
might turn out to be, once they were given exactly the
same rearing as men. Since a person's nature could be

warped in a number of ways by the formation of different types of habits, and the overemphasis on, or neglect of, various aspects of the original potential, there could be no way of knowing how women's innate abilities compared to those of men, so long as the almost total neglect of female education persisted. If men, as currently educated, could be compared to properly educated men, as cave-dwellers could be compared to those who perceive the real world, then women, confined as they were in contemporary Athens, might analogously be represented as spending their lives inside coffins, without even the benefit of enough light to throw tantalizing shadows on the walls. The contrast between the women of the society in which Plato lived and women as they might be was surely a far greater contrast than that between his fellow Athenian men and those he planned for the ideal city. Again, if the young male guardians could be seriously damaged, as we are told, by hearing of the weaknesses and follies of the male heroes of their ancestral poetry and drama, what kind of self-image could one possibly expect in a girl whose heritage was the view of her sex that prevailed in the same literature?[24] Although Plato asserts that a person who is kept in ignorance will have no option but to believe what other people tell him about himself, he does not apply this truth about self-image to the brain-washing to which Greek women had been subjected from Hesiod to Pericles.[25]

Instead, faced with the monumental task of demonstrating to his skeptical audience that women should be trained to fulfill the same elevated civic functions as men, Plato almost entirely fails to apply his own environmentalism. There is but a single, brief reference to his belief that it is not possible "to use any animal for the same things if you don't assign it the same rearing and education."[26] Apart from this, the argument he uses is designed to show that there is nothing which women, as a class, do better than men as a class, even in that sphere of things traditionally reserved for women. There is, therefore, nothing which is properly designated as women's role. Next, however, it is claimed that neither is there any role which belongs particularly to men as a class. Rather, as was indicated when the idea of the division of labor was first introduced, it is persons rather than classes of persons that have natures suited to different arts, and the generalization that men tend to be better than women at all things does not preclude that "many women are better than many men at many things."[27]

Plato claims to have demonstrated, by means of the above argument, that, the traditional sex roles being far from either rational or natural,

> there is no practice of a city's governors which belongs to woman because she's woman, or to man because he's man; but the natures are scattered alike among both animals; and woman participates according to nature in all practices, and man in all, but in all of them woman is weaker than man.[28]

Thus, via a rather convoluted route, he has demonstrated to his skeptical listeners something which could certainly have benefited from appeal to his own theory of the central importance of education in the broadest sense, in determining the level of capability reached by different persons. Why does he not make use of the significant fact that women's potential was unknown, and their current abilities distorted and cramped by their position in society? Perhaps, given Socrates' extreme hesitation in introducing his outrageous proposals about women, it may be that he chose the less radical line of attack, although it was also the less convincing.[29] As Christine Pierce has pointed out, "Plato's argument may . . . be construed as an attempt to grant as much as any misogynist could desire, and still show the logical implication to be equal opportunity for both sexes."[30] Perhaps, then, in spite of his own beliefs, Plato decided to have Socrates take the line of least resistance, in order to get women accepted into the guardian class on the same terms as men.

It is quite possible, however, that the reason Plato uses the weaker mode of argument in the *Republic* is that he was not yet convinced that women, if given the same rearing and education as men, could do just as well, except where sheer physical strength was concerned. In the *Laws*, however, he is much more forthright on the subject. Not only does he believe the old tales he has heard, but he says:

> I know now of my own observation, that there are practically countless myriads of women called Sauromatides, in the district of Pontus, upon whom equally with men is imposed the duty of handling bows and other weapons, as well as horses, and who practice it equally. . . . Since this state of things can exist, I affirm that the practice which at present prevails in our districts is a most irrational one—namely, that men and women should not all follow the same pursuits with one accord and with all their might.[31]

It certainly seems that Plato's faith in the potential abilities of the female sex had been strengthened since he had put into Socrates' mouth the contorted arguments of Book v of the *Republic*.

Not surprisingly, then, it is in the *Laws* that we find the part of the argument that seemed to be so conspicuously missing from Plato's claims for women in the *Republic*. Here, in the form of an elaborate metaphor, Plato's stress on the necessity of education and training for the development of innate potential is applied to the question of the differences between the sexes. Having just described the boys' early military training, and prescribed that "the girls also, if they agree to it, must share in the lessons, and especially such as relate to the use of arms," the Athenian asserts that "the view now prevalent regarding these matters

. . . is based on almost universal ignorance."[32] When he is asked what view he means, however, though he has not up to this time said a word about the use of hands and feet, he embarks on a lengthy discussion of the mistaken belief that one hand is naturally, and not just as a result of more use and better training, much stronger and more capable than the other, and then proceeds to extol the virtues of ambidexterity. Glenn Morrow, who probably knows the *Laws* as well as anyone, considers that there is no doubt at all as to what Plato is really talking about. He says:

> The analogy is so apt and obvious—i.e. a state that neglects the training of its women is like a man who trains only his right arm—that Plato evidently feels the discussion of the less controversial matter is the best way of preparing the reader for the acceptance of the more difficult proposal.[33]

And indeed, a reader who accepts Plato's hypothesis that righthandedness is simply the result of a one-sided socialization process, and that "in natural ability the two limbs are almost equally balanced," would be hard put to deny that much of the difference between the performances of the two sexes might be due to the fact that males were educated and trained, whereas females were confined and left untaught. At the very least, the consequence of accepting the validity of the argument about the two hands must be the admission that the vastly different rearings given the two sexes rendered it impossible to know what their respective innate potentials were.

There are several convincing reasons for us to believe that Morrow is right, and that what is apparently a discussion about the use of the limbs is in fact a discussion about the use of men and women. First, as Morrow notes, not only has Plato not mentioned the issue of ambidexterity before; he does not mention it again, either, throughout all his detailed regulations about athletics and military training. Though in all probability he was in favor of it, it certainly was not as important an issue for him as the training of women, which is stressed a number of times.

Second, it is the importance of both hands being trained for *military* purposes that is stressed, whereas in some other contexts it is considered to be of little import that the left hand plays a minor role.[34] As Plato says in the metaphorical passage, "It ought to be considered the correct thing that the man who possesses two sets of limbs, fit both for offensive and defensive action, should, so far as possible, suffer neither of these to go unpractised or untaught." This statement is closely echoed in a passage a little further on, but this time the subject is the neglect by the state of one of the sexes.[35] It is in the sphere of warfare, where strength and numbers are so crucial, that no resources should be allowed to be wasted. In certain other activities, those "of trifling importance," Plato regarded the division of labor between both hands and sexes to be of slight importance.[36]

Third, the Greeks' understanding of the symbolism of Plato's metaphor would have made it much clearer to them than it is to us. For in the Pythagorean table of opposites, familiar to them, the female was identified with the left, as well as with all sorts of other "sinister" qualities, such as badness and darkness, while the male was identified with the right, as with goodness, light, and other admired qualities.[37]

Fourth, there are several points in the discussion of the use of the hands where the subject at issue sounds much more like persons than limbs. "There is a vast difference here," the Athenian says, "between the taught and the untaught, the trained and the untrained warrior."[38] Again, at the end of the passage, the real subject is linked to the analogous one, as we are told that the aim of the children's education is "that all the boys and girls may be sound of hand and foot, and may in no wise, if possible, get their natures warped by their habits."[39]

Finally, Plato had good reason to be more cautious in the

FEMALE NATURE AND SOCIAL STRUCTURE

Laws about expressing openly his now even more radical beliefs about the potential capabilities of women. Quite apart from the fact that the subjects of discussion are no longer just women, but are also wives, the second-best city is billed, not as "a pattern . . . in heaven" but as a more modest proposal, far more likely to be realizable.[40] However, although he is aware that many of his proposals will be "abhorrent to many,"[41] Plato's Athenian stranger states his intention to "omit no detail of perfect beauty and truth" and only thereafter to decide "how far their proposals are expedient and how much of the legislation is impracticable."[42] Since, because of the family system, as we have seen, a great proportion of the reasoned conclusions about women and their role turn out to be impracticable, it is not surprising that Plato chose to disguise somewhat his most radical statement of them in all their "perfect beauty and truth." There is, indeed, a great deal of attention paid in the *Laws* to the dangers of all forms of innovation,[43] and innovation in the sphere of sexual roles and types was in all probability one of the most hazardous kinds one might propose. It was one thing to say outrageous things about women in the *Republic*, and even here Plato's sensitivity to ridicule had been great. It would have been another thing to say even more revolutionary things about women and their potential in the *Laws*, an altogether more conservative, traditional, and down-to-earth document, except by introducing them in the form of a metaphor which must have seemed altogether more credible and less offensive to the audience.

By the time he wrote the *Laws*, then, Plato had come to acknowledge that female human nature was not fairly represented by the women of his own society. Little, indeed, was known about it, though one could derive some impression of what women were capable of achieving from the example of the female warriors who in other societies held their own with the men in battle. However, as we have seen, the statements of general principle about women, in the *Laws*, are far more radical than the actual details of the society as it is drawn up. Women in fact play a role not at all equal to that of men. Moreover, in the course of the work, Plato makes several pronouncements about the "nature" of women which seem grossly inconsistent with his argument that the nature of a thing—whether it be a woman or a left hand—is unknowable as long as that thing is the recipient of discriminatory training and treatment in general. Thus, for example, in order to explain the necessity of subjecting women to the discipline of public dining, he asserts that women are "by nature" at least twice as bad as men.[44] No allowance at all is made, in this condemnation of women as doubly predisposed to evil, for Plato's own doctrine that moral failure is due to bad training and a wrong environment as well as to temperamental deficiencies—that, as he himself had said, it should be blamed on "the educators rather than the educated."[45] No reference is made to the fact that the education of women and the conditions of their daily lives were far less likely to render them filled with civic virtue and public spirit than were the parallel influences on men.

The most significant passage of all, however, relating to the nature of the female sex, occurs during the discussion of what music is suitable for the two sexes.[46] We must keep in mind, here, that "music" connotes the entire aesthetic, as opposed to the physical, aspect of the Greek education, and that, as we saw above, it was regarded by Plato as being of enormous importance for the formation of character.[47] The location in the dialogue of the passage we are about to examine is very significant. It falls between, on the one hand, a warning about the perils of innovation, especially in children's games, dances, and songs, because of the drastic repercussions that such apparently trivial changes can have, and, on the other hand, the clearest statement in the dialogue of Plato's radical proposals about the equal education and use of women. What the Athenian stranger proposes is that the words and music assigned to the boys and girls must be defined by "the natural differences of the two sexes." What very soon becomes apparent, however, is that it is not nature, but the legislator, who must "clearly declare wherein the feminine type consists." His regulation in the matter, moreover, is worded in the following manner: "Now we may affirm that what is noble and of a manly tendency is masculine, while that which inclines rather to decorum and sedateness is to be regarded rather as feminine both in law and in discourse." Such a pronouncement certainly seems at first to be hard to reconcile with the conclusion of *Republic* v—that the male and female guardians have "the same nature." We must, however, take note of the essential fact that the sentence quoted above is not a description of the natural differences between the sexes, but, rather, a *prescription* about what are "to be regarded" as the natural differences between the sexes, for the purposes of that particular society. It is a ruling about *how the two sexes must come to think about themselves and about each other.*[48]

It is essential to realize, moreover, that Plato's prescriptive use of "nature" and "natural" is by no means confined to this passage. Plato's apparently contradictory conclusions about the nature of women in his two societies become far more intelligible when we appreciate that he tends to use "natural" and "according to nature" much more as a sanction with which to underline and enforce decisions he has already made by other means, than as a standard by which to make decisions in the first place. This point is most clearly demonstrated by analysis of his use of the other animals—free from the taint of human convention or *nomos*—as an example to hold up before man.

The use of animals as examples of what is natural and therefore good, in comparison with man's often corrupted patterns of behavior, was certainly popular with the classical Greeks. Homer, as one of his most recent editors has affirmed, "has no superiority complex in relation to the animals, and admires the qualities even of wasps and flies."[49] Again, one of the main themes of Aristophanes' *The Birds* is that of how happy and orderly the life of birds is, in comparison to that of men, with all their complex and depraved institutions and customs. Plato, too, makes use of this currently popular mode of persuasion, but, as H. D. Rankin has aptly said, "Plato does not consistently employ a naturalistic basis of comparison between man and other animals in his social thinking; 'animal analogy' is more like an auxiliary support for theories already formed."[50] Thus, in the *Republic*, the guardians are said to be chosen according to criteria applicable to dogs; those with that philosophical nature which combines gentleness with fierceness in the right proportions make the best rulers just as they make the best guard dogs. Later, when Socrates introduces his proposal for the training and use of the female guardians, he refers to the absence of distinct sex roles among these same dogs, in order to persuade his audience of the unnaturalness of such distinction in the human sphere as well. Again, it is the way noble animals are bred that is held up as the example to be followed if the best guardians are to be produced. But, clearly, if such criteria were applied consistently to either of Plato's two social constructs—the *Laws*, and especially the *Republic*—each would fail miserably. For both are incredibly complex artefacts, constructed of conventions arrived at as the best for distinctively *human* society, via the merciless tests of rational argument. For every institution for which the behavior of animals can be appealed to for support, there are countless proposals which have no conceivable parallel in the animal world. The example of what the animals do is used very selectively indeed.

The area of sexual taboos is another one in which the appeal to the natural behavior of animals is striking, especially in the *Laws*. The mating of male with male or of female with female is asserted to be contrary not only to man's human nature, but even to his animal nature, since this type of sexual behavior is quite unknown among ani-

FEMALE NATURE AND SOCIAL STRUCTURE

mals.[51] The practices of birds and many other animals are raised as an example of the "dictates of nature," on which the citizens should base their sexual standard—that of totally faithful monogamy throughout their lives.[52] What Plato does *not* mention is that, as he must have known, just as many animals mate "promiscuously" as mate "monogamously," and many practice incest habitually. Those animals which can serve as examples to press a point are appealed to; the others are quietly ignored.

Plato was well aware of the disparities, made famous by Herodotus' striking findings about funeral rites, amongst the practices that different societies regard as natural, and therefore sacred.[53] The line between *nomos* and *physis* becomes blurred as the strength and age of conventional taboos increase to the point where any behavior that violates them comes to be regarded as contrary to nature. Plato was clearly well aware of this cultural relativism. At the very place where he argues the unnaturalness of homosexual intercourse, he acknowledges to his Spartan and Cretan listeners that he is "probably . . . using an argument neither convincing nor in any way consonant with your States."[54] It is almost impossible, he recognizes, to persuade people that one of their customary practices is against the laws of nature. On the other hand, on the subject of public communal dining, the Athenian points out that whereas most peoples would regard such a practice as impossible for either sex, the Spartans, while considering it quite normal for men, regard the same practice as "non-natural" if applied to women.[55] Again, in the *Republic*, Plato reminds Glaucon, who finds the idea of women exercising naked in public quite ludicrous, that it is not long since the Greeks regarded the sight of naked men as not just ridiculous, but shameful, and that many of the barbarians still think this way. Indeed, "compared to what is habitual," he says, "many of the things now being said would look ridiculous if they were to be done as is said."[56]

Thus, Plato frequently exposes what is regarded as na-

tural and necessary as nothing more than alterable convention. However, while he clearly saw that even those customs
which were supposedly sanctioned by "the dictates of nature" were in fact variable from one culture to another, and
were thus in fact matters of *nomos* rather than, as claimed,
physis, Plato was very much aware of the strength of such
taboos, and of their consequent use to the legislator. Incest
was a prime example. Plato remarks in the *Laws* that most
people never *think* of committing incest, since they have
heard it so frequently condemned as severely shameful and
unforgivable,[57] and he proposes that the same weapon of
universally held public opinion should be utilized against
other kinds of sexual irregularity, such as homosexuality
and extramarital intercourse, which the legislator has concluded are antagonistic to the welfare and virtue of the
people. The same kind of sanction is used to support the
guardians' mating system. Although the system has clearly
been constructed for basically utilitarian, eugenic reasons,
it is to be regarded by all the citizens as "sacred in the
highest possible degree."[58]

It is apparent from the total context of the Platonic
dialogues that the rational, not the natural, is their author's
central standard. Nevertheless, Plato is quite ready to use
the powerful sanction of nature, in cases where it is applicable, in order to add weight to the conclusions he has
reached by means of rational argument. What is "natural"
is, in fact, what the philosophic ruler, judging what customs
and institutions are best for the city, *tells* its citizens is
natural. The application of this use of the natural to the
subject of women is not only interesting within the context
of Plato's political philosophy, but also important because
of the continued use of very similar reasoning, though far
less consciously, by others since Plato who have written on
the same subject.

Plato knew from his own observation that there is no
such fixed quality as female human nature. He must have
looked at the Athenian and the Spartan women, and seen

two considerably different kinds of female nature; he knew
in addition that Amazons and Sarmatian women presented
types in even sharper contrast to that with which his audience was accustomed. As his Athenian stranger remarks in
criticism of the supposedly trained Spartan women, the
Sarmatian women "would seem like men beside them."[59]
Thus female nature is in fact what different societies have
made of it. Not only was Plato well aware of this; the very
different natures bestowed upon women in his own two
social constructs must be seen as his continuation of this
traditional treatment of the female sex.

In the *Republic*, because the abolition of property and
the family for the guardian class entails the abolition of
woman's traditional sphere, the natural difference between
the sexes is reduced to that of their roles in procreation.
Since the nature of the women of this class is declared to
be the same as that of the men, the radical proposal follows
that their educations and life styles are to be identical,
accordingly. Plato has prescribed an androgynous character
for all the guardians; both male and female are to be
courageous and gentle, and both, because of their education
and continued fellowship, will equally hold precious the
good of the entire community. For the purposes of this
society, therefore, the abolition of traditional sex roles is
declared to be far more in accordance with nature than is
the conventional adherence to them. In the *Laws*, by contrast, the reinstatement of property requires monogamy
and private households, which restores women to their role
of "private wives" and all that this entails. Although his
general statements about women's potential, therefore, are
considerably stronger here than in the *Republic*, Plato
cannot, because of the economic and social structure he has
prescribed, carry out to any significant extent the revolu-
tionizing of woman's role that would seem to follow logically from such beliefs. In this society, the "nature" of
woman must be different from the nature of man. She must
be pure and respectable, as befits a private wife who is to

ensure the legitimacy of the property owner's heir, while he is to retain the noble and courageous qualities which are far closer to those of the ideal guardian type. In addition, the women, who because of their prescribed role within the private household will be less inclined to civic virtue than the men, must be especially well disciplined because of this supposedly "natural" moral inferiority of the female sex. The society's needs dictate that a supposedly "natural" evil in women—which is presumably due to the fact that she is oriented toward the private sphere—be transformed into a supposedly "natural" feminine purity.

It has become clear, then, that Plato does not apply consistently to women the same arguments he applies when discussing the nature of men. In the *Republic*, in spite of revolutionary proposals regarding the female guardians, he fails to bring into play his beliefs in the power of socialization and education, thereby making his unique argument about women's potential less forceful than it might have been. In the *Laws*, on the other hand, having come to the radical conclusions about women's undeveloped capacities that he expresses in the form of the ambidexterity metaphor, he fails to follow through on these conclusions. The reason is clearly the reinstatement of the family and therefore of the role of wife—the transformation of women back into the appendages and the private property of men. The striking difference between the roles of women in the *Republic* and the *Laws*, then, is not because Plato changed his beliefs about the nature and capacities of women. To the contrary, his convictions appear to have changed in exactly the opposite way. The difference is due to the fact that private property and the family were abolished in the earlier dialogue and were reinstated in the latter. When woman is once again perceived as the privately owned appendage of a man, when the family and its needs define her function, the socialization and regulation prescribed for her must ensure that her "nature" is formed and preserved in accordance with this role.

PART II

ARISTOTLE

4

Woman's Place and Nature
in a Functionalist World

Aristotle's philosophy is strikingly different, in its aim and in its entire tone, from that of Plato. Whereas Plato, throughout the dialogues, is essentially critical, radically questioning the most sacredly held conventions of the world around him, Aristotle sets out to acquire knowledge of the way the world is, and, moreover, to explain why it is the way it is. There is probably no other philosopher, not even Hegel himself, whose work better fits the definition that Hegel gave to philosophy—that it is "its own time apprehended in thoughts."[1]

On the subject of scientific knowledge, Aristotle says: "We all suppose that what we know is not even capable of being otherwise. . . . Therefore the object of scientific knowledge is of necessity. Therefore it is eternal."[2] He sees the object of scientific inquiry as not simply correct observation of the world, but demonstration of why it is that the world and its constituent parts are, and must be, the way they are. This approach, moreover, is not peculiar to his natural philosophy, but deeply pervades his ethical and political writings also. He does not, like Plato, attempt to set out from a rational and autonomous base to examine and criticize prevailing modes of behavior, opinions and standards. Aristotle's very different method of inquiry into these areas of thought is clearly described in the *Nichomachean Ethics*, at the outset of his discussion of one of the virtues. He states:

> We must, as in all other cases, set the observed facts before us and, after first discussing the difficulties, go

on to prove, if possible, the truth of all the common
opinions about these affections of the mind, or, failing
this, of the greater number and the most authoritative;
for if we both refute the objections and leave the common opinions undisturbed, we shall have proved the
case sufficiently.[3]

He perceives his task as moral philosopher, then, as that of
redeeming prevailing moral views and standards from whatever inconsistencies or vaguenesses might mar them. The
assumption is that they are far more likely to be right than
wrong.[4] Aristotle's ethics is, to a large extent, traditional
ethics, clarified and justified. Unlike Plato, he does not
argue, in dealing with ethics any more than with biology,
that the world should be different from the way it is, but
starts from a basic belief that the *status quo* in both the
natural and the social realm is the best way for things to be.

This conservative approach, however, is not simply assumed dogmatically, but has its own rationale. Things are
the way they are, Aristotle argues, because of the function
each of them performs, and their survival is proof that they
perform their functions well. He asserts, at the beginning
of the *Politics*, "All things derive their essential character
from their function and their capacity; and it follows that
if they are no longer fit to discharge their function, we
ought not to say that they are still the same things."[5]

Aristotle's functionalist outlook is very clearly illustrated
by the account he gives of the nature of the soul. Although
psyche, soul or essence, is a characteristic found only in
living beings, it is defined in reference to two things that
are clearly instrumental or functional—an axe and an eye.
First Aristotle asserts, "If some utensil, for example an axe,
were a natural body, then 'being-an-axe' would be its substance, and this would be its soul. Apart from this, it would
no longer be an axe, save equivocally." Then he adds, "If
the eye were an animal, sight would be its soul."[6] Clearly, in
Aristotle's view, the soul of a thing is its capacity to fulfill

its function, and while this seems reasonable enough when applied to artefacts or organs of the body, he extends it further, stating, "What, therefore, holds of a part, we ought to apply to the whole living body."[7] There is obviously no recognition by Aristotle of the significant distinction between natural beings and either artefacts or the component parts of natural beings. Not only does he perceive the relationship between soul and body as an instrumental one, as when he says that "each art must use its tools, and the soul its body,"[8] but he also perceives the entire living creature in an instrumental or functional manner.

Certain prerequisites, however, are necessary, for beings to be perceived in terms of their functions. Clearly, a thing can be thought of as having a function only in relation to some other thing or things. This is why tools and parts of the body are archetypal examples of things that are thought of functionally. In order to postulate that living beings, in a manner parallel to artefacts or organs, have functions, they must be viewed in relationship to each other and to the world as a whole, in a particular kind of way. Aristotle provides such a world view.

While acknowledging that the earlier natural philosopher, Democritus, had recognized that natural phenomena are necessary, Aristotle criticized him for having omitted the concept of "final cause" or purpose. "It is of course true," Aristotle agrees, "that (all the things which Nature employs) are determined by necessity, but at the same time they are for the sake of some purpose, some Final Cause, and for the sake of that which is *better* in each case."[9] The last clause of this assertion points us to the crucially important fact that Aristotle's view of the world is completely hierarchical. His entire universe, from the lowliest plant to the human race, and beyond the human race to the heavenly bodies and the gods, is arranged in a strict hierarchy, and it is this that enables him to say, "In the world of nature as well as of art the lower always exists for the sake of the higher."[10]

Thus, frequently stressing that "nature makes nothing in vain," Aristotle argues that plants exist to give subsistence to animals, and animals to give it to men. Since man is clearly at the top of the scale of mortal beings, "all animals must have been made by nature for the sake of men."[11] The vision is not just an anthropocentric one, however. While all human beings are the highest of animals, within the human race, too, the hierarchical ordering is maintained. When Aristotle approaches the study of society, he arrives quickly at some fundamental and very firmly held premises, which are to function as the bases of his ethics and politics. These are that the Greek *polis* is the natural, and therefore best, form of political association, and that the Greek family—with its subordination of wife, children and slaves—is the natural, and therefore best, form of household and family structure. In order to see how he arrives at these beliefs, which of course gain a large part of their strength from the fact that these institutions *were* the Greek world of Aristotle's time, we must examine what he conceives the function of man to be.

Near the beginning of the *Nichomachean Ethics*, Aristotle determines that happiness is the final and self-sufficient end of human activity, and sets out to give an account of what this happiness consists in. "This might perhaps be given," he says, "if we could first ascertain the function of man."[12] Significantly, the function that is peculiar to man, unlike the functions of the lower members on the scale of being, is not found to be some purpose he serves for a being higher on the scale. While man shares some characteristics, such as nutrition, growth and sensation, with the lower animals, Aristotle concludes that what is peculiar to him alone is his reason. Since this is his distinguishing feature, man's highest good is the "active life of the element that has a rational principle."[13] Man's relationship to those above him in the hierarchy is not that of serving some purpose of theirs; though his reasoning power makes him akin to the gods, whose whole existence is spent in rational contemplation, it is clearly for his own sake, not theirs, that he emulates them. His objective is his own happiness, not the fulfillment of the needs of another. In fact, Aristotle is well aware that the gods, anthropomorphic as they are, are the idealization of the highest human virtues, reason and self-sufficiency. The gods are the way they are because man imagines them thus: "We make the lives of the gods in the likeness of our own—as we also make their shapes."[14] It is therefore hardly coincidental that man's highest virtue is also the defining characteristic of the gods, or that the gods are depicted as perpetually engaged in that activity which man has decided on as the most worthwhile for himself.

Thus, whereas most beings serve a function in relation to some higher being, and whereas most activities have an end which lies outside the activity itself and to which it is subordinate, man's proper end is his own happiness, and "the activity of reason, which is contemplative, seems . . . to aim at no end beyond itself, and to have its pleasure proper to itself."[15] The proper activity of man alone among mortals has no end or aim outside of the actor himself.

The word for "man" that Aristotle uses throughout his arguments about the nature of man, and man's highest good, is *anthropos*, the Greek word meaning "human being." It soon becomes very clear, however, that only a small minority of one sex of the human race is to share in what have been characterized as the human virtues and man's highest good and happiness. For "man" requires not only his reason, but also certain essential external goods, if he is to live the good life. He cannot be happy, Aristotle tells us, without assets such as riches, friends, many and good children, leisure, noble birth, and beauty. Some of these clearly depend on the service of other people. Thus, in accordance with his characteristic teleology, Aristotle argues that not only the entire animal kingdom, but the vast majority of humans as well, are intended by nature to be the instruments which supply to the few the necessities and comforts that will enable them to be happy in their contemplative activity. Thus, women, slaves, and artisans and traders are all subsidiary instruments for the achievements of the highest happiness of "man." "In the state," Aristotle asserts, "the conditions which are necessary for the existence of the whole are not organic parts of the whole system which they serve."[16] Human good and human happiness have been defined in such a way that the vast majority of the human race is necessarily excluded from the achievement of either.

From time to time, presumably to make his functionalism appear more palatable, Aristotle argues that the relationships between those whom he perceives as naturally ruling and naturally ruled, such as husband and wife, or master and slave, are good for both parties because the capacities of these are very different. This kind of reasoning forms a substantial part of his argument for slavery. Although the slave is characterized as an instrument or tool, we are told that "the condition of slavery is both beneficial and just" for him, that the relationship between him and his master is "for the preservation of both," and that the two of them "have an identical interest."[17] Moreover, Aristotle argues that in the relationships between soul and body, craftsman and tool, and master and slave, "the latter in each case is benefited by that which uses it."[18] In a parallel manner, he argues, first, that husband and wife have a mutually beneficial relationship—that "they help each other by throwing their peculiar gifts into the common stock," and, second, that it is in fact the woman who is the beneficiary, and the man the benefactor of their relationship.[19]

As we might expect, however, given the hierarchical structure of Aristotle's world, these illusions of mutuality and of benefits accruing to the inferior party are not consistently maintained. With regard to slaves, they very soon disappear. We are told that the relationship is primarily in the interest of the master and only incidentally in that of the slave, "who must be preserved in existence if the rule itself is to remain."[20] In general, moreover, speaking of all such pairs of the ruling and the ruled, Aristotle asserts, "Nor is the good divisible between them but that of both belongs to the one for whose sake they exist."[21] Again, in a context which explicitly includes reference to the rule of men over women, he says that "the ruled may be compared to flute-makers: rulers are like flute-players who use what the flute-makers make."[22]

Aristotle asserts that women are "naturally" inferior to men, and that they are therefore "naturally" ruled by them. However, his use of the word *physis* (nature) and its derivatives is at least as complex and ambiguous as Plato's.[23] Sometimes, clearly, he uses "natural" to refer to innate as opposed to acquired characteristics.[24] At times, again like Plato, he acknowledges that very little clear distinction can be made between the nature of a mature being and the habits it has acquired throughout its life.[25] Aristotle's most usual use of the word "nature," however, is intimately connected with his functionalist approach to the world. I have already pointed out that he considered the "essential character" of a thing to be derived from its function, and the soul of each thing to be its capacity to function. Thus, when he tells us at the beginning of the *Politics* that "what each thing is when its growth is completed we call the nature of that thing, whether it be a man or a horse or a family,"[26] we must not fail to take into account the essential connection which exists in his mind between the way a thing should grow and develop, and its function. It is noteworthy that when he first introduces the three basic relationships that exist within the household, he states his intention to examine "the nature of each and the qualities it ought to possess."[27] It is clear that, in Aristotle's world, these two factors are virtually synonymous. Thus, when he makes the extraordinary statement that "dealing with . . . animate beings, we must fix our attention, in order to discover what nature intends, not on those which are in a corrupt, but on those which are in a natural condition,"[28] it is necessary to perform a substitution of the two equivalents—the nature of a thing, and the goodness pertaining to that thing —in order to give the proposition any content. We must acknowledge Aristotle's normative use of the word "natural," and give the "natural" at the end of his sentence a distinct moral connotation. In order to be meaningfully contrasted with "corrupt," it must mean "well-ordered" or "good," and Aristotle's statement is no longer value free, as it at first appeared. Moreover, as the above discussion of his functionalism indicates, nothing is well-ordered or good unless it can perform and does perform the function ascribed to it within Aristotle's hierarchical world. Thus Aristotle has established a philosophical framework by which he can legitimize the status quo. For the conventional function of any person determines that person's goodness, and a person's nature, or natural condition, is also equated with his or her goodness. Every person, therefore, is naturally suited to his or her existing role and position in society.

Aristotle's arguments about the nature of things and beings, especially of those within the human social realm, are virtually unintelligible unless one continually recognizes his esoteric use of the term. The family exists "by nature"; the *polis* exists "prior in the order of nature to the family and the individual."[29] By saying that the family is natural, Aristotle by no means intends to imply that it has always existed, but rather that its existence is necessary for the well-ordered life of man. The reason that the *polis* is prior in the natural order is, likewise, not that it is more original or basic than the family. It is because, while the family exists "for the satisfaction of daily recurrent needs" and sustains mere life, the *polis* is the only association within which man can enjoy that self-sufficiency which enables him to live the rational life, the highest life to which he can aspire. The *polis* is more natural, in other words, because of the superiority of its aim or object, which makes it a better institution than the family.

Similarly, Aristotle's arguments about the naturalness of

slavery are incomprehensible unless one recognizes his totally teleological version of the natural. For his attempts to convince us that some people are by nature slaves are most unpersuasive if we rely on his claims that natural slaves are those men "who differ from others as much as the body differs from the soul, or an animal from a man."[30] It is only if we accept the premises that society is most properly structured when it enables the privileged few to spend their lives in rational activity, and that the functions and therefore the nature of all others must be fixed accordingly, that we can accept Aristotle's justification of slavery as natural.

The same considerations apply to Aristotle's conclusions about the nature and the natural position of women. These can be understood only by reference to the function the female sex is perceived as fulfilling in the stratified society he assumes to be the best for man. At the beginning of his discussion of the household, Aristotle informs his reader that, contrary to what the barbarians think,

> the female and the slave are naturally distinguished from one another. Nature makes nothing in a spirit of stint, as smiths do when they make the Delphic knife to serve a number of purposes: she makes each separate thing for a separate end; and she does so because each instrument has the finest finish when it serves a single purpose and not a variety of purposes.[31]

As the context makes very clear, the slave's function is the provision of the daily needs of subsistence, whereas the female's primary function is reproduction.

On the subject of woman's function, which is on the whole implicit in the *Politics*, we must turn to Aristotle's biological writings for clarification. Reproduction was a subject in which he had an intense interest, since he regarded it as the "most natural" of the operations of mature living beings.[32] In fact, however, compared with the astounding accuracy and originality of his biological findings as a whole, Aristotle's "observations" about sexual reproduction contain a number of serious errors, of which virtually all are attributable to his basic assumption that the male is always and in every way superior to the female.

The reason for the very existence of the sexual form of reproduction in most animals, Aristotle argues, is the superiority of form over matter. His "observations" of sexual reproduction informed him that the male, via his semen, always provides the form or soul of the offspring, while the female, via her menstrual discharge, provides the matter. Since "the Form, is *better* and more divine in its nature than the Matter, it is *better* also that the superior one should be separate from the inferior one. That is why whenever possible and so far as possible the male is separate from the female."[33]

Thus Aristotle explains the need for sexual reproduction in terms of his hierarchical view of the world. Indeed, he argues that it was only the need for this higher form of reproduction that made nature stray from the generic type of each species, which is clearly perceived by him as that embodied in the male. Immediately prior to explaining the appearance of "monstrosities" in nature, he accounts for the "first deviation," which occurs "when a female is formed instead of a male." This deviation from the norm, we are told, "is a necessity required by Nature, since the race . . . has got to be kept in being." Altogether, he concludes, "we should look on the female as being as it were a deformity, though one which occurs in the ordinary course of nature."[34] Even with respect to reproduction, the only reason she exists at all, the female is characterized as inferior and disabled. It is the male who performs the active role, whereas the female merely acts as a passive receptacle for the new life. It is he who provides the new life with its soul, which is after all the raison d'être of the body that she furnishes. "A woman," Aristotle concludes, "is as it were an infertile male," and even in regard to reproduction, "a male is male in virtue of a particular ability, and a female in virtue of a particular inability."[35] In all this, moreover, "what happens is what one would expect to happen," and "in all her workmanship herein Nature acts in every particular as reason would expect."[36]

The proposals made in the *Politics* for the regulation of marriage and breeding clearly reflect these biological beliefs and Aristotle's perception of woman as fundamentally an instrument for breeding men. Marriage is regarded solely as an institution for "the provision of a stock of the healthiest possible bodies (for) the nurseries of our state,"[37] and the age of marriage should therefore be when both partners are at the height of their procreative powers, with the woman in her late teens, and the man in his late thirties. Following the oracle, Aristotle recommends that the citizens "plough not the young fallow"; when mothers are too young they have great difficulty in childbirth. In keeping with his general theory of reproduction, since the mother provides only the matter for the child and the father its rational soul, it is only the father's mental prime that is taken into account, and while the mother is advised to exercise and eat well while pregnant, since the growing foetus draws on her body, her mind should be kept idle, in order that more of her strength be preserved for the child's growth. Since the child is in no way perceived as drawing on the mother's mind, the development of her mind is quite needless.[38]

In spite of her widespread inabilities, then, woman is necessary for the reproduction of man, and this is therefore seen by Aristotle as her natural function. After all, if it were not for the requirements of sexual reproduction, this particular "deformity in nature" would never have existed. Within the well-ordered society, however, reproduction is not woman's only function. Unlike the other animals, man dos not couple by chance and temporarily, since he "is not only a political but also a householding animal." For "human beings live together," Aristotle argues, "not only for the sake of reproduction but also for the various purposes of life; for from the start the functions are divided, and those of man and woman are different." While it is the man's function to acquire, it is the woman's "to keep and store."[39] The necessity of all the things and services provided by the household for daily life, taken together with the assumption that all other classes of people are intended by nature to enable the few to pursue their truly human activities, leads Aristotle to regard the entire conventional division of labor between the sexes as strictly in accordance with nature.

Aristotle's reaction to Plato's radical proposals about the family and women is extremely illuminating in this context. In Book II of the *Politics*, Aristotle argues at great length against Plato's proposal to abolish the family. He voices three major objections. First, he maintains, though not very convincingly, that the unity which Socrates regards as the supreme good for the *polis*, and which he aims to ensure by abolishing the private family and making the guardians into one big family, will have the effect of destroying the *polis*. "It is obvious," he argues, "that a *polis* which goes on and on, and becomes more and more of a unit, will eventually cease to be a *polis* at all." Rather, it will tend toward being a household, or even an individual.[40] Too much unity, or sameness, is very bad for a *polis*, which "by its nature is some sort of aggregation." Secondly, and, it seems, contradictorily, he argues that Plato's proposed extension of the bonds of kinship would have the effect of weakening them so much that they would be worthless. Since men care most for what is their own, Aristotle claims, the result would be the general neglect of people by each other, since no one would have any relatives who cared exclusively for him. Finally, it concerns Aristotle immensely that not knowing who one's relatives are would lead to an increase in breaches of "natural piety," in the form of such crimes as incest, parricide, and fratricide. These arguments against Plato are not compelling. The first can be combatted by reference to the fact that there were to be other types of diversity within the ideal state, so that the abolition of the family would by no means result in excessive sameness. Besides, Aristotle's first two arguments seem to be mutually inconsistent; if doing away with the family would severely dilute the bonds of kinship, how could it at the same time lead to much unity? The third argument seems no more convincing than Plato's contrary assertion that the formation of all the guardians into one family would result in the extension of the traditional kinship loyalties and taboos throughout the entire ruling class.

However, Aristotle certainly considers himself to have demolished Plato's case, and continues to regard the private family and household as the only, natural and necessary basis for social life. As was mentioned earlier, it was a central aspect of his philosophical method to begin by discussing previous and especially authoritative views on the subject at issue. Since Book II of the *Politics* is in large part taken up with the survey of previous writers' ideas about the abolition of the family, the equalization or communalization of property, and other such radical reforms, it is conspicuous that Aristotle has almost nothing to say about the extremely radical and unorthodox proposals of Book v of the *Republic* regarding equal education and opportunities for women. Apart from a fleeting reference, he merely comments on Plato's analogous reference to male and female dogs, which, he had claimed, are an example to humans because they do not adhere to rigid sex roles. Aristotle's answer, moreover, is virtually unintelligible unless it is recognized that both for him and for Plato, once the issue of the family is settled, that of the role of women is not an independent one. For Aristotle asserts, puzzled by Plato's ignorance of the obvious, that the analogy is quite unsuitable, since "animals, unlike women, have no domestic duties."[41] It is quite clear that, since he considers himself to have refuted the idea of the community of women and children, he does not even consider it necessary to argue against Plato's wild ideas about women and their potential as individual persons. Given the family and the private household, women are private wives with domestic functions, and there is no more to be said on the subject.

Aristotle's assumption that woman is defined by her reproductive function and her other duties within the household permeates everything he has to say about her. Indeed, Aristotle's entire moral philosophy is much affected by the existence of the hierarchy which he considers to be natural because it is necessary for the attainment of the proper objective of human life. First, all the basic relationships discussed in the *Ethics*, such as friendship and justice, are perceived as differing radically in their natures, depending on the relative positions in society occupied by the two or more persons involved. Second, none of the basic moral terms, such as virtue, temperance, or courage, are held to be universally applicable, since a person's position in the human hierarchy, and consequent function, determine the particular type of virtue, temperance, or courage that will be required of him or her. I will discuss each of these two issues in turn.

Because he perceives woman as naturally inferior to man, Aristotle asserts that all relationships between them must acknowledge and, insofar as possible, compensate for this inequality. Political justice, which he regards as the only type that genuinely deserves the name of justice, can exist only between equals, between those who have an equal share in ruling and being ruled, as fellow citizens do. In such a case, it is unjust for equals to be treated in any way other than equally. Where such parity between persons does not exist, however, justice is an entirely different matter, and can only metaphorically be called justice at all. Aristotle seems, however, to have been unsure as to the type of "metaphorical justice" that is properly applied to women. At first, he says that "justice can more truly be manifested toward a wife than toward children and chattels, for the former is household justice; but even this is different from political justice."[42] Subsequently, however, he appears to retract even this concession, comparing justice between husband and wife to that between master and slave (who is certainly a chattel) and to that between the rational and irrational parts of the soul.[43] Since he implies at times that a slave is not a human being at all, and he parallels the relationship between him and his master to that of despot and subject, we are left with the impression that, so far as justice is concerned, Aristotle has relegated woman to an altogether subhuman position.

Like the other moral relations, friendship, too, varies in accordance with the respective status of the friends in Aristotle's social hierarchy. Whereas there can be no friendship at all between a man and a slave *qua* slave (though paradoxically a man can be friends with the same individual *qua* man), the friendships between father and children and between husband and wife are categorized as friendship between benefactor and benefited. "The friendship of man and wife . . . ," Aristotle asserts, "is the same that is found in an aristocracy; for it is in accordance with virtue—the better gets more of what is good, and each gets what befits him; and so, too, with the justice in these relations."[44] The difference between various types of friendship depends both on the respective virtues and functions of the two persons and on the reasons for which they love each other. In all friendships in which the friends are not equal, the love should be proportional to the merit of the two parties, for only if the better is loved more than he loves, will equality be restored.[45] In marriage, the husband is, of course, by virtue of his superiority always the benefactor and the more useful partner. As Aristotle's disciple argues in the *Oeconomica*, one reason that a wife must obey her husband and serve him sedulously is that "he has indeed bought her with a great price—with partnership in his life and the procreation of children; than which things nothing could be greater or more divine."[46] There is no emphasis placed, in such a context, on the fact that the woman's entire life is defined in terms of the function she performs for the man. And thus Aristotle concludes that it would be ludicrous for a wife to expect her affection to be returned in a similar way, just as it would be ludicrous for man to expect the same of God; "for it is the part of a ruler to be loved, not to love, or else to love in another way."[47] Friendship and marriage are no exception to the basic principle that relationships must always reflect the respective merits and functions of those who are party to them.

The second relevant phenomenon of Aristotle's ethics— the variable application of terms and standards—was by no means new at his stage of Greek thought. As A. W. H. Adkins has demonstrated in his illuminating book, *Merit and Responsibility*, the Greeks from the time of Homer to that of Aristotle, with the notable exception of Plato, had no concept of a single standard of human morality or excellence which might be applied to anyone, regardless of his or her role or position in society.[48] Their word of highest praise, *arete* (excellence or virtue), originated in the commendation of an entirely masculine, noble, and leisured way of life, and could only be used of those who had the wherewithal, in terms of both high birth and their command of material goods and other people's services, to pursue such a life. As I noted above, in Chapter 1, "woman's *arete*" was a relative term, consisting of a set of qualities entirely different from those of men, who alone could achieve absolute excellence. This was the immense weight of custom and opinion that Socrates was combatting, both in the *Meno*, in claiming the irrelevance of sex to *arete*, and in the *Republic*, in implying that sex is no more related to the soul than baldness is. The importance of these passages in the gradual universalizing of ethical values must not be underestimated.

In his ethical and political writings, Aristotle reacts against these heresies of Socrates, and both consolidates and justifies the traditional way of thinking. Having defined the highest human virtue as reason, he constructs a functionalist rationalization of a society in which this highest virtue can be shared in only by those at the top of the class- and sex-determined hierarchy. As Adkins asserts, "Thus Aristotle leaves no hope of establishing any standard for the whole community."[49] Even free males whose work is considered menial are excluded from the possibility of participation in the higher things of life, and what is the case for artisans is, of course, even more the case for slaves, and for women of any class at all. Women's work is clearly regarded as in no way compatible with the life of excellence.[50]

What Aristotle does, therefore, is to define the goodness of each thing and each person according to its function; "let it be assumed as to goodness," he says, "that it is the best disposition or state or faculty of each class of things that have some use or work."[51] His examples extend from a coat, a ship, and a house, to a soul. While it is quite easy for us to accept this functional characterization of the excellence of artefacts, and to agree with Aristotle that "what is healthy or good is different for men and for fishes," it is jarring to the modern ear to hear the adjectives of commendation which we are accustomed to think of as constant in their meanings, applied differently to different classes of human beings. But for Aristotle, human beings have functions just as much and in the same way as artefacts do, and only those at the very top of the hierarchy have a function which is defined only in relation to themselves and not to others. There are two fundamentally different orders of human goodness. The goodness of the leisured and fully rational men is something absolute, while all the others can achieve only forms of goodness that are relative and inferior. Their goodness is determined entirely by their respective functions, and all these functions are inferior to that of those at the top. Thus, although they cannot attain the higher form of goodness, "even a woman is 'good' and so is a slave, although it may be said that a woman is an inferior thing and a slave beneath consideration."[52]

Even in the case of the free male citizen, it is "his good discharge of his function" which determines his excellence,[53] and in the good *polis* he will have two sorts of goodness, since because of his constitutional equality with his fellow citizens he must rule and be ruled in turn. He must therefore have "one sort [of excellence] which fits him to act as a ruler, and one which fits him to act as a subject."[54] Women, however, together with all the other persons who are necessary conditions but not parts of the *polis*, require only the kind of goodness which fits them to be ruled, since this is their natural and permanent role.

All the moral standards applied to woman, therefore, are determined by her function as the bearer of new citizens and the guardian of the household. Since she has a different function from that of the slave, so must her goodness be different, just as the slave's differs from that of the artisan. Aristotle asserts:

> They must all share in (moral goodness), but not in the same way—each sharing only to the extent required for the discharge of his or her function. The ruler, accordingly, must possess moral goodness in its full or perfect form because his function . . . demands a master-artificer, and reason is such a master artificer; but all other persons need only possess moral goodness to the extent required of them. It is thus clear that . . . temperance—and similarly fortitude and justice—are not, as Socrates held, the same in a woman as they are in a man. Fortitude in the one, for example, is shown in connexion with ruling; in the other, it is shown in connexion with serving; and the same is true of the other forms of goodness. . . . To speak in general terms, and to maintain that goodness consists in "a good condition of the soul," or in "right action," or in anything of the kind, is to be guilty of self-deception. Far better than such general definitions is the method of simple enumeration of the different forms of goodness. . . .[55]

Accordingly, throughout his works, Aristotle proceeds to apply distinct moral standards to the two sexes, as well as to different classes of men. He says, for example, that Sophocles' statement, "A modest silence is a woman's crown" is "a general truth—but a truth which does not apply to men."[56] Both the bodily and the moral excellences of the two sexes are differently defined. Whereas both require beauty and stature, only the male should have strength and fitness for athletic contests. Whereas both should have self-control, in the male this should be supplemented by courage, but in the female by "industrious habits, free from servility."[57] For what use is courage to one whose occupation must be the care of a house and the provision of food and clothes for her family? Moreover, Aristotle asserts that it is not at all appropriate for a woman to be "manly or clever," and criticizes Euripides for creating a female character with these unsuitable qualities.[58]

The only people who need to possess a full complement of reason, Aristotle argues, are those who rule over others. While practical wisdom is necessary in rulers, only "right opinion" is required in women, slaves, and others who are permanently ruled.[59] Thus, when he ascribes to the various members of the household different amounts of reason, we are not surprised to find that each has just that portion of rationality that is necessary for the performance of his or her function:

> It is true that all these persons possess in common the different parts of the soul; but they possess them in different ways. The slave is entirely without the faculty of deliberation; the female indeed possesses it, but in a form which remains inconclusive; and if children also possess it, it is only in an immature form.[60]

Why should nature, who makes nothing in vain, have given woman full rationality, when her function does not require it?

Thus, Aristotle has established the standards of physical, mental and moral excellence in woman according to the functions she performs for man. To be the best of women, she must have many qualities, such as quietness and modesty, that are undesirable in a man. On the other hand, she must *not* have many qualities, such as manliness, strength or cleverness, that are required of a good man. Having prescribed for the two sexes separate and frequently conflicting standards of excellence, however, Aristotle proceeds to weigh perfection in woman against perfection in man, and to conclude that woman, even the best possible woman, falls short.

In the *Eudemian Ethics*, it is asserted that "the state of human character called human goodness is of two kinds." "Let us assume," Aristotle continues, "that man is one of the things that are excellent by nature," and he concludes that man's form of goodness is "good absolutely," while that of the others who are not excellent by nature is good only relatively—"only good for that thing."[61] The two examples chosen to illustrate this are the goodness of a man as compared with that of a woman, and the goodness of a gifted man as compared with that of a dull one. In each case, the latter is clearly an inferior kind of goodness. This same point is repeated several times in the other works—for example, in the *Rhetoric*, when we are told that "virtues and actions are nobler, when they proceed from those who are naturally worthier, for instance, from a man rather than from a woman."[62] What has happened is that Aristotle arrives at the conclusion that woman is inferior to man by a completely circular process of reasoning. Because he perceives woman as an instrument, he has assigned her an entirely separate scale of values, and then he measures her against the scale of male values, and finds her inferior. But the functionalist treatment of women is itself founded on the assumption of the Aristotelian hierarchy, in which woman is "naturally" placed in an inferior position.

Aristotle's view of society as rigidly hierarchical, patriarchal, and functional allows him to "prove" things about its various classes by drawing on assumptions that already presuppose the things he claims to prove. If it were not for his initial assumption that the free and leisured male is the highest of mortal beings, there would be no grounds from which to argue that all other members of the human race are naturally defined by their functions in relation to him. Objectively speaking, there is no more evidence for the proposition that women are intended by nature to reproduce men than that men are intended by nature to beget women (as the Amazons may have argued in their version of the *Politics*).

Aristotle determines that woman is inferior by considering the functions she performs and the relevant qualities she manifests in Athenian society. This was a society, however, in which she was thoroughly disadvantaged and oppressed—a society dominated by men, in which her role and all the qualities valued in her were dictated by men. Aristotle is not interested in the qualities of women apart from this context. Thus, in spite of his expressed beliefs in the power of the environment to shape and alter the human character and abilities, he is no more interested in applying these beliefs to women than in applying them to slaves. Except for the free and leisured man, Aristotle is not interested in the potential of any living being, but only in those "natural" and "naturally inferior" characteristics which enable each person to perform his or her proper function in the social system which has his approval and which he sets out to justify.

The fact that Aristotle treats the vast majority of people as instruments, and condemns them to a necessarily less-than-human existence, has been treated in various ways by students of his works. A few, even at this point in time, feel no compulsion to take issue with the way in which he disposes of either women or the majority of men. Harry Jaffa, for example, is content merely to summarize what Aristotle says about women, and actually seeks to justify his argument that there are natural slaves.[63] At the other extreme, John Ferguson, in his recent book on Aristotle, points to "the extraordinary mixture of sound scientific observation and grotesque class prejudice" which resulted in the philosopher's teleological conclusions about all relations within the household. Ferguson realistically suggests, moreover, that "those who reject Aristotle's view of the political inferiority of 'servants' and women must be sure that they do not suffer from residual prejudices and are offering an equality that is practical as well as theoretical."[64]

Ferguson's attitude, however, is exceptional among scholars of Aristotle. A number of them, in more recent years, have indeed felt impelled to dissociate themselves from the arguments for slavery. W. D. Ross, for example, says, "What cannot be commended in Aristotle's view . . . is his cutting of the human race in two with a hatchet."[65] No one, Ross objects, can be legitimately treated as both a tool and a man. He objects, too, to Aristotle's regarding the class of mechanics as merely a means to the existence of the *polis* and the happiness of its privileged class. "Society cannot," he argues, "in fact be split into two parts of which one is merely a means to the welfare of the other. Every human being is capable of a life worth living for itself."[66] In the middle of all this dissent, however, Ross upholds Aristotle's defense of the family against Plato, and points out his recognition of it as "a natural and normal extension of personality, a source of pleasure and an opportunity of good activity."[67] Nowhere does he recognize that Aristotle's "family" involves the treatment of women as mere means to the welfare of men, or that this "natural and normal extension" of the man's personality entails the obliteration of the woman's. Compared with the opportunities available to Plato's female guardians, the Aristotelian household can hardly be regarded as "a source of pleasure and an opportunity of good activity" for its *female* members. Because of his own prejudices, Ross does not see that this other cutting in half of the human race, according to sex, is just as indefensible as that separating master and slaves.

Similarly, D. J. Allan, though he praises Aristotle for his "breadth of vision" and his "humanity," does acknowledge that his ideal *polis* does not appear to be "perfect" from the points of view of either the slave or the artisan.[68] He too, however, completely ignores the fact that Aristotle relegates women to a similar condition. Third, G. E. R. Lloyd also is critical of Aristotle's antiegalitarian ideas about slaves, workers and barbarians. Asserting that Aristotle was, in these areas, hardly if at all in advance of contemporary opinion, he concludes that "the effect of his work was to provide some sort of rational justification for some deep-seated Greek prejudices." He simply summarizes, however, without comment, Aristotle's belief in the natural superiority of males to females.[69]

What may initially seem to be a coincidental lack of perception on the part of these scholars becomes totally intelligible in the light of one very significant fact. A large part of Aristotle's "social teleology"—that is, his functional treatment of most men—is no longer acceptable. Given the development, beginning in the seventeenth and eighteenth centuries, of modern concepts of equality and the rights of man, it is no longer regarded as justifiable to designate some men as by nature the instruments of others, or to set up different moral standards for different classes. Thus, those who wish to redeem Aristotle's political and moral philosophy as a whole are obliged either to go out of their way to argue anew for his treatment of slaves and workers, or else explicitly to dissociate themselves from this part of his thought, in order to free the remainder from its taint.

By contrast, the perception and treatment of women in purely functional terms has remained so prevalent that these intelligent scholars have not felt the need to argue against Aristotle's disposition of the female sex. In fact, it is fairly clear that they are unable to see that the injustice of his treatment of slaves, women and workers is all of a piece. The continuing existence of a double standard of values, which has replaced Aristotle's multiple one, allows them to regard his treatment of women as far more rational and defensible than his treatment of the majority of men. The birth of modern egalitarianism by no means brought with it the demand for the equal treatment of women, as the following analysis of Rousseau's thought on the subject will demonstrate.

PART III

ROUSSEAU

5

Rousseau and the Modern Patriarchal Tradition

The ideas of Jean-Jacques Rousseau on women—on their nature, their education, and their proper place in the social and political order—are worthy of thorough examination for three important reasons. The case he argues is, in a qualified sense, representative of the whole Western tradition regarding women; his views are, unusually, very consciously held and adamantly justified, in spite of the fact that they violate all the major principles of his ethics and social theory; and their effects are tragic, even within the context of his own philosophy.

Albeit in an exaggerated way and sometimes with almost hysterical fervor, Rousseau argues all the most commonly held assertions that have, as part of our patriarchal culture, rationalized the separation and oppression of women throughout the history of the Western world. He argues, to begin with, that woman's sharply distinct position and functions are those that are natural to her sex. It is interesting, since Rousseau was so much an advocate of the natural, to see how different his reasoning is about what is natural in and for women from about what is natural in and for "man." In keeping with a long tradition that as we have seen, reaches back to Aristotle and beyond, Rousseau defines woman's nature, unlike man's, in terms of her function—that is, her sexual and procreative purpose in life. While man has been categorized in terms of a generally limitless potential, for rational thought, creativity, and so on, woman has been viewed as functionally determined by her reproductive role, and her actual and potential abilities perceived as stunted, in accordance with what have been regarded as the requirements of this role. Woman's function is seen as physical and sensual, whereas man's potential is seen as creative and intellectual. For centuries, the extreme disparities between the method and extent of the education of the two sexes have been conveniently glossed over, as they are by Rousseau, as the case is made that women, while intuitive and equipped with a talent for detail, are deficient in rationality and quite incapable of abstract thought.[1]

Equally in keeping with a tradition that has invented Pandora, Clytemnaestra, Lilith, Eve, succubi and witches, Rousseau saw women as a major source of the world's evil. As a recent historian of patriarchal attitudes has said, "Woman as a source of danger, as a repository of externalized evil, is an image that runs through patriarchal history."[2] In Rousseau's writings about women, we can clearly discern his consciousness that it was woman who aroused in him that sexuality which produced in him feelings of both fear and guilt,[3] and who by her ability to arouse him endangered his independence and self-sufficiency. Since she is seen, in this sphere, as unlimitedly powerful, the conclusion drawn is that woman must be thoroughly subjugated in other spheres if even a balance of power, let alone man's superiority, is to be maintained. Since she is depicted as the source of sin and evil, her subjection is seen as her justified desert, and consequently Rousseau had his own version of God's cursing Eve with the pains of childbirth.[4]

As man's sexual object, woman must not only assume a subordinate position; she is also radically dichotomized. Man, with his passionate impulses and desire for pleasure, wants the female to be seductive and arousing; at the same time, out of fear of his own sexuality, he asks her to be responsible for controlling what he conceives to be his unlimited desires. Hence the demand for her to be asexual and chaste. Either different classes of women, or the same woman in a Jekyll and Hyde manner, have been required to be both highly desirable and icy pure, hypersexual and asexual. For Rousseau (who had an exaggerated terror of syphilis even in an age that was so concerned with it),[5] the solution that would provide two different types of women to fulfill the two functions was untenable. He represents, instead, a classic example of the demand for the individual woman to be both filled with shame and modesty about sexuality and as enticing as an eastern houri, to be as chaste as marble but to be made for love, to be sober and confined after marriage though coquettish and gay before, to refrain from the least gesture of flirtation with other men but to be everlastingly seductive toward her husband— in short, to be both virgin and prostitute.

Finally, the problem of establishing paternity—a matter of considerable importance in a number of other accounts of the status of women—was an obsession with Rousseau. He refers frequently in his works to the need for a man to be absolutely certain of the faithfulness of his wife in order to insure that his children are indeed his own, thus setting entirely different standards of morality for the two sexes. On this basis Rousseau justifies the absolute rule of men over their wives, the confinement of women in the home after marriage, the desirability of segregation of the sexes even within the household, and a moral education for women that is the complete opposite of what he proposes for the moral education of men. The standard of excellence in a man is a complex one, but the only important virtue in a woman is chastity.

Given the predispositions and general trends of thought indicated above, it is hardly surprising that Rousseau, the philosopher of equality and freedom, should not have applied these basic human values similarly to both sexes. As we shall see, when he undertook to explore the origins of inequality among men, it was literally men that were the subject of his investigation; the inequality of the sexes was assumed in passing, as though it did not also need to be investigated. Rousseau's failure to apply his most cherished ideals to the female sex will be analyzed in Chapter 7.

Rousseau's patriarchal theories about women are of course representative of a long tradition. They cannot, however, be glossed over as mere biases or assumptions of the contemporary scene or as anachronistic prejudices to which he gave little thought, which have slight bearing on the main body of his work, and which, in all deference to his genius, should be tactfully ignored. This is so for a number of reasons. *Emile*, in which the ideal education for women is described at length, was claimed by its author to be "the best and most important of all my works," and the one with which one should begin, in order to understand his whole philosophy.[6] The essentials of his thought, he asserted, are contained within *Emile* and the *First and Second Discourses*.[7] Moreover, it was Book 5 of *Emile*, about half of which is concerned with the rearing and education of the ideal woman, Sophie, which Rousseau claimed to be his favorite part of the work. And, as Pierre Burgelin has said of Book 5, "Quant au ton, ce qui concerne Sophie est écrit avec un frémissement que le reste ne comporte évidemment pas."[8] Again, the importance to Rousseau of his ideas and assertions about women is testified to by the fact that he wrote to a critic that the whole object of his *Letter to M. d'Alembert*, which we generally consider to be about the theater, was to demonstrate how women are to blame for the corruption of society.[9]

Rousseau was certainly not disposed, in general, to accept contemporary opinion or prejudice.[10] It is by no means predictable that such an iconoclast should take a not merely conservative, but positively reactionary stance on the issue of the position of women. He openly challenged those philosophers who regarded his views about women as old-fashioned prejudice and deceit, maintained by men to protect their patriarchal privileges, and took it upon himself to show that the subordination of women was not the result of mere prejudice or convention but was part of the natural and necessary order of things.[11] Thus while an independent man like Emile should not take account of the opinions of those around him with respect to other matters, the prejudice, so-called, that held a man accountable for his wife's misconduct was a unique and justifiable one, because the whole order of society depends on its being maintained.[12] Indeed, Rousseau claimed that the inequality between the sexes which is reflected in law and custom "is not of man's making, or at any rate it is not the result of mere prejudice, but of reason."[13]

In the period in which Rousseau wrote, there was no lack of discussion of the subject of women, their status in society, and the question of whether their subordination to men was their natural position or rather the result of centuries of discrimination practiced against them in the interests of patriarchal culture. In the *Lettres persanes*, Montesquieu had raised some of the central issues, such as the socialization of women, the importance of their sexual fidelity, and the institution of monogamy itself.[14] In the *Esprit des lois*, moreover, he states unequivocally that it is nature which has distinguished men by their reason and strength and women by their charms, and that the sexual boldness of men and shame and resistance of women are likewise dictated by nature.[15] On the other hand, Helvétius, in *De l'Homme et de l'éducation*, gives a very different explanation of the contemporary differences between the sexes. Referring to the examples of famous women in several important spheres of life, he argues that they are not naturally disadvantaged in comparison with men. "If women be in general inferior," he says, "it is because in general they receive a still worse education."[16] However, the first substantial application of Enlightenment theories about the importance of environment and education to the case of women is to be found in the chapter "Des Femmes" of Baron d'Holbach's *Système sociale*. "From the way in which women in all countries are brought up," he asserts, "it seems that it is only intended to turn them into beings who

retain the frivolity, fickleness, caprices and lack of reason
of childhood, throughout their lives."[17] The refusal of contemporary European society to give them a sensible education, he argues, is just another instance of the universal enslavement to which women have always been subjected. In
the *Encyclopédie* of the *philosophes*, too, there are a number of articles under the heading "Femmes," in which the
case is argued for and against the naturalness of various
female characteristics and of the subordination of women
to the authority of men.[18]

Moreover, not only was Rousseau not writing about wom-
en in a vacuum, but he himself had in his early adulthood
held views on the subject that were very different from
those he so adamantly asserted in his major works. He had
collaborated with a Mme. Dupin on a proposed book about
the condition of women in society, of which only a few pages
are known to be extant, and which was clearly to constitute
a violent and revolutionary attack on the position forced on
women.[19] His two brief essays on women, which date from
the 1730s when he was living at Chambéry, likewise reveal
Rousseau as having held far more radical opinions about
women and their proper role in his youth than in his middle age.[20] The latter then, for all the above reasons, are
certainly not unquestioned assumptions, but constitute a
consciously thought-out position.

The final major reason for the importance of Rousseau's
arguments about the proper education and role of women
is that the results of his proposals are tragic, even within
the confines of his own social theory. They are tragic, moreover, not only for women themselves, but for those two
institutions which he depicted as the ideal modes of human
experience. As we shall see in Chapter 8, a woman socialized
in the way Rousseau approved of, and subject to the constraints that he claimed were right for her, would have an
extremely high propensity for undermining the monogamous family and the ideal republic, and, moreover, for
being destroyed herself in the process. We have only to fol-

low and reflect on the fates of the two ideal women he created—Julie, in *La Nouvelle Héloise*, and Sophie, in *Emile* and its unfinished sequel—to see that his theory of the education and treatment of women, in practice leads to tragic conclusions. Rousseau's perceptive recognition of the conflicts of loyalties with which human beings are faced led him to pessimistic conclusions about the fate of man, but his conclusions concerning the fate of the only type of woman he could conceive of are even worse.

6

The Natural Woman
and her Role

The most prevalent argument used to justify the perpetuation of a distinct and subordinate sex role for the female is that such a role is natural. Far from being anything imposed on or developed in her by particular social, economic and cultural institutions, the passive, dependent, chaste, subrational, sensitive, nurturing characteristics of the female have been regarded as bestowed on her, directly and unmistakably, by nature.[1] Since Rousseau is the archetypal modern instance of this mode of argument, and since glorification of the natural is a theme that pervades his entire philosophy, it is important to examine with care exactly how his case is made.

A substantial part of Rousseau's writings in general is devoted to what amounts to a deification of the natural, in mankind and its mode of living, and to the rejection, or at least devastating criticism, of most of those results of civilization which his contemporaries were inclined to laud unambivalently as constituents of progress. The epigraph he chose from Aristotle's *Politics* to introduce the *Discourse on the Origin and Foundations of Inequality among Men* reads: "Not in corrupt things, but in those which are well ordered in accordance with nature, should one consider that which is natural." It may well be considered one of his most fundamental principles, and the refrain that "nature never lies" occurs throughout most of his works.[2] Just as Emile's education is so carefully planned in order to enable him to be a natural man in a corrupt world, so is

Sophie, his proposed wife, to be educated as a natural woman. Advising her to honor her position as a woman, Rousseau tells Sophie, "The essential thing is to be what nature made us. We are always too much inclined to be what men want us to be."[3] Since Sophie's education is such a complete contrast to Emile's, it is essential to see what reasoning is employed to discover the natural man and how it differs from that used to discover the natural woman.

Rousseau used two principal means to separate what is natural in man from the characteristics he has acquired from social life and civilization. One way was to try to separate the innate characteristics of the individual from those that are the product of his environment. The real purpose of *Emile* is to show what a man could be like, educated independently of popular prejudice. Rousseau claims to develop in Emile those innate qualities usually so stunted and warped by a corrupt society that we no longer know what man is really like. The sharp contrast between the ways he applies the nature/nurture distinction to the two sexes will be discussed below.

The other method for discovering natural man, through an hypothesized "state of nature," was of course by no means uniquely Rousseau's. The concept of the state of nature has been used by many philosophers in an attempt to strip away the historical accidentals and effects of social and/or political life, in order to find out what human nature and human relations are like in their most fundamental state. By some philosophers, for example Locke, the concept has been used simply to examine man in a state of lawlessness. In some versions, however, including Rousseau's, it is aimed at separating the effects on human beings of education, technological advance, the division of labor, private property, and a multitude of other social and political institutions, from a human nature that is construed as prior to all these accretions, logically if not chronologically. Then, at least usually, the theorist makes use of the conclusions reached in this manner to argue for a social and political order which is justified and legitimated by the human characteristics that have been established as natural.

This is the type of philosophical voyage of discovery that Rousseau embarks on in the *Discourse on the Origin and Foundations of Inequality among Men*. As he argues in the Preface to the work, in which he justifies his method, we cannot discover the source of inequality amongst men unless we know what man is really like. We must consider, not that disfigured and unrecognizable statue of Glaucus which so many factors in the history of society have distorted, but man "as nature formed him," in "his original constitution," with "his true needs, and . . . the principles underlying his duties." Only thus can we "succeed . . . in separating, in the present constitution of things, what divine will has done from what human art has pretended to do."[4] Making it very clear that he has no pretensions to historical accuracy, but aims only to clarify the nature of things by means of hypothetical reasoning, Rousseau sets out to discover the natural state of mankind. No previous philosopher claiming this discovery had, he asserts, actually penetrated as far back as natural man.

As has been noted,[5] Rousseau's discourse does not postulate a single, simple state of nature, but rather a series of several, culturally distinct stages. Of these, he suggests to the reader, "you will seek the age at which you would desire your species had stopped."[6] It is important to note both that the stage of mankind as isolated brutes, which is what he calls "the state of nature," is not the age at which he desires that his species had stopped, and, more importantly in the present context, that he refers back to different hypothesized stages in order to assert the "natural" status of different qualities and states of affairs. This is particularly true with respect to both the natural woman and the natural status of the family.

In the first section of the *Discourse on Inequality*, Rousseau draws a picture of what we will henceforth refer to as his "original state of nature." This was the stage at which, he hypothesizes, human beings of both sexes had lived isolated and nomadic lives, totally devoid of cooperation except for the momentary and chance encounters that satisfied their sexual impulses. Male and female copulated, with no preference for one individual over another, since they had no capacity for comparison. Then, each going his or her own way, they would not recognize each other if they met again. Thus, it is argued, natural and instinctual sexuality is radically different from sexual love as experienced in civilized society—from that terrible and impetuous passion which "in its fury, seems fitted to destroy the human race it is destined to preserve."[7] In the state of nature, sexuality was a simple animal appetite, analogous to hunger and the need for rest, an instinct designed to ensure the perpetuation of the species, and readily satisfied by any willing member of the opposite sex who chanced to pass by. What savage man experienced was just the physical part of the feeling of love, as opposed to the moral part, which attaches itself to one preferred object, and is "an artifical sentiment born of the usage of society."[8]

Since no one in this original state of nature had any contacts with, or even any means of recognizing, anyone else, the females were in practice the only parents of their offspring. Though not endowed with any maternal instinct, the female would suckle the child at first for the sake of her own comfort, and later because habit had endeared it to her. As soon as the child could subsist alone, it left her, and the two would no longer recognize each other. The human female, Rousseau argues, is well equipped to nourish her child and feed and protect herself as well, since she can carry it easily and without slowing her own pace. Indeed, he goes to great lengths, in a note, to argue fiercely against the "specious objection" that Locke had raised against the idea that natural man lived in isolation—the contention, that is, that the conjunction of the two parents in marriage is necessary for the survival of the human species, and that therefore no state of nature can reasonably be hypothesized that does not suppose the existence of the nuclear family.[9]

Without going into all the details of either Locke's argument or Rousseau's counter argument, it is important to point out several assertions in the latter that radically conflict with Rousseau's subsequent claims about the natural status of the family. First he claims that, in a natural state, prior to cohabitation, pregnancies would be likely to occur less frequently and children would be tougher and sooner able to fend for themselves, so that mothers, unlikely to have more than one dependent child at a time, would be quite capable of rearing them unaided. Second, in the original state of nature, since male and female separate after copulation, and no man therefore knows which children are his, there is no logical reason for him to help a female to rear her child. The assumption that he would is held up by Rousseau as a prime example of the failure of Locke, no less than Hobbes, to get beyond the centuries of society to the real state of nature, in which no one had any reason to cohabit or cooperate with anyone else. Third, Rousseau criticizes Locke's state of nature methodology in an even more devastating way. Locke is attacked on the grounds that he has used "moral proofs" in his argument for the natural existence of the family; he has referred to the male as "bound to take care for those he hath begot" and therefore "under an obligation" to stay with the female until the children can subsist on their own.[10] Such moral arguments, Rousseau objects, "do not have great force in matters of physics, and . . . they serve rather to give a reason for existing facts than to prove the real existence of those facts."[11] From his next statement it is clear that he is disinguishing between what a philosopher may want to justify as good, and what he can prove to be necessary in the natural order of things. For he says, "Although it may be advantageous to the human species for the union between man and woman to be permanent, it does not follow that it was thus established by nature; otherwise it would be necessary to say that nature also instituted civil society, the arts, commerce, and all that is claimed to be useful to men."[12] And this, clearly, would utterly undermine the purpose of the state of nature concept, for one could define into it any human institution one found desirable.

In Rousseau's original state of nature, then, there is no sexual love apart from indiscriminately and mutually satisfied instinct, and no marriage, family, or any other sign of dependence of one sex on the other, or inequality between them. When he says, in *Emile*, that "there is, in the state of nature, in fact, a real and indestructible equality, since it is impossible in that state for the bare difference between one man and another to be sufficient to make one dependent on the other,"[13] he has no legitimate reason for excluding the female half of the species. Indeed, considering that the isolated, natural woman was supposed capable of feeding herself and her offspring, while man had only himself to preserve, it would be difficult to argue that she was anything less than equal.[14]

Rousseau's attitude to the original state of nature was by no means one of unambivalent rejection. While its inhabitants were in a grossly undeveloped and primitive state, they were undoubtedly free, and independence was one of the most important, if not the most important, of values for him. "What type of misery [can there] be," he asks, "for a free being whose heart is at peace and whose body is healthy?"[15] While the original state of nature is not his chosen age, he asks that we at least suspend judgment on it until we have seen what is to follow. Moreover, it was the only era completely free of the evils of selfishness, as distinguished from a healthy degree of self-love. As soon as there was any regular contact among individuals, selfishness had begun to contaminate mankind, and it is to the original state of nature that Rousseau looks back in order to prove that man is naturally good.[16] He is good because he has no need for anyone else, does not compare himself with anyone else, and has no reason to fear that anyone will seek to hurt him.

The decisive events which separate the natural state of mankind from the beginning of civil society in the *Discourse on Inequality* are the establishment of private property in land, and the division of labor between agriculture and metallurgy. It was from this point on, Rousseau asserts, that some men began to enslave and exploit others, since each was no longer self-sufficient, and all the evils of social inequality had germinated and grown. Rousseau's preferred stage in man's hypothetical history is the long period which lies between the original state of nature and the era of inequality which he saw as resulting from the division of labor—that is, the "golden age" of the patriarchal nuclear family. It is very clear, both from his praise for it in the discourse itself and from the numerous attempts he made to recreate the situation, in *Emile*, in *La Nouvelle Héloise*, and in his idealized descriptions of the Swiss mountain people, that the self-sufficient, rural, patriarchal family was for Rousseau at least one of the two best possible modes of life for man, and the only one possible in a corrupt age. He called it "the veritable prime of the world."[17]

As Lovejoy has remarked, "For Rousseau, in short, man's good lay in departing from his 'natural' state, but not too much."[18] However, the extent of the departure from self-sufficiency and independence that was required in order to enter Rousseau's nuclear family was considerably greater for the woman than for the man. Suddenly, in a single paragraph, and virtually without explanation, he postulates "a first revolution," in which, together with rudimentary tools and the first huts, which together constituted "a sort of property," appears the very first cohabitation, in the form of the monogamous nuclear family. Suddenly, also without justification, he introduces a complete division of labor between the sexes. Whereas previously the way of life of the two sexes had been identical, now "women became more sedentary and grew accustomed to tend the hut and the children, while the man went to seek their common subsistence."[19] This division of labor, of course, meant that the entire female half of the species was no longer self-sufficient, and since it had been this very self-sufficiency which had been the guarantee of the freedom and equality that characterized the original state of nature, one might expect, though one will not find, some commentary on the inequality which has thus been established. On the one hand, this first family is described as united only by the bonds of "reciprocal affection and freedom."[20] On the other hand, however, the male has been assigned the only work Rousseau considers to be productive of property,[21] and it is made very clear that the family goods belong only to the father: "The goods of the father, of which he is truly the master, are the bonds which keep his children dependent on him, and he can give them a share of his inheritance only in proportion as they shall have properly deserved it from him by continual deference to his wishes."[22] There is no reason to assume, since the goods are his and the work assigned to his wife is not considered to be productive labor, that the woman's necessary posture is any less deferential to her husband than her children's. As we shall see, the necessarily patriarchal character of the golden age family and the economic dependence of women on men are confirmed in many of Rousseau's subsequent works.

The important thing to note at this point is that the assumption of patriarchy is not remarked on by Rousseau as constituting an inequality between two adult human beings. Clearly the human inequality with whose origins the discourse is concerned is solely the inequality between one male and another. A brief hint of this is given when, quite early in the work, women are referred to without a qualm as "the sex that ought to obey."[23] It is evident that until the second great revolution instituted landed property and the division of labor among men, Rousseau considers the human race, in spite of the patriarchal nature of the family, to have been living in a state of perfect equality. It was only when "one man [i.e. male] needed the help of another" and "they observed that it was useful for a single person [male] to have provisions for two," that equality is considered to have disappeared.[24]

In all his subsequent writings, Rousseau treats the nuclear family as a natural institution and monogamy as a God-given destiny for mankind. "The most ancient of all societies and the only one that is natural is the family," he says at the beginning of *The Social Contract*.[25] And in describing man in his primitive state in *Emile*, he asserts that "he is destined by nature to be content with one female," and that "mating leads to a kind of moral bond, a type of marriage" in which "the female, belonging by choice to the male to whom she has given herself, generally refuses all others." In complete contradiction with his refutation of Locke, Rousseau here uses the argument that children are helpless for so long that they and their mother could "with difficulty do without the father's affection and the care that results from it."[26]

Moreover, it is not just the monogamous family, but the patriarchal family that is assumed henceforth by Rousseau to exist according to the dictates of nature. Emile is advised that it is "the patriarchal rural life" that is "man's original life, the most peaceful, the most natural, and the most pleasant for those whose hearts are not corrupted."[27] Sophie is correspondingly told: "When Emile became your husband, he became your master; it is the will of nature that you should obey him."[28] In the *Discourse on Political Economy*, and in a parallel passage in the Geneva Manuscript version of *The Social Contract*, Rousseau gives three reasons for the necessity that the male rule within the family. First, there must be a single, final authority to decide issues on which opinion is divided; second, since women are sometimes, however infrequently, incapacitated by their reproductive functions, this single authority must be that of the male; and third, the issue on which the matter clearly turns, the man must have authority over his wife because it is essential for him to know that the children she bears and he maintains are his own.[29] The requirement of the certainty of paternity is therefore seen as the unquestionable justification for the natural subordination of women. Thus Rousseau claims:

> The relative duties of the two sexes are not, and cannot be, equally rigid. When woman complains of the unjust inequality which man has imposed on her, she is wrong; this inequality is not a human institution, or at least it is not the work of prejudice but of reason: that one of the sexes to whom nature has entrusted the children must answer for them to the other.[30]

Again, in the *Letter to d'Alembert*, Rousseau exclaims, "As if all the austere duties of the woman were not derived from the single fact that a child ought to have a father."[31] How could the same moral code be applied to both sexes, when chastity is for this reason so much more essential in a woman than in a man? The unfaithful husband is, admittedly, cruel and unjust to his wife, but the adulterous wife, who exposes herself to the possibility of bearing a child that is not her husband's, is positively treasonous; "she breaks up the family, and rends all the natural ties,"[32] and her wretched child is the sign of her husband's dishonor and the thief who robs his children of their property. The need for a man to know that his children are his own, and to have others also believe this to be so, is the basic reason why Rousseau completely separates both morality and moral education for women from what he prescribes for men.

It is necessary to make something of a digression at this point, and to return to the subject of Rousseau's ideas about sexuality, in order to understand fully his characterization of the natural woman. At the beginning of his prescription of the education of Sophie, he states, "In everything that does not depend on sex, a woman is a man; she has the same organs, the same needs, the same faculties."

He very swiftly adds, however, that "where sex is concerned man and woman are in all respects complementary and in all respects different" and that "the difficulty in comparing them is due to our inability to decide, in the constitution of either, what is a matter of sex and what is not."[33] What very soon becomes apparent is that, to Rousseau's mind, virtually everything for a female is a matter of sex. Thus he argues in three short paragraphs from the statement that "in everything that does not depend on sex, a woman is a man," to the conclusion that "a perfect woman and a perfect man should no more resemble each other in mind than in face."[34]

Since Rousseau argues that the role of woman in the sexual act itself, in addition to her function as a mother in a patriarchal family, has immense implications for her entire personality and the way she should be educated, it is essential to see how his ideas about sexuality changed from those set down in the *Discourse on Inequality*. There, he had seen sexual intercourse as an instinctual and need-fulfilling activity, freely engaged in by both sexes, and any other form of sexual love was regarded as the product of society. What he later saw as the natural characteristics of the two sexes is based on a view of the sexual act as not a mutually shared one, but one in which the male is the attacker and the female the aggressed upon. It is from this revised theory of sexuality, sexuality in its social form, which in itself has two inconsistent versions, that Rousseau deduces all those necessarily female characteristics—shame and modesty, passivity and conquerable resistance—which dictate so much of the course of Sophie's education.

Though he never denies that men and women have similar sexual needs, in his first revised version of human sexuality, Rousseau implies that the male will be aroused only if the female makes herself especially pleasing to him, and lures him by means of her bashfulness, coquetry, and either genuine or simulated resistance to his advances. The mutuality and spontaneity of the original state of nature completely vanish in the *Letter to d'Alembert*, where it is argued that the man must necessarily be the pursuer, since it is his sexual arousal upon which the successful performance of the sexual act depends. If women did not veil their desires with shame or at least feign resistance, "the passions, ever languishing in a boring freedom, would have never been excited."[35] Far from repressing the desires of the male, "chasteness inflames them." Because, then, of what appears to be a dubious faith in the natural potential for sexual arousal in the male, Rousseau concludes that whereas it is not essential for the man to please the woman, beyond displaying his strength, woman, on the other hand, is "specially made to please the man." Since the best way to arouse him is to resist his advances, chasteness and shame are natural concomitants of the female's role in the sexual act. And this, Rousseau says, in spite of the theory of spontaneous and instinctual sexuality he had postulated in the *Discourse on Inequality*, "is the law of nature, which is older than love itself."[36] It is no mere result of certain societal or cultural variables.

Concurrent with this account of the nature of human sexuality, however, there appears in *Emile* another, completely incompatible version, although it, too, requires that women be modest and bashful. According to this second view, presented along with the first as if there were no inconsistency between the two, the human potential for sexual arousal is frighteningly limitless. God has endowed both sexes with "unlimited passions," but he has given reason to man, and modesty to woman, in order to restrain them. Here, then, female resistance becomes essential not in order to entice and arouse the male, but as a curb to the boundless desires of both sexes. Without this restraint— of necessity imposed by the woman, both because of the greater consequences which the act may entail for her, and because the requirement of his potency makes the man naturally the aggressor—"the result would soon be the ruin of both, and the human race would perish by the means established for its preservation."[37]

These two conflicting accounts of sexuality are of great significance, because they are at the root of the two conflicting demands Rousseau makes of women. Women must, on the one hand, allure, and on the other hand, control and restrain; they must be sensuous, lovable and passionate, but on the other hand scrupulously chaste. It is the tension between these two "natural" functions of woman that ultimately leads to the tragedies of both Rousseau's ideal women, Sophie in *Emile* and its unfinished sequel, and Julie in *La Nouvelle Héloise*.

Unwilling to acknowledge that many aspects of the relations between the sexes as he presented them were the results of many centuries of patriarchal culture and of the economic and social dependence on men of women and their children, Rousseau argues that the consequences of her sex are inevitably much greater for a woman than maleness is for a man. "The male is only a male at certain times, the female is a female all her life or at least throughout her youth."[38] While admittedly she does not spend her whole life bearing children, yet "that is her proper purpose."[39] A woman's education must be founded on the principles that "woman is made to please and to be subjected to man" and "it is according to nature for the woman to obey the man."[40] Clearly, the "natural" status of these precepts depends on the correctness of Rousseau's assumptions that both the patriarchal family and his version of sexuality are natural. Once these premises are accepted, he can proceed to define woman solely in terms of her sexual and reproductive functions, and structure her position in society and her education accordingly. As Julie writes to her lover Saint-Preux, taking issue with Plato's single model of perfection for the two sexes, "The attack and defense, the boldness of men and the modesty of women, these are not conventions as your philosophers think, but natural institutions which are easily explained, and from which all the other moral differences can readily be deduced."[41] Thus it is not, Rousseau claims, prejudice or convention that makes him prescribe for Sophie an education that, in complete contrast to Emile's, is designed exclusively to form her into a highly alluring sex object for her man, his chaste and obedient wife, and the devoted mother of children that are unquestionably his. To the contrary, that Emile should be educated to be his own man, while Sophie is educated to be his own woman, is in accordance with the dictates of nature.

A grand summary of this view of the place of the "natural" woman in a patriarchal world is made near the beginning of Book 5 of *Emile*, and warrants quotation in full:

> Man and woman are made for each other, but their mutual dependence is not equal: men are dependent on women on account of their desires; women depend on men on account of both their desires and their needs; we could do without them better than they could do without us. In order for them to have what is necessary for their station in life, we must give it to them, we must want to give it to them, we must find them worthy of it; they are dependent on our feelings, on the price that we place on their worth, on how we esteem their charms and their virtues. By the law of nature herself, women, as much for themselves as for their children, are at the mercy of men's judgment.[42]

Here we have a very obvious case of the selective use of the concept of the natural, employed to justify and legitimate what the author deems to be good and useful for mankind. It is of course the very method of reasoning for which Rousseau had attacked Locke. The nature which lays down as law all the above aspects of woman's dependence on men is clearly not the original state of nature, in which the sexes were scarcely differentiated, with regard to life style or capacity for self-sufficiency. It is, rather, the "natural" state of patriarchy, the golden age of isolated families, with their sexual division of labor and their rudimentary property owned by the male, that is the reference point used to define the natural woman. Moreover, the transition between the two eras had been accomplished in Rousseau's mind without the least concern about why women would have agreed to such a change. If, indeed, "all, being born equal and free, alienate their liberty only for their own advantage,"[43] one might well ask how the patriarchal family, in which the woman's equality and freedom are sacrificed to the man's need to assure himself of his children's paternity, could ever have come into being. While he felt it was necessary to postulate a contractual origin, albeit a fraudulent one, for the first civil society, in order to refute the idea that "proud and unconquerable men" would ever have rushed into slavery,[44] Rousseau did not feel at all compelled to explain why proud and unconquerable women should have done that same unreasonable thing.

The whole issue of whether or not the patriarchal family is natural or conventional is therefore of critical importance for Rousseau's treatment of the subject of women.[45] Since the works in which the subject is most thoroughly aired, the *Discourse on Inequality* and *Emile*, are both works aimed at penetrating beyond all social and cultural institutions and practices in order to find out what the human race is originally or "naturally" like, the fact that he ignores all other possible types of sexual and marital custom—all forms of polygamy, polyandry, communal tribalism, and matriarchal or matrilineal forms of society—and concludes that the patriarchal nuclear family is natural and inevitable, is even more striking than it would be otherwise. There is no recognition in Rousseau's later works, in spite of his attack on Locke for the same prejudice, that this type of family system, with the radical division of labor between the sexes, the dependent position of the woman, and the overriding concern with female chastity, has any relation to particular social and economic arrangements and power relationships.

It is all presented as according to nature. Thus when Rousseau refers to the natural man and to the natural woman, he has two distinct reference points in mind. Natural man is man of the original state of nature—totally independent of his fellows, devoid of selfishness, equal to anyone else, and imbued with the natural goodness of pity for any suffering fellow creature. Natural woman, however, is woman defined in accordance with her role in the golden age family—dependent, subordinate, and naturally imbued with shame and modesty. Thus, the very minimal functions which would necessarily follow from the physiology of femaleness without this assumption of the patriarchal family are expanded to such an extent as to make Rousseau accept entirely different models of perfection for women and for men and consequently radically different methods for socializing the two sexes.

Insofar as I am aware, Rousseau expressed doubt about the "natural" status of the requirement that women be subordinate and confined only twice: once in the very early essay, "Sur les Femmes"; and again in the *Letter to d'Alembert*, where the doubt is presented not as the author's, but rather in the form of an additional argument to convince the skeptical. In the early essay he had written:

> First, let us consider women deprived of their liberty by the tyranny of men, the masters of everything, for crowns, offices, employments, the command of armies, all is in their hands, they have monopolized them from the very earliest of times by some natural right that I have never been able to understand and which well could have no other foundation than greater strength.[46]

The patriarchal nature of society and the division of labor according to sex are certainly not regarded as the natural order of things in this youthful statement. Clearly, Rousseau later came to very different conclusions.

In the *Letter to d'Alembert*, addressing himself to those who objected that the domestic confinement of women is merely a dictate of popular prejudice, and that chasteness is "only an invention of the social laws to protect the rights of husbands and fathers and to preserve some order in families,"[47] Rousseau at first argues at length, as above, that the female virtues and characteristics are dictated by nature. Then however, possibly out of concern that his case is not sufficiently convincing, he eventually seeks refuge in the argument of social expediency:

> Even if it could be denied that a special sentiment of chasteness was natural to women, would it be any less true that in society their lot ought to be a domestic and retired life, and that they ought to be raised in principles appropriate to it? If the timidity, chasteness, and modesty which are proper to them are social inventions, it is in society's interest that women acquire these qualities; they must be cultivated in women, and any woman who disdains them offends good morals.[48]

It is impossible to say how necessary Rousseau considered this supplementary, safeguarding argument to be, but it clearly reveals the motives behind his derivation of the natural man and the natural woman from different stages of his hypothetical history of mankind. Society requires the patriarchal family, in Rousseau's judgment, and thus that is as far back as he will choose to look in defining the natural woman. The important point to note is that this method of reasoning, from social expediency to the rights and obligations of the individual, is in complete contradiction to Rousseau's general philosophical method. There is only one other circumstance in which he argues in a similar manner, and that is when he considers the issue of Greek slavery.[49] Just as his philosophical rejection of slavery is qualified by the requirements of the ideal republic and its citizens, so it is the same social expediency, rather than nature's laws, that prevents Rousseau from postulating any theory of human nature and human rights that is independent of sex. If society is necessarily founded on the male-ruled family, as he argues, then the inconveniences that result must inevitably be borne by women. His inflexible attachment to the patriarchal family results in a philosophy of woman that, in all its most important respects, contradicts his philosophy of man.

The second way in which Rousseau seeks to discover the natural man is by attempting to separate out those characteristics that are innate in the individual from those acquired in the course of rearing and education. Here again, his reasoning about women is radically different from his reasoning about men.

In his works, from the *Discourse on the Origin of Inequality* on, we can find innumerable instances of Rousseau's strong belief in the power of the environment to alter human characteristics and abilities. The attribution to physical causes of what is in fact due to moral ones is, he says, in *Emile*, "one of the most frequent abuses of the philosophy of our century."[50] And in the discourse, the point is made at greater length:

> In fact, it is easy to see that, among the differences that distinguish men, some pass for natural that are uniquely the work of habit and the various types of life men adopt in society. Thus a robust or delicate temperament, and the strength or weakness that depend on it, often come more from the harsh or effeminate way in which one has been raised than from the primitive constitution of bodies. The same is true of strength of mind; and not only does education establish a difference between cultivated minds and those which are not, but it augments the difference among the former in proportion to their culture.[51]

We therefore err seriously if we take civilized man as exemplary of the true characteristics of the species, for ' in becoming sociable and a slave he becomes weak, fearful, servile; and his soft and effeminate way of life completes

the enervation of both his strength and his courage."[52]
Civilized children, for example, are weaker and attain self-
sufficiency later than their primitive counterparts, who are
required to fend for themselves as soon as possible.[53] On the
other hand, puberty and sexual maturity are reached earlier
among educated and sophisticated races than among the
primitive, since the cultural influences which impinge on
the individual in the former cases stimulate his precocious
development.[54] Environment can be seen to win out over
temperament, Rousseau argues, in countless such cases.

Probably the most striking example of Rousseau's belief
in the power of environmental influence occurs in his argument against slavery. In asserting that slavery was the
natural condition of some men, he argues, Aristotle had
mistaken the effects of slavery for the cause. "If there are
slaves by nature it is because there have been slaves against
nature. Force made the first slaves, their cowardliness perpetuated the condition."[55] The environment in which a man
is raised, especially if it is one so differentiated from that of
those around him, is bound to develop and accentuate some
of his innate characteristics, at the cost of suppressing and
distorting others. Thus, one certainly cannot tell from enslaved peoples, which all the civilized world must be considered, to a greater or lesser degree, what is the natural
potential of man. We know only the point of departure, in
the weakness and ignorance of infancy, and we cannot know
all the possible destinations that man may achieve. Early in
Emile, Rousseau makes this point very clearly. "I do not
know of any philosopher who has yet been rash enough to
say: here is the limit which man can reach but beyond
which he cannot go. We do not know what our nature
allows us to be; none of us has measured the possible
distance between one man and another."[56] Thus we have
no alternative but to acknowledge that the limits of man's
potential are unknown.

The objective of Emile is not to provide a treatise on
educational method in any practical or positive sense;

rather it constitutes a radical critique of what contemporary civilization and its socialization techniques have done to the natural man. Emile is to become a natural man, not in the sense of being reared for savagery, but by being educated in a way that is free from the prejudices and opinions of any particular time or place. The method followed is professed to be "nothing other than the course of nature."[57] At the beginning of the work, Rousseau pays homage to the great power of education in the broadest sense of the term: "Men are shaped by education as plants are shaped by cultivation. . . . We are born weak, we need strength; we are born lacking everything, we need help; we are born stupid, we need judgment. Everything that we do not have at birth and that we need when adult, is given us by education."[58] By assuming total responsibility for and authority over the child, the tutor's task is to isolate him from the misleading and distorting prejudices of the world around him, and to use his natural tendencies, especially his curiosity, to develop in him powers of independent judgment.

One of the fundamental principles of Emile's education, then, is that the child should never be told things on authority but should rather be helped to find them out for himself. For reason is not by any means a strong and natural human quality that will spring back up again if repressed, but a delicate potential that must be nurtured if it is to flourish. "Naturally, man thinks but little. Thinking is an art that he learns like all the others, but with even more difficulty. In both sexes I know only two really distinct classes; people who think and people who do not, and the difference is almost entirely due to education."[59] Only by guiding the child's attention subtly away from popular prejudices and trivial concerns will the tutor be able to develop his precious powers of reason and prevent him from coming to rely on the opinions of others. For "if ever you substitute authority for reason in his mind, he will no longer reason; he will become simply the plaything of other people's opinion."[60] The careful isolation of Emile and the painstaking care devoted to every aspect of his education are aimed, above all, at making him develop independence of judgment and his powers of reason.

Rousseau's stress on the importance of education is also strikingly apparent in his advice to rulers, whom he considered to have a great deal of responsibility for the character of the people they govern. "Make men, therefore, if you would command men," he advises the would-be preservers of a republic. The only way to make citizens is to educate them as children. For "it is too late to change our natural inclinations when they are developed in us, and when selfishness is reinforced by habit."[61] The intensely community-oriented socialization which Rousseau designed for the Polish children would be so effective in instilling in them virtuous, republican ways of thinking that, after such an education, strict laws would scarcely be necessary to make them do what was best for their country as a whole.[62]

Rousseau had little feeling but contempt for the men of his day, but it was not their innate faculties he denied; rather he saw the education they were given and the environment in which they lived as the source of their failings. In particular, Rousseau attributed men's lack of manliness and creativity to women, who, due to their sexual hold over men, always dictate the environment in which they live. How could contemporary men achieve great and noble works, as the ancients had, when they were so bound up with the trivial business of amusing women? It was the insidious influence of women which was making men into effeminate gallants, devoid of physical exercise or mental stimulation, and incapable of sustaining themselves against the elements. The result of all the time spent in female society was that the men around him seemed to Rousseau to be turning into a breed of lap dogs. "Given to these puerile habits," he says, "to what that is great could we ever raise ourselves? Our talents and our writing savor of our frivolous occupations." "Men were coarser in my time," he laments, and it was their rearing that made them so.[63]

Thus, without going as far as Helvétius' "l'éducation peut tout," Rousseau thought that education in the broadest sense of the term was responsible for most of the characteristics of the adult male, and for the difference between the peoples of various times and places. With regard to the natural versus the current prevailing qualities and abilities of women, however, he declines to apply his theories in anything like the same way. The statement quoted above[64] is certainly not consistent with what he says about women's talents. Just as he had refused to seek as far back in primitive time for the natural woman as he did for the natural man, so he does not acknowledge for girls to the same extent as for boys that their behavior, abilities and achievements are a function of the total environment in which they are reared.

Rousseau considers a lengthy list of "feminine" qualities to be indisputably innate in women. Shame and modesty, love of finery and embellishment, the desire to please and to be polite to others, and skillful shrewdness tending to duplicity—all these characteristics are presented as inborn and instinctive in the female sex.[65] As for the quality that makes a woman submit to injustices and wrongs done to her, this, too, "is the natural amiability of her sex when unspoiled." Boys, on the other hand, could never be accustomed to such treatment: "Their inner feelings rise up and revolt against injustice; nature has not made them able to put up with it."[66] Rousseau was unable to perceive the relevance of the objection he had made to Aristotle's argument for natural slavery, to his own conclusion that servility is natural in all women. This selective blindness persists in spite of the fact that in a number of passages Rousseau makes it very clear that unless a woman possesses all the characteristics he has labeled innate or natural in the female sex, she is unlikely to fare at all well, or perhaps even to survive, in the male-dominated culture in which she has to live. At times, indeed, Rousseau suggests in teleological fashion that such characteristics as duplicity and tolerance of injustice are innate in women *because* of the subordinate position in life for which they are naturally destined. Since a woman in love, for example, has the same desires as a man, but not the same right to express them, she must be equipped with the alternative language of deceit with which to make her feelings known indirectly. Similarly, since "woman is made to submit to man and even to put up with his injustice," it is useful for her to have an innate capacity for amiability in order to cope with such treatment.[67]

In direct contradiction to his emphasis on nurture and life style, to explain why contemporary men and little boys were the way they were, Rousseau tended to accept much of the character of contemporary women and little girls as immutable fact. Thus, even in spite of his recognition that the Spartan women were strong and healthy because of the physical education they underwent, and its undeniable corollary that indeed women's bodies might be very different from those of the eighteenth-century French ladies, he ignores this possibility when arguing that women are incapable of engaging in occupations outside the domestic sphere. Instead, he draws the ridiculous picture of a woman "who has never been exposed to the sun and who scarcely knows how to walk after fifty years of indolence"[68] attempting to transform herself overnight from a nursing mother into a soldier.

In the same vein, the tastes of the two sexes in toys and entertainment are treated as innate and not conditioned by surrounding attitudes: "Boys seek out movement and noise," whereas "the doll is the girl's special toy; there we see her taste obviously determined by her purpose in life." "Almost from birth," girls love adornment, and as soon as they can understand what people say, they can be controlled by what people will think of them. However, anyone who is silly enough to try this means of control with a small boy will fail completely, since "provided they can be free and enjoy themselves they care very little about what people think of them."[69] This distinction between the sexes seems hardly consistent with the fact that a great deal of care is taken to isolate Emile from the effects of opinion. Moreover, it proves nothing at all about the innate characteristics of boys and girls and merely testifies to the fact that little girls are very soon made aware that it is by pleasing and being pretty that they will achieve attention. It leads to no conclusions about how they might behave if given the same treatment, the same freedom and opportunity to enjoy themselves, as little boys. The dubious foundation of all Rousseau's conclusions about the innate difference between the sexes is illustrated by the fact that, when he invites the reader to look at a boy and a girl who are "so to speak, only just born," in order to see how differently they handle a given situation, his examples turn out to be no less than six years old.[70] Apparently, environmental influences up to the age of six are, in this context though not in others, considered trivial.

Rousseau treats intellectual capacities similarly. His emphasis on the importance of education and environment does not apply to women, in spite of his isolated assertion that the ability to think is, in both sexes, almost entirely the result of education. In a footnote to the very paragraph in which he attributes the lack of solid intellectual achievement of contemporary men to their life style and the trivia that occupy their minds, he says categorically that "women, in general, do not like any art, know nothing about any, and have no genius. They can succeed in little works which require only quick wit, taste, grace, and sometimes even a little bit of philosophy and reasoning," but they never have the "celestial flame" of genius.[71] Even though the environmental theory was surely most applicable to the almost entirely uneducated women of his day, Rousseau could only see their comparative lack of achievement as an immutable fact.

Rousseau does not, however, first assert that woman is mentally inferior to man and then draw conclusions from this about her proper function and position in society. Rather, his method is to begin by assuming that woman's role is to be a desirable and faithful sexual object for man, his wife and the mother of his children, and then to draw conclusions as to what her intellectual capacities *should* be like, in order to fit her for her proper function. It seems quite likely, in fact, for several reasons, that Rousseau was by no means completely convinced that women are necessarily and innately inferior in mind to men.

First, it is interesting to note that in the early essays on women he had expressed ideas about the abilities of women that are very different from those he espoused later. He had argued that, if history had not been written with such a masculine bias, there would not have been such a vast preponderance of heroes over heroines in its pages, and the balance would have been much more even. Although, given the conditions that prevailed, the number of men who had excelled would still be greater, "we should see in the other sex models of civic and moral virtue that are as perfect in every way."[72] Moreover, the remaining disparity could be explained in terms of the lesser opportunity afforded women to demonstrate their courage or heroism in positions of leadership. Of those who had the honor of being advanced to such positions, almost all distinguished themselves brilliantly. Thus, with a final flourish, Rousseau concluded: "I repeat that, with due allowance made, women would have been able to show the highest examples of greatness of soul and love of virtue, and in greater numbers than men have ever done, if our injustice had not taken away with their liberty all the occasions on which they might have manifested it in the eyes of the world."[73] In addition, he pointed to the existence of a number of talented female writers to suggest that, with greater opportunities women could show their true intellectual potential. At this stage of Rousseau's thought, then, it was clearly lack of opportunity that explained the discrepancy between the achievements of men and women throughout history.

Second, unlike Locke,[74] Rousseau did not cite the inferior abilities of women as a reason for giving absolute rule over the family to the man. Instead, asserting that there must be a single source of authority and that women are sometimes indisposed by their reproductive functions, he concluded that the man must rule because "when the balance is perfectly even, a straw is sufficient to turn the scale."[75] It would be strange to regard the balance as so even, surely, if he had thought that women were always and innately less capable of reason than men.

In spite of this, however, both in *Emile* and in the *Letter to d'Alembert*, Rousseau asserts, in accordance with a long tradition that extends at least as far back as Aristotle and is still very much alive,[76] that women have a kind of intellect different from and inferior to that of men, and lack the capacity for abstract reasoning and creativity. "Reason in women is a practical reason," he says, "which enables them easily to discover how to arrive at a given conclusion, but which does not enable them to reach the conclusion themselves."[77] Women cannot discover principles, as men can, but they have better heads for detail. However, as is obvious from the following quotation, the paradox in Rousseau's thought about the abilities of women can at least partly be explained by the fact that he was far less interested in what they could achieve than in what they should achieve:

The search for abstract and speculative truths, for principles, for axioms in science, everything that involves the generalization of ideas, *is not within a woman's province*: their studies *should concern* practical things;

it *is their task* to apply the principles discovered by man, and it *is up to them* to make the observations that lead man to discover these principles.[78]

Here, and again when we are told that "the art of thinking is not foreign to women, but they *should* only skim the surface of the science of reasoning,"[79] we realize that for Rousseau, in the main body of his writings, woman's potential is in fact irrelevant. What is important is that she *should* be, in mind as well as in body, what man wants her to be— his laboratory assistant no less than his concubine—and that she will certainly not benefit by attempting to be anything else. Julie, writing to her lover, Saint-Preux, is undoubtedly expressing Rousseau's position when she echoes this functionalist, rather than descriptive, account of the qualities of women. Fiercely rejecting Plato's argument that since the differences between men and women are minimal, they should be educated alike, Julie protests that it is clear from "the purpose of nature" and the "intentions of the creator" that the two sexes should not be alike. Since God and nature have clearly destined women for wifehood, child-rearing and domestic affairs, and men for labor and the pursuits of the outside world, "these vain imitations by one sex of the other are the height of foolishness; they make the wise man laugh and they banish love. . . . A perfect woman and a perfect man *should* be no more like each other in soul than in face."[80]

It is clear that Rousseau in his maturity was not at all interested in discovering what woman's natural potential might enable her to achieve, but was simply concerned with suiting her to her role as man's subordinate complement in the patriarchal family. Beyond this narrow and purely prescriptive view of woman's capacities he does not look. Several times, Rousseau asserts that the intelligence of little girls is more precocious than that of little boys and the explanation given is a purely functional one; it all has to

do with that precious jewel of virginity that a girl is entrusted with guarding. As Julie explains: "If reason is ordinarily weaker and fades sooner in women it is also formed
earlier, as a frail sunflower grows and dies before an oak.
We find ourselves from the very beginning entrusted with
such a dangerous treasure that the care of preserving it
soon awakens our judgment. . . ."[81] Once woman's reason
has developed sufficiently for her to know how to preserve
her virginity and to realize how essential it is for her to do
so at all costs, we may infer that it can then safely be allowed to stagnate, except insofar as it is required to make
her a good wife and mother. Again, when the question "Are
women capable of solid reason?" is explicitly asked, it is immediately followed by: "Is it essential for them to cultivate
it. . . . Is this culture useful for the functions imposed on
them, is it compatible with the simplicity that suits them?"[82]
If women are capable of reason, clearly they should be
trained to reason only if it helps them to perform their
proper functions better and does not make them any less
appealing to men.

Rousseau sees the fitting characteristics of the two sexes
in both the moral and the intellectual spheres as essentially
complementary. Individually incomplete, together they
form a whole and harmonious being. With regard to intellect, "woman has more wit, and man more genius, woman
observes while man reasons; from this cooperation results
the clearest enlightenment and the most complete knowledge that the human mind on its own can achieve."[83] This
is no less true in the moral realm: "The social relation of
the sexes is a wonderful thing. From this association results a moral person of which the woman is the eye and the
man the arm, but with such dependence of one on the other
that the man teaches the woman what she should see and
the woman teaches the man what he should do."[84] Likewise, in the supposedly admirable marriage of Julie and
Wolmar, Julie says that the two have but a single mind, of

which "he is the understanding and I the will."[85] Julie feels, and motivates and inspires people, while Wolmar reasons and makes decisions. As Judith Shklar has pointed out, Rousseau, while eschewing the traditional medieval use of the "body politic" metaphor in the political sphere, applies it in a slightly adapted form to the sphere of the family, to describe the complementary nature of the sexes in marriage.[86] If men and women were not complementary in nature, Rousseau argues, the institution of marriage would be in danger, and with it the basis of social stability. For if men and women were each endowed with a complete set of talents, instead of being mutually dependent, "they would live in never-ending discord, and relations between them would be impossible."[87]

Thus the reason for Rousseau's refusal to apply his beliefs about the vast influence of environmental factors to women as he did to men, and to conclude as he would have had to that their potential was equally undiscovered, was that his strong conviction of the virtues of the patriarchal family made him unwilling to consider women as independent persons or in any other context than the family. Arguments about the equality or inequality of the sexes are simply vain disputes, he asserts, once one recognizes what a woman should be like, in order to fulfill her natural sexual and maternal function.[88]

Whereas Rousseau stipulated two distinct and very different educational systems for boys, depending on whether it was intended to turn them into citizens or into independent and natural men, he set out only one type of education as suitable for women. As we shall see, it did not fit her to be a citizen, in Rousseau's sense of the word, and it certainly did not fit her to be an independent person. What is called the education of the natural woman is a training in modesty, domesticity, and complete submissiveness to prevailing opinion. The education of Sophie, complete failure that it turns out to be, is the logical consequence of the narrow role that Rousseau considered to be the only legitimate one for women.

As has been suggested, *Emile* is a critique, not just of contemporary educational practice, but of all that civilization has done to the natural man: "Everything is good when it leaves the hands of its creator. It degenerates in the hands of man. . . . He mutilates his dog, his horse, his slave. . . . He wants nothing to be as nature made it, not even man; he breaks him in like a horse, and makes him conform to his taste like a tree in his garden."[89] Emile, an unexceptional but healthy male child, is to be educated so as to be free of the prejudices of the world around him—the world that would strip him of his natural goodness and honesty, and shape him to the tastes and needs of a corrupt civilization. The only way to find out what man's potential is, is to look to his origins, in infancy, and to encourage him to develop all his natural capacities as they manifest themselves. Thus, Rousseau's definition of a natural man is an extremely open-ended one; he must be free to become whatever he can and will.

Woman, by contrast, is defined in a totally teleological way, in terms of what is perceived to be her purpose in life. Her education, therefore, is totally dictated by her function and by the characteristics considered essential in her life if she is to fulfill it properly. Having argued that the family is essential to society, and assuming, as he does, that woman's subordinate position within it is dictated by the necessity that paternity not be in doubt, Rousseau concludes that the prescriptions for female education follow from this directly. As has been acknowledged by several Rousseau scholars, the consequent education proposed for women is based on principles that are in direct and basic conflict with those that underlie his proposals for the education of men.[90] This contrast between the education of Emile, founded on man's unknown potential, and that of Sophie, founded on her narrowly defined female function, is clearly summarized in the following quotation, which should be compared with the philosophy of the first four books of *Emile*:

> The entire education of women must be relative to men. To please them, to be useful to them, to be loved and honored by them, to rear them when they are young, to care for them when they are grown up, to counsel and console, to make their lives pleasant and charming, these are the duties of women at all times, and they should be taught them in their childhood. To the extent that we refuse to go back to this principle, we will stray from our goal, and all the precepts women are given will not result in their happiness or our own.[91]

Having considered the possibility of not giving woman any intellectual education at all, but confining her training solely to "the labors of her sex," Rousseau concludes that this solution would be satisfactory only for a very simple, uncorrupted, and isolated living situation. A woman's duties are simple enough, to be sure. Her subordination to her husband's absolute authority and the devotion she owes her children are such natural consequences of her position in life that it requires no complex reflection on her part to recognize them. Thus, in a rural and moral environment, a woman might without danger to her virtue be left in profound ignorance. However, in the corrupt world of the city, with so much to tempt her and so many subversive prejudices to lead her astray, she would require a somewhat more sophisticated education, involving both the development of her own conscience and a thorough knowledge of the prevailing value system. Since she must necessarily preserve all the proprieties, as her husband's honor depends upon it, she must be educated to a level where she can reconcile the dictates of her own conscience with the demands of public opinion, consider all prejudices seriously, and reject them only when her conscience is in definite conflict with them. This difficult reckoning "cannot properly be done without cultivating her mind and reason."[92] As will be argued below in chapter 8, moreover, the fates of Rousseau's two heroines suggest that the reconciliation of conscience and public opinion is indeed an impossible task.

On the question of the proper position and assigned life style of women, Rousseau was sure that the Greeks (in this case, however, excluding the Spartans) had the only correct answer.[93] Especially after marriage, "there are no good morals for women outside of a withdrawn and domestic life."[94] He cited with approval Pericles' dictum that a good woman should never be spoken of, and quoted Aristotle's views on women in a subsequently discarded passage of *Emile*. As the ancient philosopher had said, while woman alone should regulate the domestic aspect of life, she must limit herself to the home; while mistress of her own sphere, she herself must remain "under the absolute law of her husband."[95] The Greek pattern of complete seclusion and domestication, Rousseau thought, "is the mode of life that nature and reason prescribe for the female sex."[96]

Nature, according to Rousseau, not only dictates a totally different education and life style for the two sexes, but also prescribes that they live for the most part separated from each other. As he says in the *Letter to d'Alembert*, "Let us follow the inclinations of nature, let us consult the good of society; we shall find that the two sexes ought to come together sometimes and to live separated ordinarily."[97] This, too, was the praiseworthy system of the ancients. It was also the reason Rousseau so much admired the Genevan clubs, for they constituted a way in which the men could free themselves of the shackling demands and chatter of their women, and talk about important things, while the latter could amuse themselves with gossip which, though probably malicious, was considerably less harmful than some alternative pursuits they might have devoted themselves to. According to Rousseau, too much association of the sexes leads not only to the decline of morality, but to the loss of men's virility, since "unable to make themselves into men, the women make us into women."[98] When a critic objected to the clubs, Rousseau's response was to tell him: "find some other way in which men can live separately from women, and I will abandon that one."[99]

In *La Nouvelle Héloise*, this principle, "on which all good morals depend,"[100] is developed at greater length. Although Julie and her husband live together, they never do the same things, since "the inclinations which nature gives them are as diverse as the functions she imposes on them."[101] Both Wolmar and Julie agree that this separation of life styles and complete division of labor is the best and the most natural way to live, both for love and for marital harmony. The servants, moreover, except for their meals and certain supervised festivities, live totally segregated according to sex, in order to ensure their honor and chastity, which are held to be the basis of all morality. The "admirable order that reigns" at Clarens testifies to the truth of the precept that "in a well-regulated house the men and women should have little association."[102]

It is interesting to note that Saint-Preux, in praising the Wolmars' segregated mode of living, argues that with the exception of the French and those who imitate them, it is in fact the universal custom of the people of the world. He concludes: "Such is the order the universality of which shows to be natural . . . and even in the countries where it has been perverted one still sees vestiges of it."[103] This argument is strikingly uncharacteristic of Rousseau, who, in many ways an iconoclast, was certainly not accustomed to argue that contemporary practice in the world exemplified what was natural and necessary for the human race. As he had said earlier of Locke's claim that the family was natural, so also this argument of his would lead to the assertion that "nature also instituted civil society, the arts, commerce, and all that is claimed to be useful to man."[104]

Rousseau had failed to apply in the case of women both

types of argument he had used to define the natural man, instead finding her naturally located in her subordinate role in the patriarchal family and naturally endowed with all those qualities considered essential to her functioning in that role. Here he undermined his own reasoning about the natural once more, so as to use what he considered to be prevailing world practice as a support for his preferred, sexually segregated life style. Having proposed a form of education for women that would make them appealing sexual objects and submissive wives, Rousseau was faced with the dilemma that the women so educated were not fit to be the everyday companions of the type of men he thought society needed. His only solution was to conclude that it is not only socially expedient but according to the very dictates of nature for the two sexes to live, for the most part, separated from each other.

7

Equality and Freedom
— for Men

The two most prevalent values that coexist, however uncomfortably at times, in Rousseau's social and political philosophy are equality and freedom. While he considered these characteristics to be essential for men, he denied their relevance for women. This contrast in approach is the subject of the following chapter.

One of Rousseau's most abiding concerns was the inequality that prevailed in the society around him, and one of the most constant objects of his philosophy was to discover the principles of a political system that would minimize inequality between persons. His deep hatred for inequality originated in his own experience. As Judith Shklar has said, "Inequality for him was always an intensely personal experience, a display of cruelty on one side and corresponding servility and fear on the other."[1] The shock of the subservience required of him first as an apprentice and then as a valet, after a childhood in which, as he says, "I was accustomed to living on terms of perfect equality with my elders," brought him quickly to the conclusion that "every unequal association is always disadvantageous to the weaker party."[2] He felt that he knew the darker side of inequality intimately, and it repelled him.

The *Discourse on Inequality* is the result of Rousseau's reflections "upon the equality nature established among men, and upon the inequality they have instituted."[3] Certainly there were natural differences among individuals in any setting—differences in their bodily and mental strengths and talents, and therefore in their capacities for production and acquisition. However, the various political relations established among men could either exaggerate and perpetuate, or minimize and compensate for, these original inequalities.

As has been noted, the golden age of independent and therefore substantially equal patriarchal families was regarded by Rousseau as "the happiest and most durable epoch" and "the best for man." Surely only some fatal accident, he thought, could have brought man out of this state of "real and indestructible equality."[4] The fatal events which had resulted in ever-increasing inequalities among the members of the male sex were, he concluded, the institution of private property, the division of labor and the exchange of commodities, for the combined effect of these developments was that some men possessed what others needed, and thus grew rich at their expense. The step from here to political and institutionalized inequality is explained in the second part of the *Discourse on Inequality* as having originated from the seduction of the poor by the rich into a false, pseudomutual contract. The poor, who "ran to meet their chains, thinking they secured their freedom," merely succeeded in legitimizing the exploitation of themselves by the rich. Rousseau concludes:

> Such was, or must have been, the origin of society and laws, which gave new fetters to the weak and new forces to the rich, destroyed natural freedom for all time, established forever the law of property and inequality, changed a clever usurpation into an irrevocable right, and for the profit of a few ambitious men henceforth subjected the whole human race to work, servitude, and misery.[5]

The result is that all existing governments, in spite of their various claims to legitimacy, are based on fraud. In spite of the "vain and chimerical equality of right"[6] that civil societies claim to have substituted for the real but unguaranteed equality of the golden age, in fact the power of the community is co-opted by the strongest, so as to enable them to oppress the weak both more thoroughly and quasi-legitimately. Thus:

> The multitude will always be sacrificed to the few, and the public interest to private interest. Those specious words, justice and subordination, will always serve as the instruments of violence and the weapons of injustice; thus it follows that the upper classes which claim to be useful to the rest are in fact only serving themselves at the others' expense.[7]

Greater strength or wealth, Rousseau argues, can in no way create legitimate right. "To yield to force is an act of necessity, not of will; it is at the most an act of prudence. In what sense could it be considered a duty?"[8] Thus, since no man has by nature authority over any other, and no authority can derive from force, he concludes that the only legitimate solution to the problem of political authority is the true social contract, which makes the will of the people sovereign. Without such a contractual foundation, the undertakings of a political system can only be "absurd, tyrannical, and subject to the grossest abuse."[9] To the contrary, as the first book of *The Social Contract* concludes:

> Instead of destroying natural equality, the fundamental compact . . . substitutes a moral and legitimate equality for that physical inequality that nature has established among men, and which, though they may be unequal in strength or intelligence, makes them all equal by convention and right.[10]

By giving everybody an equal share in legislative power, therefore, a properly constituted political system could make civil society a state of greater equality than naturally exists among men.

It is clear from his advice to the Polish leaders about the lack of representation of the mass of their people, still serfs, in the legislature, that Rousseau regarded political inequali-

ties as never legitimate, and to be tolerated only temporarily. While acknowledging that emancipation would not
be easy to accomplish, he asserts that

> the law of nature, that sacred and imprescriptible law
> . . . does not permit us to confine the legislative author-
> ity in such a way, and to make the laws binding on any
> person who has not cast his vote on them in person,
> like the deputies, or at least through chosen representa-
> tives. . . .[11]

Since the serfs, too, were men, he tells the nobles, who
"have in them the makings of becoming everything that
you are," they must be freed first in soul, then in body, and
raised to full political equality.

In the light of the above principles, it seems scarcely
necessary to mention that Rousseau regarded slavery as
totally illegitimate.[12] It is degrading to his essence, and offensive to both nature and reason, for a man to give up his
life, freedom, and right to himself, to another. Nature,
which makes man's self-preservation his first duty, and
his conscience, which is responsible for regulating his behavior in accordance with morality, cannot possibly con-
done such a drastic renunciation of human autonomy.
Existing slavery can be based on nothing but force confirmed by habit. However, as has frequently been noted,[13]
Rousseau's favorite Greek republics, for all their civic equality, were founded on the enslavement of multitudes of people. Moreover, when he himself confronted this fact, he
acknowledged that since civil society, like all departures
from nature, must have its disadvantages, it might unfortunately be the case that the enjoyment of true self-government by some could be maintained only by means of the
enslavement of others. "There are some such unfortunate
circumstances," he says, "in which people can only preserve
their liberty at the expense of that of others, where the
citizen cannot be perfectly free unless the slave is completely
a slave."[14] As we turn to Rousseau's treatment of women,

and find that his most fiercely held principle of equality
does not apply at all, it is worth remembering this conclusion. For it seems that, just as the liberty and equality of
the Spartan citizens were dependent on the radical enslavement of the helots, Rousseau's ideal republic of free
and equal heads of patriarchal families is necessarily built
on the political exclusion, total confinement and repression
of women.

The principle of equality, together with its corollaries—
the rejection of the right of the strongest and the legitimacy
of those governments alone which were based on the general
will—were all held by Rousseau to be of crucial importance
for men. However, the violation of every one of them where
women were concerned was perpetrated without question.

First, Rousseau violates with respect to women his repudiation of the right of force. If women do not become the
kind of sexual objects men want them to be, "the less they
will be able to control them, and then men will be really
the masters."[15] Being so much weaker and less able to provide for herself, characteristics regarded as independent of
the economic and social structure, woman has only her
charms, her wit and her intuition in order to compensate.
Rousseau never suggests, of course, that *men* who are weaker than others need special natural talents in order to
compensate, for it is the task of the social contract to substitute civil equality for natural inequality, among men.
Any superiority of strength which nature has given men
over women, however, clearly has a purpose, and is not
perceived by Rousseau as requiring any kind of institutionalized alleviation or compensation. That men are stronger
and women dependent on them for their subsistence are
simply facts of life that the latter must learn to live with.

Second, the principle of political equality, as a means to
self-government, is not applied to women. Clearly, Rousseau
never envisaged that women should be enfranchised citizens
whose voices contribute to the formulation of the general
will. Though he told the "amiable and virtuous women of

Geneva" that their fate was to govern men, from what follows this assertion it is clear that he saw only one legitimate way for them to use their influence, and that was through the agency of their husbands. No civilized man, according to Rousseau, could resist the exhortations to honor and reason voiced by a tender wife. Thus, the women's "chaste power" was to be "exercised solely in conjugal union," where they should "continue to exploit on every occasion the rights of the heart and of nature for the benefit of duty and virtue," and "for the glory of the state and the public happiness."[16] It was, then, only through their domestic influence on their husbands, exerted through making full use of the latter's feelings for them, that women were to have any power in Rousseau's ideal republic. No contract-based civic equality was to replace the natural differences bestowed upon women. Unlike the Polish serfs, women had no right by virtue of their humanity to political participation, and that "sacred and imprescriptible" law of nature which mandates participation, or at least representation, for all who can legitimately be obliged to obey the laws, apparently was seen by Rousseau as having no application to any member of the female sex.

Finally, within the sphere of the family, Rousseau was most explicit in denying women equal partnership with men. Like Aristotle, Locke and Hegel, to name three obvious examples, he made a clear typological distinction between the family and the state. Apart from the occasion examined above, in which the natural status of the family is denied, the family is consistently referred to in his works as a natural institution, founded on feeling, and thereby distinguished from all larger, political associations, which are based on conventions and reciprocal rights and duties. Those who claimed, as Filmer had, that political authority is based on the prior authority of the family patriarch over his children were therefore committing a seriously misleading fallacy in their attempts to legitimize absolute government.

Thus the rule of husbands over their wives is claimed to be a natural order in no way comparable with the requirements of equality in the political realm. For "the law of nature bids the woman obey the man" and a wife must "keep her person always under the absolute law of her husband."[17] Any power that the woman wields within the family is to be acquired by her manipulation of her husband to do what she wants, and by her use, specifically, of her status as "arbiter of (his) pleasures."[18] When Rousseau actually enumerates the three reasons for this immense violation of his dearly held principle of equality, however, we can see clearly that they owe far more to the requirements of an orderly, property-based, patriarchal society, than to any state of affairs that could reasonably be construed as natural.[19]

Authority in the family cannot be divided between the father and the mother, Rousseau argues, because in every division of opinion there must be a single will that decides. One might perhaps expect that the creator of the concept of the general will would be the last of political philosophers to require absolute government within the family. A very intimate group of people—one that is distinguished by Rousseau himself from the larger society by the fact that it is held together by affection and mutual concern— would seem to be an exemplary context in which to apply the principle of rule by the general will. Surely a nuclear family should be able to establish what is in the best interests of the whole, if a republic of many thousands can do it. But no, one alone—the man—must govern.

The second reason given for familial patriarchy is that women have periods of inactivity, because of their reproductive function. Though these may admittedly be slight, Rousseau says, "it is a sufficient reason for excluding [women] from this authority," and for placing permanent rulership over the family in the husband's hands. Needless to say, Rousseau does not resort to similar reasoning in order to exclude certain groups of men, who may be inconvenienced by lameness, for example, or by the fact that they live too far from the meeting, from sharing in decision-making. The argument is, at any rate, fatuous, except perhaps in the case of decisions which *must* be made during the final stages of childbirth. We can only conclude that the actual process of self-government, so important according to Rousseau for men and their character, is considered of no value for women.

The third reason is undoubtedly the most important one, since Rousseau returns to the issue again and again[20]—"the husband must be able to supervise his wife's conduct: because it is essential for him to be certain that the children, whom he is compelled to recognize and maintain, belong to no one but himself." Rousseau does not recognize certainty of paternity as the prescript of a certain type of society, with its sacred institutions of private property and inheritance;[21] he attaches so much importance to it that in order to assure it, he, of necessity, excludes women from all the otherwise inviolable rights to equality and self-government.

However, neither Emile's conduct with regard to his family, nor that of Julie's father, Baron d'Etange, nor Rousseau's own, constitutes any evidence for Rousseau's claim that not only the children in their stage of dependency but the wife throughout her life can safely be trusted to the absolute authority of the patriarch, because of his natural family feelings. Emile, deserting his innocent son no less than his guilty wife, could scarcely be said to demonstrate paternal affection: he would rather see his son dead, he says, than Sophie with another man's child. Julie's father's record of habitual adultery, subsequent harshness to his wife (which we are told is a frequent accompaniment to a husband's infidelity), violence to his daughter sufficient to provoke a miscarriage, coercion of her into a marriage against her will, and claim that he would have killed her if he had known she had lost her virginity—all this is no more encouraging. And whether or not Rousseau actually did dispose, as reported, of Thérèse le Vasseur's children, against her will, into a foundling home, he does not regard the act, despite his subsequent guilt, as an instance of tyranny toward either the children or their mother.[22]

Just as there are conflicting interests within civil society, which Rousseau was only too well aware of, so in any group of individuals, not excluding the family, there must of course be times when there are radical conflicts of interests. In fact Rousseau indicates that he is under no illusion as to the abuses of paternal power that were perpetrated without compunction in the society of his day.[23] However, whereas with regard to political inequalities, he acknowledges that "in general it would be very foolish to expect that those who are in fact the masters will prefer any other interest to their own," and that tyranny will necessarily exist "wherever the government and the people have different interests and consequently opposing wills,"[24] he refuses to recognize, even in the light of his own fictional and personal examples, that such conflicts of interests, and such resulting tyranny, require as radical reform of the family as he advocates for the state. To the contrary, the overriding need for paternity to be certainly established abolished any notion he may have had that justice or equality is pertinent in this context also.

There are many indications in Rousseau's writings that he had an additional reason for refusing to apply his principle of equality to women. This was his strong fear that if women were not subordinated to men in certain important ways, they would predominate over them altogether. For, since woman, he believed, has the capacity to stimulate man's sexual desires to the extent that they can never be fully satisfied, and since nature has made her strong enough to resist his advances when she chooses to, it follows that, with respect to his sexual needs, man is "by an unvarying law of nature" dependent on the good will of woman.[25] As he says in the *Letter to d'Alembert*, "Love is the realm of women. It is they who necessarily give the law in it, because, according to the order of nature, resistance belongs to them, and men can conquer this resistance only at the expense of their liberty."[26] Thus woman was clearly, as Rousseau saw it, in command of a critical area of man's life. This tremendous sexual power over man was what made him so adamant that women should not, in addition, "asurp men's rights," or, in other words, make themselves the equals of men in those other areas which men have traditionally reserved for themselves. "For, to leave her our superior in all the qualities proper to her sex and to make her our equal in all the rest, how is this different from transferring to the wife the primacy which nature has given to the husband?"[27]

Fear of the power of women, and the related belief that the female sex is the source of the major evils of the civilized world are not, of course, peculiar to Rousseau. They are, however, very strongly articulated in his writings. In a poem entitled "Sur la Femme," he addresses woman as the "seductive and deadly one, whom I adore and detest," and goes on to say that she "makes man into a slave, . . . makes fun of him when he complains, . . . overpowers him when he fears (her), . . . punishes him when he defies (her), . . . and raises storms that torment the human race."[28] It is interesting to note in this context that, like Hesiod in his womanless Age of Gold, like Plato in the *Statesman* and the *Timaeus*, and recalling the Garden of Eden before the creation of Eve, Rousseau in the *Discourse on Inequality* looks back to an original state of nature which, although not without women, was a period in which the isolated life style meant that there was no social relationship between the sexes. Men were not only free of dependence on other men, they were also in a significant way independent of women, or at least of any particular woman, since their sexual urge was spontaneously satisfied by any passing female.

This simple and unemotional version of sexuality was to come to an abrupt end with the appearance of the monogamous family at the beginning of the golden age. Significantly, woman's economic dependence on man is introduced simultaneously with man's dependence on one woman for his sexual pleasures. The power she consequently would have over him must apparently be counterbalanced. Thus, although Rousseau did not postulate, like the Manichaeans, a hermaphroditic period of human innocence, at the end of which all the evils of sexuality emerged as mankind was divided into male and female, he did see the original state of nature as a time of purely instinctive and conflict-free sexuality. Only later, with settled living patterns, the comparison of oneself and one's woman with others, and the consequent onset of selfishness, did the combination of sexuality and individual love begin. This was the fatal connection that resulted in jealousy, conflict, and "duels, murders and worse things."[29] In line with St. Augustine's account, then, Rousseau postulated an event in history, equivalent to the Fall, which had transformed sexual feelings and behavior from a simple and conflict-free means of procreation into a furious passion intimately bound up with envy, guilt, fear, and sin. What he referred to as the moral as opposed to the simply physical element of love was to some extent the inevitable result of the move from nomadic isolation to the settled living patterns of society. However, it was women who were accused of having nurtured carefully the emotional side of love and of playing up its importance, so as to establish their dominance over men.[30] The blame for the guilt and fear experienced in relation to sexuality was laid on the female sex, as the arouser of the passions.

Thus the vast influence that women in society derived from their sexual power over men was held to be a fact independent of time and place. However, its particular direction and its consequences were not. In contemporary France, Rousseau considered the dominance of bold and licentious women to be not only responsible for the poor quality of the artistic and intellectual achievements of the time, but the root cause of all social evil. This evil influence of women is a major theme of the *Letter to d'Alembert*. It was because the real world offers no examples of virtuous women that the idealized ones depicted on the stage were so dangerous, for they seduced men into believing in the romance and innocence of something that was in reality so likely to lead to their damnation. In the actual world, it would be a miracle if a single truly pure woman could be found in London or Paris, as Saint-Preux's lengthy letter from the French capital confirms. Though intelligent and educated, the women of Parisian society shocked and repelled him on account of their boldness and lack of modesty. Being so much like men, they might make a good friend, but never a wife or a mistress.[31] Rousseau's only commentary on this judgment is to remark that it is hardly likely to please the ladies themselves, since it credits them with qualities they scorn, and denies them those they most aspire to.[32]

Since he believed that "men of sound morals are those who really adore women" and "women are the natural judges of a man's merit,"[33] Rousseau considered that the depravity of the women around him had dire consequences. The only way to preserve the adolescent Emile's character, therefore, was to isolate him scrupulously from all married women and prostitutes, who are bundled together in the same debauched category. Since all other women in French society are depicted as a multitude of whores, the only women with whom he can safely come into contact are chaperoned virgins.[34]

However, Rousseau wavered between blaming women themselves for the faults and evil influence he attributed to them and acknowledging, more in line with his reasoning about contemporary men, that social and legal circumstances were to a large extent the cause. On the one hand, in the *Letter to d'Alembert* and a subsequent letter to a M. Lenieps, it is made clear that women alone are to blame. When Lenieps comments in criticism of Rousseau's position in the former work, that perhaps it is not women's fault, but men's own fault, if they are corrupted, Rousseau answers: "But my whole book is taken up with showing how it is their fault, and I don't think there is anything to answer to that."[35] According to this account, women have abused their powers, in order to corrupt men and undermine the morals of society. In *Emile*, however, Rousseau's ambivalence about whether to blame women or whether to blame the conditions and institutions of the time is obvious, as in a single sentence he appears to do both. "Under our senseless institutions," he says, "the life of a good woman is a perpetual struggle against herself; it is right that her sex should share the pain of the evils that she has caused us."[36] Here, woman is depicted as the victim, but legitimately so; she is the justly banished Eve, the rightly burned witch.

On the other hand, probably because he obviously felt sympathy for his heroine, Julie, in her hopeless predicament, Rousseau is far more prepared in *La Nouvelle Héloise* to recognize that if women have strayed far from his chaste ideal, this is to a large extent due to the abuse of the powers wielded over them, particularly by their fathers. Allowing them to be forced into ill-assorted marriages for the sake of property and snobbery, the laws and customs which deprive women of the disposal of their own hearts and persons can to a large extent be blamed for their subsequent misconduct. Lord Bomston, who serves as a confidant for Saint-Preux and also at times as a kind of Greek chorus, argues at length against the right of fathers to give their daughters in marriage against their wills. He concludes that "there is no knowing to what extent women in this brave land are tyrannized by the laws. Need we be surprised that they revenge themselves so cruelly by means of their morals?"[37] The confirmation that these are indeed the opinions of the author can be found in the Second Preface to the work, which is of invaluable help in clarifying some of the major morals and messages of the novel.

Agreeing with his critic that the morals of married women are scandalous, Rousseau, in contrast to his response to M. Lenieps, answers: "But be fair to women; the cause of their misconduct lies less in them than in our evil institutions."[38] Natural feelings, he continues, are being stifled by the extremes of inequality in society, and it is the "despotism of fathers" that leads to the sins and misfortunes of their children. According to this account, then, the bad conduct of contemporary women and the consequent evil of the influence they exerted over the whole of society were by no means unchangeable, since they could, at least in large part, be traced to specific and identifiable causes.

Thus, although there is no hope of escape from the influence of women, it need not be an influence for evil. On the contrary, as Rousseau asserts in the *Discourse on the Arts and Sciences*, "I am far from thinking that this ascendancy of women is in itself an evil. It is a gift given them by nature for the happiness of the human race; better directed, it could produce as much good as today it does harm."[39] Women have been respected by every virtuous nation, and the age in which they lost this position and in which men no longer looked to their judgment would be "the last stage of degradation." What great things their influence might achieve if it were properly directed, both on the individual and the national levels! The inspiration of being loved by a really good woman is seen by Rousseau as able to work miracles in a man: "It is certain," he says, "that only women could bring back probity and virtue among us."[40]

It is clear, however, that Rousseau could envisage only one way in which women should exercise their vast influence for good. Only by being chaste, retiring, and devoted wives and mothers, should women exert their proper "subservient domination" over their men, and restore virtue to society. Governed absolutely in their domestic lives and excluded totally from civic life, Rousseau's women were to be the permanent subordinates of men. For this generally egalitarian philosopher, sex was the only legitimate ground for the permanent unequal treatment of any person.

Closely related to the ideal of equality, in Rousseau's works, is the importance of freedom. He stresses continually the value of freedom from dependence on other persons or on their opinions and prejudices. "It is only among free people," he says, "that man's worth is apparent; freedom [is] the most noble of man's faculties"; and "To renounce liberty is to renounce being a man, to give up the rights of humanity, and even its duties. Such a renunciation is incompatible with man's nature, and to take away all his freedom of will is to deprive his actions of all morality."[41] Both in the original state of nature hypothesized in the first part of the *Discourse on Inequality*, and in the education prescribed for Emile, independence from others and their opinions is clearly the central value. Like equality, freedom was also a very personal ideal for Rousseau. In *The Confessions* and *The Reveries of a Solitary*, he expresses his repugnance at being dependent upon anyone, or obligated to do anything, even if the required activity in itself might be a pleasant one.[42] Eventually he concludes that his need for independence in fact renders him quite unsuited to the needs of civil society: "So long as I act freely I am good and do nothing but good; but, as soon as I feel the yoke, whether of necessity, or of men, I become a rebel or, rather, restive; then I am nothing. . . ."[43] Although in his political theory Rousseau had to try to reconcile man's natural need for independence with the requirements of life in a social state, his original state of nature is an idealization of complete independence. It was designed to prove that man is naturally good when he lives in isolation from and independence of his fellows, and that it was the development of society, with its multiplication of needs and conflicts of interests which, by making men mutually dependent, had fostered their selfishness and caused all the harm they inflict on each other. As Rousseau asserts:

> Everyone must see that, since the bonds of servitude are formed only from the mutual dependence of men and the reciprocal needs that unite them, it is impossible to enslave a man without first putting him in the position of being unable to do without another; a situation which, as it did not exist in the state of nature, leaves each man there free of the yoke and renders vain the law of the stronger.[44]

However, the state of nature was fated to come to an end, and, as soon as one man needed another, "slavery and misery were seen to germinate."[45]

The principal concern of Rousseau's political philosophy is the restitution of man's freedom within civil society.[46] For, while any constraint laid on a person's will by another individual makes the former no longer free, constraint of some kind is of course necessary for social harmony. The only solution to the great social problem of the dependence of man on man, which, according to Rousseau "causes all manner of vices and depraves both master and slave,"[47] is through the substitution of the rule of law for that of any individual will. For when the general will is sovereign, "every man in obeying the sovereign is only obeying himself, and . . . we are freer under the social pact than in the state of nature."[48] Anyone who, within civil society, sets aside the law which accords with the general will and claims to subject another person to his personal will, thereby puts himself and the other back into the pure state of nature, in which the latter has no obligation to obey him. The state of war exists between them.[49] Personal absolutism and subservience then, in principle, have no place in Rousseau's political theory.

Just as abhorrent to Rousseau as personal dependence, was dependence on the opinions of others or on the prejudices of one's time and place.[50] Eventually, he found it necessary to retreat from almost all personal contacts and into the realm of nature, in order to free himself from "the yoke of opinion."[51] Likewise, according to the *Discourse on Inequality*, one of the most regrettable things that the end of the golden age brought with it was the need to impress others, which led to deception, dissimulation, and all the vices that follow from these.[52] Since then, our fate has been sealed, "all our wisdom consists in slavish prejudices; all our customs are nothing but subjection, coercion and constraint. Civilized man is born, lives and dies in slavery."[53]

The roles people were obliged to play in contemporary society were regarded by Rousseau as the most intrusive and personal form of tyranny. What disgusted him so much about actors was their prostitution of themselves by slavishly taking on roles and becoming the toys of the spectators —an occupation far too debasing for a creature as noble as man.[54] What repelled him above all about Parisian society was its slavish conformity to the prevailing prejudice or fashion of the moment. The customs of contemporary city life were altogether a sham; politeness, decorum and the art of pleasing had so far taken over that one no longer had any way of distinguishing the genuine from the assumed. The inevitable result was that there were "no more sincere friendships; no more real esteem; no more well-based confidence."[55] The appalling decline in morals that Rousseau perceived around him, he attributed very largely to this cancerous servility to opinion and dissimulation that was taking over society. It was only by leaving behind the cities, the empire of opinion, and living in rural isolation—as he himself did, as his ideal Wolmar family did, and as he urged Emile and Sophie to do—that one could hope to be truly happy. Only thus could one freely reject that false conception of honor and virtue that was based on prejudice, and discover and devote oneself to the true and eternal principles of morality. "What good is it to seek our happiness in the opinion of others if we can find it within ourselves?"[56]

Emile's education is designed to make him into an independent man in a corrupt world. This is not as paradoxical as it seems, since ultimately, Rousseau believed that "liberty is not found in any form of government, it is in the heart of the free man, he bears it everywhere with him."[57] Emile is to be such a man. First, although of independent means, he must be self-sufficient in a more personal way. He must never need to be economically dependent on anyone or any circumstance, and so is trained in the universally useful trade of carpentry. Secondly, and of far deeper significance, he is to be educated in such a way that he never feels subjected to another person's authority. The result of this is that, at the time his intellectual education begins, Rousseau tells us that the boy has "the confidence of independence," "he follows no rule, yields to no authority or example, and acts and speaks only as he pleases," for "does he not know that he is always his own master?"[58] In fact, as the whole of Book 2 testifies, he is controlled in many ways by his tutor throughout his childhood, but this control is exerted in such a way as to disguise the fact that it emanates from another person. In order to preserve him from dependence on the opinions or authority of others, he is not told what he ought or ought not to do, nor influenced by what people will think of him or by the prevailing prejudices.[59] Instead, his tutor contrives to manipulate circumstances in such a way that Emile learns how to behave by responding to the fortunate or unfortunate results of his actions. Children should never receive punishment as such, Rousseau teaches; the harm that befalls them should always appear to be the natural consequence of their fault. Thus, while the tutor is, covertly, very much in control of Emile's training, this is not perceived by the child. His independence of judgment suffers far less from his submission to consequences which seem to be "the heavy yoke of necessity under which every mortal being must bow" than from obedience to "the caprices of man."[60] Only because he is artificially preserved from the influence of authority and prejudice is Emile enabled to develop his own reasoning powers and to become able to distinguish for himself between good and evil. With this background, when the time comes for him to respond to the society around him, since he is "free from the yoke of prejudice, but ruled by the law of wisdom," he will care only about the opinions of the most honorable people, those most like himself.[61] He will be an independent man, so far as circumstances permit.

In society, Rousseau asserts, sexuality leads inevitably to the deep and extensive dependence of each sex on the other. "In every station, every country, every class, the two sexes have so strong and so natural a relation that the morals of the one always determine those of the other."[62] However, in the cases of both Emile and Sophie, and in general, Rousseau was far less inclined to stress the effects on their morals and character of women's dependence on men, than the influences of the dependence of men on women. As for the first—a dependence vastly intensified of course by the economic and social disparities between the sexes in a patriarchal society—he was completely unconcerned. He recognizes it, admittedly, in several passages, but only to confirm its necessity, not at all to question its rightfulness or its social effects. Several times he threatens women with the prospect of becoming merely the slaves of men, if they do not assume the sex-defined role and character required of them. Without her cunning wit, which compensates for her lack of physical strength, "woman would be man's slave, not his partner. . . . She has everything against her, our faults and her own weakness and timidity; her beauty and her wits are all that she has." Since beauty must inevitably fade, her only lasting resource is her wit, and the only way she can control man is by "manipulating us and taking advantage of our own strength."[63] Thus the only route to power that a woman has is to use her sexual hold over man to persuade, trick or cajole him into deciding to do what she wants.

Similarly, when he advises mothers to be sure to make their daughters into well-socialized women, and not to try to defy nature and make them like men, Rousseau says "be sure it will be better both for her and for us."[64] It is made very clear, however, that women are in no position to consider anything better for themselves if it is not also what men want of them, for women's complete dependence on men's approval is thrown up at them in the same discussion. Having suggested, ironically, that there is nothing to stop mothers from educating their daughters in any way they please and that men are not responsible for the fact that girls are educated only for trivia and flirtation, Rousseau proceeds to acknowledge at length that it is only by successful exploitation of their feminine charms that women can exert any power at all. Thus the philosopher who abhorred the rule of force and the reign of public opinion over the individual could acknowledge without any sign of disapproval that unless women educate themselves, structure their personalities and regulate their lives totally in accordance with man's liking, they can expect only to be enslaved by their more powerful opponents.

Rousseau's fear of women and their influence undoubtedly provides an important part of the explanation for this paradox. He was so convinced of the extent of man's sexual and emotional dependence on woman that he felt it was only by disadvantaging and oppressing her in other areas that his supposedly natural predominance could be restored to the male. Thus, in direct contrast to his assertion that the central need of the man is to be free, Rousseau argues that a woman is formed by nature for dependence and constraint.[65] Since he depicts her life as necessarily controlled by the requirements of the patriarch, the family is the one place where Rousseau's principled stand against personal power and subservience is not applied. Clearly, no woman can be enabled to live her own life as Emile is educated to live his. To the contrary, she can find her happiness only via the happiness of a good man, and thus she must direct all her energies toward pleasing and being respected by men, necessarily submitting to all their judgments, their needs and their injustices. Thus "the first and most important quality in a woman is gentleness; created to obey a being as imperfect as man, often so vicious and always so full of faults, she must learn at an early age to suffer injustice, and to put up with the wrongs of a husband without complaint."[66] Opposition or bitterness can only make things worse for her. While many of the qualities needed for this role were seen by Rousseau to be innate in women, Sophie's entire education is designed to reinforce them, and above all, to ensure that she will fulfill the requirements and never wish to upset the hierarchy of the patriarchal family.

Far from being an autonomous or even a distinct person, Rousseau's ideal woman should be strong only so that her sons will be strong, reasonable only to the extent required to preserve her chastity, converse with her husband and rear his children wisely, and even attractive only to the point where she appeals sexually to her husband but does not threaten his peace of mind. All her thoughts, "apart from those directly related to her duties, should tend toward the study of men or toward that pleasant learning which has the formation of taste as its aim."[67]

Thought, or the use of her reason, for any other purposes than these, are not only unnecessary but distasteful in a woman: "A female wit is a plague to her husband, her children, her friends, her servants, and everybody. From the exalted height of her genius, she scorns all her duties as a woman, and always sets out to make a man of herself. . . ."[68] Thus women "should learn many things, but only those things that are suitable."

Sophie is educated, therefore, just to the point where it is agreeable for Emile to converse with her without being in any danger of being threatened by her. Her mind is "pleasing but not brilliant, and thorough without being profound, a mind that inspires no comment, because it never seems brighter nor duller than one's own." She is deliberately left with great gaps in her knowledge which Emile, tutor as well as lover and husband, will have the pleasure of remedying.[69] Intended solely as a wife and mistress for man, any woman who was not considered desirable according to these criteria was judged by Rousseau to be worth nothing at all, however happy or successful she might be in her own right. Such a woman was willfully defying nature and trying to be a man.[70]

Only once in his mature writings does Rousseau consider Plato's radical proposals about the equal education of women in a positive way, and it is noteworthy that on this occasion, too, his concern is entirely with the implications that such a change would have for men. Perhaps, he speculates in a footnote to the *Discourse on the Arts and Sciences*, since "men will always be what is pleasing to women," it would only be by educating women to recognize and appreciate greatness of soul and virtue that these ancient qualities might be reestablished among men. Thus, even in suggesting that Plato's thought on the issue should be further developed, Rousseau held to his basic principle that women and their education must be suited to what were their only proper functions in a patriarchal culture.[71]

Because of her natural and predestined station in life, chastity is by far the most important moral quality for a woman to possess. Whereas the dignity of men consists in their freedom, the dignity of women "consists in modesty, [and] shame and chasteness are inseparable from decency for them." A woman who has lost her honor must be regarded as totally lacking in morality of any sort.[72] While virtue is a concept that, as Pierre Burgelin has pointed out, is scarcely mentioned in the context of Emile's education, since it always implied to Rousseau struggle against the self and a threat to freedom, it is the central value in the education of Sophie.[73] For it is only through the successful struggle against the self, or at least the passionate part of the self, that a woman can hope, by guarding that precious treasure, her chastity, to acquire and keep a husband. Love of virtue "is a woman's glory," it is "the only way to true happiness, and . . . she sees nothing but poverty, abandonment, unhappiness and infamy in the life of an unseemly woman."[74] Indeed, Sophie's ultimate fate is the clearest possible confirmation of this belief.

Rousseau had two reasons for considering it essential that woman's moral code should be not only different in content but also based on an entirely different principle from that applicable to men. First, she can achieve satisfaction in life only to the extent that others, notably men, find her pleasing. Secondly, not only must she be scrupulously chaste, but her chastity must be utterly unquestioned, by her husband or anyone else. Since the least breath of scandal is an "indelible stain" on a woman's character, and a man's honor depends less on his wife's actual conduct than on what people think about it, she must be sure not to compromise her reputation in any way. Thus, for women,

> it is not enough to be estimable, they must be esteemed; it is not enough to be beautiful, they must please; it is not enough to be good, they must be recognized as such; their honor is not in their conduct alone but in their reputation, and it is impossible for a woman who is really virtuous ever to allow herself to be thought vile. In order to act rightly, a man is his own master and can defy public opinion, but by doing the right thing a woman has only completed half her task, and what people think of her matters to her as much as what she really is. It follows from this that the principle of her education must be in this respect contrary to that of ours: opinion is the tomb of man's virtue and the throne of woman's.[75]

Thus, unlike Socrates and Plato but like the rest of the Greek world, Rousseau clearly regarded female morality and male morality as essentially different. It is not simply a matter of the familiar "double standard"; what he thought to be necessary was not two standards on the same ethical scale, but the construction of two radically different scales. Because women were viewed by him entirely in terms of the function they perform in a male culture, their standard of goodness is defined solely in terms of the requirements and prejudices of that culture, whereas goodness in men, who were not viewed functionally in this way, is defined as independently as possible of social prejudice. While there are many more or less equivalent ways in which a man might manifest his morality and worth, the preservation of her chastity is a woman's all-important moral goal.

Sophie's moral education is, as a result, a travesty of that prescribed for Emile. Indeed, if Rousseau's attitude to women were not so manifest, both in *Emile* and elsewhere, one might be tempted to interpret the description of her rearing as a satirical commentary on the contemporary culture and its educational methods, against which the work as a whole is directed.

Virtually everything Sophie does, and is encouraged to do, is for the sake of appearance. Unlike the free and casual child Emile, the girl takes endless pains over her toilet (in order to achieve the "natural look"), she learns the spinet for the purpose of showing off her white hands against the darkness of the keys, and everything she says is gauged, not according to its sense or usefulness, as Emile's conversation is judged, but according to the effect it will have on the listener. Though she is quite lacking in originality, "she always says what pleases the people who talk to her."[76] Her moral education is devoted to reinforcing her innate female tendency to be submissive and constrained, and teaching her to dissimulate, in order to conform exactly to what society expects of her. For girls, in contrast to boys,

should be restricted from a young age. . . . They will be subjected all their lives to the most severe and perpetual restraint, that of propriety: one must impose restraint on them from the start, so that it will never be a hardship for them, so as to master all their fantasies and make them submit to the wills of other people. . . . This habitual restraint results in a docility in women which they need all their lives, since they will always be in subjection to a man or to men's judgments, and will never be allowed to set themselves above these judgments.[77]

One of the major paradoxes of Sophie's education is due to the requirement that, while she must behave with the utmost reserve and self-control both before marriage and toward all men but her husband after marriage, she must be well versed in all the arts of coquetry and seduction, in order to maintain her husband's sexual interest in her. Rousseau blames the teachings of the Church for the fact that women frequently lose their amiableness and cause their husbands to become indifferent to them. To solve this problem, he says, "I wish that a young Englishwoman, would cultivate the talents which will delight her future' husband as carefully as a young Eastern woman cultivates them for the harem. . . . Surely that will add happiness to her husband's life and will prevent him, exhausted after he leaves his office, from seeking out amusements away from home?"[78] In keeping with this wish, the education of the ideal woman includes advice on how to maintain and elevate the future husband's sexual interest, alongside the strictest prohibitions against any other form of sexual expression. Sophie is indeed to be both concubine and nun.

In all respects, Rousseau argues that the constraints placed on women should be stricter after marriage than before. It is only among corrupt peoples, he asserts, that married women are allowed more freedom than young girls; with those who have preserved their morals, the opposite practice is followed.[79] The correct status of a married woman is described by Julie, speaking of her cousin Claire:

When she was unmarried, she was free, she had only to
answer to herself for her conduct . . . but now all is
changed; she must account to another for her conduct;
she has not only pledged her trust, she has renounced
her freedom. . . . A virtuous woman must not only de-
serve her husband's esteem but must obtain it; if he
blames her, she is blameworthy; and if she has acted
innocently, she is guilty as soon as she is suspected; for
even preserving appearances is part of her duty.[80]

Thus upon marrying, woman, truly for Rousseau a "femme
couverte" in the moral as well as the legal sense, loses all
her autonomy of judgment and conscience.

The extreme to which Rousseau extends his denial of
personal autonomy to women is his refusal to allow her to
formulate her own religious beliefs. While Emile is, when
old enough, encouraged to think for himself about religious
matters, "just as a woman's conduct is subject to public
opinion, so is her faith subject to authority."[81] A daughter
must unquestioningly adopt her mother's religion (which
is, of course, her father's too), and a wife her husband's.
Rousseau assures his readers that no woman will be made
to suffer for this, since "if this religion should be false, the
docility which makes the mother and daughter submit to
the natural order effaces the sin of error in the sight of
God."[82] Faith and doctrine are apparently unimportant for
women; they are redeemed through submission. This pronouncement, analogous to the Mohammedan belief that a
woman has no soul, is to make her, of course, in a religious
world, the ultimate non-person.

Although Rousseau could not conceive of any alternative to the rigid and prejudice-based code of ethics he prescribed for women, neither was he entirely comfortable
with it. After laying down a pattern of conduct for Sophie
which, totally in conformity with social prejudice, violates
every principle of Emile's education, he admits concern,
briefly, about what he is making woman into:

Perhaps I have said too much already. What will we reduce women to if we give them no law but public prejudices? Let us not debase to that level the sex which governs us, and which honors us when we have not made it vile. There exists for the whole human species a more fundamental law than opinion. . . . This law is our inner conscience. . . .[83]

Since the opinion of society should be obeyed only when it is in accordance with the dictate of conscience, he concludes, rather belatedly, that whereas women must do their best to reconcile the two, if this cannot be done, they should follow their consciences. "If these two laws do not coincide in the education of women," he acknowledges, "it will always be defective." When one considers, however, that the conflict between what is right and good and the prejudices of a corrupt society is what Emile and most of the rest of Rousseau's writings are all about, the results of Sophie's education seem doomed. There appears to be not much hope that public opinion and conscience will constantly coincide, as Rousseau believes they must if the education of women is to be successful. If we consider the outcomes of the stories of Emile, Sophie and Julie and the results of the kind of socialization of women Rousseau advocated as the only proper one, we have to conclude that, for him, the problem of women remained an insoluble dilemma.

8

The Fate of
Rousseau's Heroines

Rousseau was acutely aware, perhaps more than any other political philosopher, of the conflicts of loyalties in people's lives, and the incompatible demands made by the various personal and group relationships in which people participate. A moderate degree of self-love, love of another individual, love of one's family, of one's fellow countrymen, of humanity as a whole—all these he perceived as by no means easily reconcilable. All, however, he valued as important in their own way, and it was his ultimate conviction of their incompatibility that made his philosophical conclusions so deeply pessimistic. After outlining the denouements of *Emile* and *Les Solitaires* (its unfinished sequel), and *La Nouvelle Héloïse*, I will draw on the fates of Rousseau's characters to explore the repercussions of his ideas about women on the already conflicting demands of the human condition as he perceived it.

In accord with his tutor's plan, Emile on attaining adulthood rejects all existing governments and chooses to be an independent man.[1] All he wants, he says, is a wife and a piece of land of his own, and the one chain he will always be proud to wear is his attachment to Sophie. However, Rousseau points out that it is not so easy to be an independent man, since although his need for a mate and companion is perceived as natural, in becoming the head of a family, he becomes necessarily the citizen of a state.[2] "As soon as a man needs a mate, he is no longer an isolated being; his heart is no longer alone. All his relations with his species, all the affections of his soul are born with this

one. His first passion soon makes the others develop."[3]
Moreover, citizenship of a state is not treated, even in the
case of Emile, as a necessary evil. Rousseau convinces Emile
that he owes much to the laws of the country in which he
resides, however far they may fall short of that genuine
law that originates in the social contract and popular
sovereignty. He is indebted to them not only for protection, but also for "that which is most precious to man, the
morality of his actions and the love of virtue."[4] While a
man in the depths of the forest might have lived more
happily and more freely, "having nothing to struggle
against in order to follow his inclinations . . . , he would not
have been virtuous. . . ." In civil society, on the other hand,
a man can become motivated for the common good: "He
learns to struggle with himself and to win, to sacrifice his
interest to the general interest."[5] The laws do not prevent
man from being free; rather they teach him to govern
himself.

With this introduction of virtue and civic duty as ideals,
not just necessities, for Emile, one wonders just what has
happened to the natural man whom Rousseau had set
out to educate. In the last part of Book 5, he seems to
be trying to do what he had said was impossible—to
make Emile into a natural man and a citizen at the same
time. It is decided that Emile should live where he can
serve his fellow men best, which is not, in this corrupt
world, by immersing himself in town life, but by presenting
an example of rural simplicity.[6] The important point is
that the rural life is not decided on simply because it is
best for Emile and Sophie themselves, but because of the
example it will provide others. Moreover, while it is unlikely that he will be called upon to serve the state, since
a corrupt world has little use for such a man, if he *is* called
upon, like Cincinnatus he must leave his plow and go.[7]
Thus Rousseau clearly attempts to make of Emile a citizen,
as well as a natural and independent man.

The impossibility of these demands—that the naturally

educated man should also fill the roles of husband, father and citizen—is clearly asserted by Rousseau in the two letters that were all he completed of *Les Solitaires*. It very soon becomes apparent that it was only through the covert authority of the tutor and his continual manipulation of the environment that the illusion of Emile's success as a natural man in society was maintained. The adult Emile is in fact still hopelessly dependent on his tutor, and when left by him to lead his own life he fails as a husband, a father and a citizen, and feels unequivocally free only when he has divested himself of all these attachments and responsibilities and become an emotional isolate. The conclusion that he eventually draws from his experience is a complete confirmation of the irreconcilability of the man/citizen dichotomy. "By breaking the ties that attached me to my country," he says "I extended them over all the earth, and I became so much more a man in ceasing to be a citizen."[8] And, as Judith Shklar has noted, "What is impossible for the perfectly reared Emile, who possesses every virtue except the quality that controls men and events, is certainly not possible for lesser men."[9] Rousseau's conclusions about the man and the citizen could not be more clear.

Emile's education, however, is both a failure and a success. It has failed to make him into both a natural man and a citizen, but Rousseau had already told us at the outset of the work that this was impossible.[10] As Emile himself acknowledges, he cannot fulfill his duties as a husband and father without the constant help of his tutor. He is fitted neither for emotional closeness and dependence nor for the loyalty of a patriot, as his desertion of his family and his country makes clear. On the other hand, however, the end of his story shows that, in the sense of forming an autonomous, internally free man, his education has been a success. When he becomes literally enslaved, it is vitally important to him that, although his work and his hands can be sold from one master to another, his will, understanding, and real essence are inviolable.[11] He rejoices that, because of his unique education, he has, as Rousseau intended, internal freedom, of which no one can deprive him. His personal, moral autonomy renders him essentially free even when his body is enslaved. His education has failed to do the impossible; but it has, Rousseau concludes, succeeded in making Emile into a universal man, adaptable to any situation and free of all restricting attachments.

What, though, of Sophie? Her ideal female education, as we have seen, was designed to endow her with that combination of alluring charm and chaste modesty that befits the wife of the patriarch. Like Emile, she "has only a natural goodness in an ordinary soul; every way in which she is better than other women is the result of her education."[12] The outcome described in *Les Solitaires* is therefore undeniable testimony to the failure of the ideal female education, just as it is to the failure of the attempt to make a natural man fit for social life.

First, Sophie, who has not been taught like Emile how to accept necessary evils, is so upset by her daughter's death that Emile has to take her to Paris in order to distract her from her grief. Inevitably Paris, the cesspit of civilization, proves their downfall. Emile, corrupted by the city, breaks his marital vows by faltering in his love and devotion for Sophie. She, whose whole life has been made to revolve around love, whose entire self-esteem depends upon whether she is pleasing to men, cannot cope with her feelings of rejection, commits adultery, and finds herself with child by another man. Even though Emile is convinced by her honesty and remorse that Sophie's heart has remained pure throughout, and he is aware that the temptations she faced were greater than any he could ever be expected to resist, he is unable to see any alternative to leaving her and their surviving child. Neither is it conceivable that she could accept his pardon, were he to offer it; she sees herself after her adultery as irredeemable. Instantaneously, in her own eyes, and in those of Emile and Rousseau, she has fallen from the pedestal of the madonna to the gutter of the prostitute. Having fallen once, there can be no possible guarantee that she will not do so again, since when a woman has lost her chaste reputation, she has no virtue left to preserve: "the first step toward vice is the only painful one." Emile does, in fact, consider whether, being such an independent man, he should ignore that social prejudice which holds a wife's crime against her husband's honor. He concludes, however, that it is indeed a reasonable prejudice that deserves to be heeded. For any such crime *is* her husband's fault, either for choosing badly or for governing her badly. Though thus acknowledging that he is largely to blame, Emile decides that it is impossible for him to take Sophie back as his wife. The final decision is made when he reflects on the horror of her being the mother of another man's child, for in sharing her affection between the two children, his son and this usurper, she must likewise share her feelings between their two fathers. His feelings of revulsion against this are such that he exclaims: "I would sooner see my son dead than Sophie the mother of another man's child."[13]

Here we are presented with a very clear case in which the feelings of the natural man and the interests of his family and country are in direct conflict. His feelings prevailing, Emile is of course far better able to cope with the consequences of the break-up of his family than is Sophie, with the responsibility for two dependent children. Though saddened by what he sees as the irreparable loss of the woman he loves, he leaves his family and country and goes off, independent and self-sufficient, to be a real "solitaire." Soon reveling in his new-found independence, he owes no one anything, and finds himself at home and self-supporting wherever he goes. "I told myself," he relates to his tutor, "that wherever I lived, in whatever situation I found myself, I would always find my task as a man to do, and that no one needed others if each lived agreeably for himself." "I drank the waters of forgetfulness, the past

was erased in my memory."[14] Sophie, however, is in no
position to forget the past; she has two children, of whom
one soon dies, no status in society, and no respectable
means of support unless she relies on Emile. Surely neither
her self-respect and shame nor his obvious lack of responsibility make this a viable solution. She has no alternative
but to die, which she obligingly does, charming to the
end.[15]

The importance of this fictional denouement arises, of
course, from the fact that *Emile* and its sequel are not just
novels, but the account of the fates of a man and a woman
educated to be paragons of their respective sexes. Sophie's
adultery, which together with what is regarded as Emile's
inevitable reaction to it destroys this ideal family, is of
supreme importance because, after all, *not* to commit
adultery was the aim of her entire education. As Emile
acknowledges, "If Sophie soiled her virtue, what woman
can dare rely on hers?"[16] Sophie's failure is indicative of
the failure in the society of Rousseau's time, of the best
possible education he thought a woman could have. She is
designed to be very conscious of her charms, "consumed
with the single need for love,"[17] and ruled by the judgment of public opinion. As Burgelin has pointed out, it is
Eucharis, the seductive nymph, with whom Sophie identifies when she fantasizes about Telemachus, not the chaste
wife, Antiope.[18] It is hardly surprising, then, that, neglected
by her husband in a licentious city, she acts according to
its lax moral code. The narrowness of what is considered
to be her proper sphere, and the contradictory expectations
placed on her—not least that she behave like a concubine
with her husband and like a nun with all other men—
make it inevitable that she will "fall" as she does. The
corrupt city certainly compounded the problems that resulted from Sophie's education, but an examination of the
fate of Julie, who never leaves the idyllic countryside, reveals that the issue is more complex than this.

Julie is Rousseau's ideal woman—the kind of woman he

himself would love.[19] She is extremely sensitive and emotional; she abounds in those qualities—modesty, romanticism and sexual attractiveness—without which Rousseau considered a woman to be worthless. The central theme of *La Nouvelle Héloise* is the conflict between her feelings and her duty which Rousseau believed a sensitive woman must confront. Julie is torn between her passionate feelings for her tutor, Saint-Preux, and her strong sense of duty to her mother, and to her impossible father, who will have nothing to do with the commoner and wants to marry his daughter to a noble friend.[20] When Julie's violent love for Saint-Preux overpowers her devotion to her duty to preserve her virginity, as one would expect of such a passionate character, she feels that she is utterly destroyed. In a desperate letter to her cousin and confidante, she writes: "Without knowing what I was doing I chose my own ruin. I forgot everything and remembered only love. Thus in a wild moment I was ruined forever. I have fallen into the depths of shame from which a girl cannot recover herself; and if I live, it will be only to be more wretched."[21] Having lost her virginity, she feels that she has no further worth as a person, and, overwhelmed with guilt, cries out to Saint-Preux, "Be my whole being, now that I am nothing."[22]

Through Julie, who in spite of her exaggerated piety is a far more real and intelligent character than Sophie, Rousseau acknowledges to the reader that her plight is a terrible one, and one that no man could ever suffer from. As Julie writes to her lover:

Consider the position of my sex and yours in our common misfortunes, and judge which of us is more to be pitied? To feign insensitivity in the turmoil of passion; to seem joyful and content while prey to a thousand sorrows; to appear serene while one's soul is distressed; always to say other than what one thinks; to disguise what one feels; to be obliged to be false and to lie through modesty; this is the customary position of all girls of my age. Thus we spend out finest years under the tyranny of propriety, which is at length added to by the tyranny of our parents' forcing us into an unsuitable marriage. But it is in vain that they repress our inclinations; the heart accepts only its own laws; it escapes from slavery; it bestows itself according to its own will.[23]

Apart from forced marriages, all of these misfortunes are regarded by Rousseau as inevitable consequences of being born female. While Saint-Preux is affected as much emotionally by their enforced separation, he is not, like Julie, degraded by shame or obliged to hide his feelings. Neither is he forced to marry someone whom he does not love, but instead can go off on journeys and exploits, and enjoy an autonomous existence insofar as he can without the woman he loves. Since Julie was not married when she committed her terrible crime, and the child she conceives miscarries, there is still hope for her moral redemption. Whatever course of action she chooses, however, she cannot herself be happy, and the choice is never put in terms of what *she* wants to do, but always as a contest between the wills of the three men who surround her—her lover, her father, and later her husband. "Whom shall I give preference to, out of a lover and a father?" she asks, when deciding whether to elope or to marry the man of her father's choice; ". . . whichever course I take, I must die both wretched and guilty."[24] Again, while she cannot marry Saint-Preux without her father's consent, she promises her lover that she will not marry anyone else without *his* consent.[25] On the occasion of her reluctant marriage, Julie describes her fate in this male-ruled world in which she lives: "Bound by an indissoluble chain to the fate of a husband, or rather to the will of a father, I am entering into a new way of life which must end only with death."[26]

By placing her duty to her parents before her love for

Saint-Preux and marrying the man her father forces on her, in Rousseau's eyes Julie has redeemed herself. The whole of the rest of the novel, however, consists in her never-ending struggle against her feelings, and her repeated attempts to convince herself that she has conquered her passion. Slowly, she recovers her honor and virtue, in the role of wife and mother which, she says, "elevates my soul and sustains me against the remorse resulting from my other condition."[27] Nevertheless, by her own account she is not happy, despite the worthy Wolmar, her husband, who treats her like a delightful child, despite her healthy children, her religion, and her reunion (on a strictly non-physical level) with Saint-Preux. Though the rural domestic situation in which she lives is described as the happiest possible life on earth,[28] and Julie herself as the perfect mother and most tasteful mistress of the house, she confesses to Saint-Preux, toward the end of her life, her inexplicable unhappiness. Though she sees only reasons for happiness around her, she says, "I am not content," and then "I am too happy; happiness bores me." Tormented by a "secret regret," she laments "my empty soul reaches out for something to fill it."[29] The final denouement, Julie's pseudo-accidental death, and her posthumous confession of her still unconquered passion for Saint-Preux, can only be seen as tragic commentary on her deluded sense of victory over her feelings. As she at last realizes, "Great passions can be stifled; rarely can they be purged."[30]

Julie has behaved as she ought to have done, ever since her first great sin. She has preserved her virtue intact throughout her marriage, although she was deluded in believing that she was cured of her love. When, therefore, she realizes that she has always been and still is in danger of succumbing to temptation, her death is the only way out of the dilemma. Any reunion between her and Saint-Preux from that point on would be so dangerous that God takes the matter out of their hands. Indisposed after saving her son from drowning, Julie loses the will to live. Thus her passion has escaped destroying the ideal Wolmar family, but only by destroying her instead.

As Judith Shklar has asserted, Julie, as the human sacrifice, is a Christ figure.[31] Since, however, she is the ideal woman, loving and lovable, honorable, kind, and struggling always to be virtuous, the fact that she is sacrificed has profound implications for Rousseau's whole theory of women. Julie is his heroine, it must be recognized, *because* in spite of her rigid and repressive upbringing and her love of virtue, she is passionate and, like the original Héloise, "made for love." However, given this personality, she is doomed to spend her entire adult life fighting her natural feelings, for the sake of her all-important chastity, her duty to her class-conscious parents, and her obedience to the prejudices of an inegalitarian world. Rousseau asserts in *Emile* that "in our senseless conditions, the life of a good woman is a constant struggle against herself,"[32] but his own ideas about women's education and proper position in society, taken together with his convictions about love and marriage, make it clear that in any conditions he was prepared to envisage, the kind of woman he idolized would not only be condemned to perpetual struggle, but might very well be required (not only in the corrupt city, but even in the pure countryside) to sacrifice her life for the sake of virtue. The ancient two-fold demands made of woman—that she be both the inspiration of romantic, sexual love, and the guardian of marital fidelity—are seen at their most tragic in Rousseau.

There are three important sets of conflicting claims on the human individual which are discussed in Rousseau's works, and which must be reviewed in the light of his theories about women and the examples of ideal womanhood that he created. The first is the conflict between the impulses of the individual and the requirements of the republican state. Rousseau says that men must be educated as either individuals or citizens, but his education of women does not fit them to be either. The second is the conflict between the consuming commitment to a dyadic love-relationship and the needs of the wider world—whether family, state, or mankind as a whole. The third set of claims, which Rousseau considers but ultimately does not acknowledge to be in conflict, consists of the demands made by the family and those made by the ideal republic. It is my contention that, however problematic these second and third conflicts of loyalty are for man, it is woman, educated and defined as Rousseau would have her, who will opt for what he considers to be the less valuable of each pair of alternative commitments, and whose inevitable tendency will be to subvert both of his ideal institutions—the patriarchal family and the patriotic democratic republic.

The central theme of Rousseau's social theory is the conflict between the ideal of the independent, natural man, and that of the man who is part of a large whole, his country—between the man and the citizen. At the beginning of *Emile*, he frankly states the dilemma which to him is the necessary starting point of any honest social theory: no person can be both man and citizen: "The natural man is altogether for himself; he is the unit, the absolute whole, who has no relation to anyone but himself or those like him."[33] In educating the natural man, the essential thing is to let nature take its course: "The whole [education] consists in not spoiling the natural man by making him conform to society."[34]

The education prescribed for the citizen, however, is very different. Rousseau considered that he had proved through his construction of an hypothetical state of nature that man's natural tendency is to be good, in the sense that he finds it pleasant to be kind to his fellows, so long as they do not thwart his needs or desires. The citizen, however, is required to have far more moral fiber than this. Living in close proximity to and mutual dependence on others, he will be required to perform duties that may well be disagreeable to him and involve considerable sacrifice. Thus it is not sufficient for him to rely on his natural tendency to be kind because it makes him feel good; he must, in short, learn to be virtuous.

> The citizen is but the numerator of a fraction which belongs to the denominator, and whose value is in his relationship with the whole—the social body. Good social institutions are those which best know how to denature man, to take away his absolute existence and to give him a relative one, and to move the individual self into the community; so that each does not think of himself as one, but as part of the whole, and has feelings only as a member of that whole.[35]

The education of a real citizen, such as Rousseau considered the Spartans and the Romans to have been, thus involves no less than the destruction of most of man's natural tendencies, and the transformation of his personality. As examples, he cites Brutus, who condemned his sons to death for their betrayal of the Republic; Pedaretes, who was rejected for membership of the Spartan Council and rejoiced that there were three hundred citizens better qualified than himself; and the Spartan mother, who ran to thank the gods for her country's victory though her five sons had all been killed in the process of attaining it.[36] The citizen socialized as Rousseau advocates would live for his country; he would think neither of his individual self nor of humanity as a whole, but solely of his fellow-citizens. He would be a patriot "by inclination, with passion, by necessity."[37]

Rousseau held up Plato's *Republic* as the outstanding account of true public education. In the *Discourse on Political Economy* and in *Considerations on the Government of Poland*, we have his own treatments of the subject, and in the *Letter to d'Alembert* he asserts that the only way of proving that education has improved is by showing that it makes better citizens. In *Emile*, however, stating that there are neither fatherlands nor citizens in his time, he argues that there can therefore be no public education, and that he will discuss the other alternative—private and domestic education.[38] His essential point is that the choice must be made; the socialization process must combat either society, in order to make a natural man, or nature, in order to make a real citizen.

> He who wishes to preserve the supremacy of natural feeling in civil life does not know what he is asking. Always in contradiction with himself, always fluctuating between his inclinations and his duties, he will never be either a man or a citizen; he will be no good to himself or to others.[39]

At this point in his argument, Rousseau poses the problem of how a man educated for himself, as he intends to educate Emile, could live with others. He says that "*if* perhaps the double aim proposed could be reunited into a single one, by getting rid of man's contradictions one would remove a major obstacle to his happiness."[40]

Rousseau's denial of the possibility of such a reunion of the two aims is expressed by what becomes of Emile. For Emile is not intended to be by any means an isolate, but rather to be "a natural man living in society, . . . a savage made to live in town."[41] He must know how to live, if not *like* its other inhabitants, at least *with* them. His choice to be a husband and father entails the obligations of the citizen.[42] Emile's failure in all these three roles is the proof of the irreconcilable conflict between manhood and citizenship. His education has fitted him to be his own man, but not to tolerate any attachments, personal or patriotic. The denouement of Emile's story is simply a confirmation of what was stated at the beginning of Book 1 —one must choose to educate a man or a citizen, but not both.

There is, however, for Rousseau, only one possible method of educating a woman. She is not, like Emile, educated to be her own person, with independent judgment, economic self-sufficiency, and an acquired ability to accept necessity and adapt to any situation in which she finds herself. Neither is she, like the Polish children, to be first and foremost her country's citizen, socialized so as to think of the fatherland in every waking moment and to subordinate her wishes always to the public welfare. There is no mention of such alternatives with respect to Sophie's and Julie's educations. They are educated, instead, to be the appendages—the obedient and submissive daughters, wives, and mothers—of the men on whom they will depend for livelihood and for self-respect. The relationships they are prepared for are entirely personal ones; because their only proper means of influence or power are through the men who are closest to them, they are taught to manipulate them for their own ends.

It seems extraordinary, therefore, that Rousseau should have expected the Genevan women to utilize their single means of power in the world to expedite civic virtue and the public interest. For them or any other women educated in the mode he regarded as proper—having had no public socialization and sharing no part of the duties or rights of the citizen—to place the public welfare before their own or that of the persons closest to them, would certainly be remarkable, according to Rousseau's own reasoning. At the beginning of *The Social Contract*, he attributes his conviction that it is his duty to study governments and public affairs to the fact that he was born a citizen of a free state and voting member of the sovereign.[43] No woman he could envisage would ever be so motivated. Nothing in his prescribed education for girls leads to the expectation that patriotic loyalties will take precedence over personal or selfish ones.

The second conflict of loyalties that Rousseau's social theory confronts is that between the exclusiveness of intimate love and the welfare of the outside world—whether family, fatherland, or humanity. Although he admired romantic love and pined for it, he depicts it as founded on mere illusion.[44] It creates its own love objects, by covering those in the real world with a veil of fantasy. "We are," as Julie says, "far more in love with the image we conjure up than with the object to which we attach it. If we saw the object of our love exactly as it is, there would be no more love in the world."[45] The one time Rousseau himself fell in love, with Mme. d'Houdetot, was the result of his investing her with the qualities of Julie, whom he was currently creating. Similarly, Emile is carefully prepared in advance for his meeting with his future wife by having an idealized Sophie presented in detail to his imagination, and it is not, we notice, on their first meeting that he falls in love with her, but on hearing her name and realizing that this girl is indeed the embodiment of his fantasies.[46] Based as it is on illusion, love is necessarily evanescent. As Julie writes to Saint-Preux, though one may feel it so violently that it seems indestructible, love will inevitably fade, and boredom and oversatiation follow. Love "wears out with youth, it fades with beauty, it dies under the iciness of age, and since the beginning of the world two lovers with white hair have never been seen sighing for each other."[47] (The love of Julie and Saint-Preux, of course, is no exception, since they were parted at such an early stage that there could be no question of oversatiation. The tone of their letters, indeed, suggests strongly that their passion was kept alive by being thwarted.)

While love lasts, however, Rousseau does not question its intensity. How exclusive and all-consuming he considered a dyadic love-relationship to be is clearly expressed in *The Confessions* as well as in his other writings.[48] Plato is referred to as the true philosopher of lovers because of his conviction that "throughout the passion, they never have another."[49] The exclusive nature of love is clearly illustrated in the melodramatic outbursts of Saint-Preux, who lives for his passion alone. After he and Julie finally contrive to spend the night together, he writes to her: "Oh, let us die, my sweet friend! Let us die, beloved of my heart! What is there to do, henceforth, with an insipid youth, now that we have exhausted all its delights."[50] He gives up himself and his will totally to Julie's disposal, discounting any connection except with her. When separated from his love, he cries out to her cousin, Claire, "Ah, what is a mother's life, what is my own, yours, even hers, what is the existence of the whole world next to the delightful feeling which united us?"[51] The anarchistic tendencies of exclusive love are pointed out by Lord Bomston, Saint-Preux's confidant, as he talks of the bond between two lovers. "All laws which impede it are unjust," he says, "all fathers who dare to form or break it are tyrants. This chaste or natural bond is subject neither to sovereign power nor to paternal authority, but only to the authority of our common Father, who can govern hearts. . . ."[52] The rights of the family and of the state are seen by Bomston as having no precedence over those of love.

It was the absolute demands made by love, as Rousseau conceived of it, and as described by Bomston and exemplified by the complete self-abandonment of Saint-Preux, that led him to see it as such a threat to the other loyalties required of us. The worth of a man who speaks in the way Saint-Preux is quoted above, as a member of a family, a country, or even of the human race, is surely questionable. All he can think of is his passion for Julie. However, although Rousseau conceives of romantic-sexual love as so all-consuming and intense, his conclusion seems to be that, like all passions, love is good if we are the masters of it and do not let it master us. A man is not guilty, he tells Emile, if he loves his neighbor's wife, so long as he controls his passion and does his duty; but he is guilty if he loves his own wife so much that he sacrifices everything else to that love.[53] In a letter, his thoughts on the subject are summarized, thus:

> We are justly punished for those exclusive attachments which make us blind and unjust, and limit our universe to the persons we love. All the preferences of

friendship are thefts committed against the human race and the fatherland. Men are all our brothers, they should all be our friends.[54]

If even friendship is a theft, then *love* and wider loyalties are far more liable to clash. Where there is opportunity to devote oneself to groups and causes outside the narrow circle of intimacy—to fatherland or humanity—then exclusive dyadic love is to be eschewed as a threat to civic or humane loyalties. This is why Rousseau was so opposed to introducing the romantic love of the theater into Geneva, since he believed that city to have a level of morality and civic feeling that could only be lowered by the fostering of personal and sexual intimacy.[55] For although "it is much better to love a mistress than to love oneself alone in all the world . . . the best is he who shares his affections equally with all his kind."[56]

Because he perceived romantic love to be so exclusive and marriage to be an essential and functional *social* institution, Rousseau was by no means sure that the continuation of intense passion was compatible with marriage. Certainly at times he expresses the wish that they were. He laments the fact that, although if the happiness of love could be prolonged within marriage we would have a paradise on earth, this has never been seen to happen. Unfortunately, "in spite of all precautions, possession wears out pleasures, and love before all others."[57] He advises Sophie to forestall the fading of Emile's amorous interest in her as long as possible, both by continuing to be alluring and by granting her sexual favors sparingly. In spite of this, however, the time will inevitably come, as in any marriage, when the husband's ardor will cool. Thus, the feelings on which marriage is based must ultimately be tenderness and trust, mutual esteem, virtue, and the compatibility of the partners, strengthened by the extremely important bond that children form between their parents—"a bond which is often stronger than love itself."[58]

In *La Nouvelle Héloise*, however, Rousseau has Julie argue not just that romantic love cannot last in marriage, but that it has no place in a good marriage. As she writes,

> Love is accompanied by a continual anxiety over jealousy or privation, little suited to marriage, which is a state of joy and peace. People do not marry in order to think exclusively of one another, but to fulfill together the duties of civic life, to govern their houses prudently, and to bring up their children well. Lovers never see anyone but themselves, are concerned only with each other, and the only thing they can do is love each other. This is not enough for married people who have so many other cares to attend to.[59]

Marriage, then, is a serious social institution, which by no means succeeds easily; it *should* be based on honor, virtue and compatibility, and is indeed better off without the disturbances of passion. While Saint-Preux has been an ideal lover, Julie (and her creator) doubt that he could be a good husband, for Rousseau believes that the combination is extremely rare.[60] Between Julie and her husband, Wolmar, a man totally without passion, there is none of that illusion which maintains such a state of heightened tension between her and Saint-Preux. It is Wolmar, moreover, who is billed as the ideal husband, father and head of household. The marriage of the Wolmars is depicted as admirable and orderly, and the family they form as a model for others. However, the achievement of this model is founded on the overriding of passionate love, which entails the sacrifice of Julie's feelings, and eventually of her life.

Thus, while in one respect Julie's impossible position might have been alleviated if the laws and customs which gave fathers so much power over their daughters were different, the important conflict between love and marriage would not thereby be resolved. Without the despotism of fathers and the requirements of the property system, Julie would have married her lover, but we are not given the impression that such a solution would have been either a happy or a socially useful one. After all, at the height of their passion, what they had thought of as the climax of their relationship was to die together, more than to live together, and Rousseau was very skeptical about the fate of their kind of love if it was subjected to the trials and disillusionments of many years of day-to-day life. It is made very clear to us that although it was Saint-Preux whom Julie always loved so passionately, Wolmar was undoubtedly the best man to be her husband and her children's father. In fact, then, for the sake of virtue and her social duties, the only alternative for Rousseau's ideal woman is to do exactly as she does, even without the coercion of her father. She must marry, without love, a worthy and dispassionate man, and make an orderly and happy home for him and his children, even though she is all the while in torment herself, and finally her only means of victory over love is to die.

Julie, however, is an exceptional paragon of virtue—a Christ figure. This is why, though she must be destroyed, she is able to place her duties to her family and to society above the feelings of love which possess her. Sophie, on the other hand, though she has received the ideal education for her sex, succumbs to the temptation of illicit love after marriage, thereby dooming both herself and her family. The attempt to create a woman in the image of a seductive nymph, Eucharis, and then have her behave like the virtuous wife, Antiope, is as much a failure as the attempt to make a natural man into a citizen. The ideal woman's need to please and to be loved continually, and her dependence on men's approval for her self-esteem and on public opinion for her moral code, make it virtually certain that in conditions of stress, sexual love will prevail over the demands of monogamy, which is the basis of all social order. Since "love is the realm of women,"[61] and virtually their sole means of power, they can only be expected to exaggerate its importance, whether at the expense of the calmer affections on which marriage should be based, or to the detriment of their families, fellow countrymen or fellow humans.

Rousseau's conviction that intimate dyadic relationships are threatening to the larger community has been asserted by many other leaders or theorists of groups which demand their members' undivided loyalty. As a recent sociological study by Lewis Coser documents, libidinal withdrawal has been perceived as a threat by close-knit communities and sects as diverse as the Church and its religious orders, the early Bolsheviks, and many of the early American utopias. In order to prevent the drawing off of energies and affections from the common purpose, such groups have tended to require of their members either celibacy or promiscuity, which, as Coser points out, "though opposed sexual practices, fulfill identical sociological functions."[62] Citing much evidence of this type of reasoning from the writings of theorists of the three groups named above, Coser also points to a finding that all except one of the successful nineteenth-century American utopias practiced either free love or celibacy at some time in their history. Of the twenty-one unsuccessful communities, however, only five did so, and of these, four permitted couples to form if they wished.[63] Thus, for the type of community in which total allegiance of the members is perceived as essential, it would seem that there is good reason to place controls on dyadic relationships.

Rousseau gives a small scale example of such practice, in the sexual segregation in the Wolmar's household at Clarens. Masters who are at all concerned with being well served by their servants should realize that "too intimate relations between the sexes never produces anything but evil," and that therefore, "in a well-regulated household the men and women should have little to do with each other."[64] The ruin of the richest families, he warns, has been brought about by the intrigues of the men and women in their service. Thus segregation, in addition to preserving the chastity of the female servants, will also ensure that servants of both sexes perform their duties to the household faithfully and without distraction. On the republican level, arrangements such as the Genevan clubs perform the same function of preventing the distractions of sexual intimacy from harming the greater cause of civic life.

It is important to note, at this point, that those "greedy" communities which Coser analyzes are not only antagonistic to intimate sexual love relationships but also decidedly hostile to the family. The Catholic priesthood, the early Bolshevik militants and the successful utopias in America either bluntly prohibited, or at least strongly discouraged, their members from committing themselves to the demands of family life. A number of philosophical creators of utopian communities made similar recommendations. Plato in the *Republic*, Campanella in his *City of the Sun*, and Fourier in his projected *Phalansteries*, all extended their wariness of intimate relationships to the family.[65] In the light of this fact, Rousseau's treatment of the possible conflicts between the family and the republic and his conclusion that the family must indeed be preserved as the basis of society, are extremely interesting. Almost alone among creators of close-knit utopian communities, Rousseau was so far from hostile to the family that he idealized it.

In spite of his distinction between the natural basis of the family and the conventional basis of political society, Rousseau envisaged his ideal, small, democratic republic as, in many respects, like a big family. In the *Letter to d'Alembert*, for example, he refers to the public balls which he regards as so salutary for the peace and preservation of the republic as "not so much a public entertainment as . . . the gathering of a big family."[66] Again, he recommended to the Poles that republics should be small enough so that the citizens' behavior can be supervised by their rulers and their peers alike, which is far closer to his description of a family than to that of a political society.[67] Finally, in a single noteworthy sentence in the *Discourse on Political Economy*, he refers to the state as a loving and nourishing mother, and its citizens when children as each other's "mutually cherishing" brothers, and when adult as the fathers and defenders of their country.[68] While the metaphor is somewhat strained, its implication is unmistakable. The highly community-oriented method of socialization administered to the citizens of the ideal republic was intended to produce a family, a brotherhood, rather than a collection of individuals.

While discussing the dilemma that one cannot be both a man and a citizen, Rousseau had made a sociological observation, very like the arguments put forward by other utopians, about the functioning of groups and their tendency to demand all of their members' loyalties and emotions. "Every partial society," he writes "when it is close-knit and well united, alienates itself from the larger society. Every patriot is harsh toward foreigners; they are only men, they are nothing in his sight. . . . The essential thing is to be good to the people with whom one lives."[69] Moreover, just as patriotic loyalty detracts from one's love for humanity as a whole, one's membership of and loyalty to subgroups within one's country was recognized by Rousseau as being likely to detract from the patriotic loyalty required of the true citizen. Thus, since "the same decision can be advantageous to the small community and very harmful to the large one," it follows that "a person could be a devout priest, a brave soldier, or a zealous professional, and a bad citizen."[70] In *The Social Contract*, therefore, since the aim is to develop real citizens joined in one "moral and collective body"[71] with a general will, and the ascendancy of particular interests over the common interest is perceived as an ever present danger, the existence of partial societies is distinctly frowned upon. For "when particular interests begin to make themselves felt and the smaller societies to have an influence over the greater, the common interest changes and finds opponents, unanimity of opinion no longer reigns, the general will is no longer the will of all. . . ." With the growth of particular and group interests, each will come to focus on his own particular benefit, and will neglect the decline of the public welfare.[72]

It would seem that one of the most obvious applications of this theory of conflicting interests would be to the family. This is a group, surely, which requires its members to have a very strong loyalty to its needs and wishes, which may well conflict with the good of the greater society. Since the family's "principal object," as Rousseau says, is "to preserve and increase the patrimony of the father, in order that he may one day share it amongst his children without impoverishing them," and since private property and inheritance are regarded by him as the most sacred rights of citizenship,[73] there must obviously be many occasions on which the interests of individual families will be opposed to the needs of the country as a whole. Any circumstances requiring taxation, the absence of the breadwinner for public duties, or the regulation of private property for the general good, for example, are more than likely to cause conflict between family and patriotic loyalties. However, in spite of the fact that Rousseau's conflict of interest theory is applied to the level of patriotic feelings versus humanitarian ones, and to *some* partial groups within the republic, he refused explicitly to recognize that it can be applied also to the tension between the demands of the greater society and those of the family.

It is important to point out, at this point, two occasions in his writings when Rousseau does come very close to recognizing the potential conflicts of interest between his two ideal institutions—the democratic republic and the property-owning patriarchal family. First, the most striking examples he cites of Spartan and Roman patriotic devotion are those of citizens who subordinated their family feelings and attachments to the requirements of their fatherlands. Even though Brutus and the Spartan mother must have privately grieved over their children's deaths, they were undoubtedly citizens before they were parents. These two real citizens were sufficiently able to abstract themselves from their family feelings to hold the state always dearer, but the conflict of interest and loyalties was undeniably present in both cases.

Second, and even more significantly, Rousseau did not consider the family to be a trustworthy dispenser of the education required by the citizens of a republic. He regarded public socialization of children from the earliest possible age as "one of the most fundamental principles of popular and legitimate government."[74] It is by this means that the young citizens will develop in such a way as to transcend that individualism which is so threatening to the general will. In the rough draft of the *Discourse on Political Economy*, moreover, Rousseau was more explicit than in the final version as to *why* this type of socialization could not be entrusted to families. In the final draft, the reasons given are that, just as his civic duties are not left up to the individual to decide upon, so the education of children should not be left up to the individual father's ideas and prejudices, since its outcome is of even more importance to the republic than to the father. He, after all, will die, and often does not experience the fruits of his work, but the state endures forever, and the effects of its citizens' education are its lifeblood.[75] However, the significant reason that is not included in the final version, but was written and subsequently crossed out in the earlier one, is that fathers cannot be entrusted with the task of education in a republic because "they could make [their children] into very good sons and very bad citizens."[76]

In these two examples, then, Rousseau was to some extent in agreement with those other utopia builders who recognized the threat of the family to the cohesion of the larger community. In general, however, his theory of the relations between the family and the state is in direct opposition to this tendency. He refers to marriage as "certainly the first and holiest of all the bonds of society," an institution which "has civil effects without which society cannot even subsist."[77] Thus in a republic it is inconceivable that it be left to the clergy alone to regulate.[78] His belief in the central place of the family in society was what made Rousseau so disgusted by the plots of Greek drama. *Oedipus* and other such plays depicting incest and parricide were likely to corrupt the spectator's imagination with "crimes at which nature trembles." Molière's comedies were equally deplorable, because so satirical about the very most sacred of relationships. By ridiculing the respectable rights of fathers over their children and husbands over their wives, he "shakes the whole order of society."[79]

In Book 1 of *Emile*, Rousseau makes it clear that he regards the family as the principal socializing unit for the preservation of social order. It is with mothers that one must begin, in order to "restore all men to their original duties." When mothers resume nursing their children, "morals will be reformed; natural feelings will revive in every heart; the state will be repopulated; this first step alone will reunite everybody." The best counterpart to bad morals, he asserts several times, are the attractions of domestic life.[80] When mothers become devoted to their children again, men will become just as good in their roles of husband and father, which is crucial. For a "father, in begetting and providing nourishment for his children accomplishes only a third of his task. He owes men to the species, sociable men to society, and citizens to the state."[81] In agreement with this, Saint-Preux affirms that the principal duty of man in society is to rear his children well and provide them with a good example. The Wolmar family is certainly a model in this respect, laying great stress on the education of its young.

This whole trend of thought, which seems so inconsistent with Rousseau's insistence that one must choose to educate a child to be either man or citizen, and with his acknowledgment that educating him to be a loyal family member by no means coincides with making him into a loyal citizen, is brought to a climax in the attack, in Book 5 of *Emile*, against Plato's proposal that the family be abolished. This objectionable suggestion, Rousseau claims, constitutes the

> subversion of the tenderest natural feelings, sacrificed to an artificial feeling that cannot exist without them; as if one had no need of a natural attachment in order to form the bonds of convention; as if the love that one has for those nearest to one were not the basis for that which one owes to the state; as if it were not through the little fatherland that is the family that one's heart becomes attached to the great one; as if it were not the good son, the good husband, the good father who makes the good citizen.[82]

Here, no tension is seen to exist between family interest and republican interest, and the arguments for public education seem to be completely undermined. Given Rousseau's belief that human nature had to be deformed in order to make men into citizens, his calling upon natural feelings to aid in the development of the artificial ones of patriotism is highly puzzling. An individual reared in a very private atmosphere, with affections for and loyalty to just a few people, is scarcely likely to grow up feeling that all his compatriots are equally his siblings, the state his mother, and all the members of its ruling generation his fathers.

If the men who are members of nuclear families will have difficulties in becoming the sort of citizens Rousseau requires for his republic, the conflict for women, as he would have them, must inevitably be worse. Since the family is regarded as their only proper sphere of influence, and they receive no preparation for civic participation, it is not reasonable to expect them to use the powers that they have over their husbands for the promotion of any but the most narrow interests—those of their immediate households. Since their children are explicitly seen as their vital link with a husband whose affections may be otherwise inclined, they are hardly likely to sacrifice the interests of these children, let alone their lives, for the sake of a republic which can have very little reality in their own purely domestic lives. No woman educated and confined as Julie and Sophie are would ever be able to behave like the Spartan mother whose patriotism Rousseau so much admired.

Thus, Rousseau's women are even more vulnerable than men to the conflicts of loyalties that he was so much aware of in the human condition. They were, moreover, almost bound to lend their support to the side he considered the less desirable. For in spite of his yearnings for isolation and independence, he believed that the wider one extended one's affections, the better one was as a person. "The most vicious of men," he asserts, "is he who isolates himself the most, who most concentrates himself in himself; the best is he who shares his affections equally with all his kind."[83] Women, however, socialized in the restricted way he considers suitable for them, and placed in the only position he believes proper, have no reason to choose their country before their families, and have few defenses that would make them able to prefer any wider sphere of loyalty than that of sexual love, which provides them with their only means of power. Thus, in addition to the fact that Rousseau's prescriptions for women are in flagrant contradiction with those values, equality and freedom, which he regards as so crucial to humanity, the women he envisages are not only likely to be destructive of themselves, but are also likely to be subversive of his two most idealized institutions, the patriarchal family and the small democratic republic.

Rousseau's philosophy as a whole is by no means optimistic. What he asserts is the ultimate insolubility of the dilemma of being a man in society. However, he did construct a republic of denatured men, transformed into devoted patriots, and his intentions that this should not be considered simply an intellectual game are manifest in his works on Corsica and Poland. On the other hand, the end of the story of Emile is not totally pessimistic either. Emile survives the abortive attempt to make him into a husband, father and citizen, and becomes what he was always intended to be—a natural and autonomous man. The fates of Rousseau's women, however, could not be more tragic. Though ideals of their sex, they cannot be allowed to live in the patriarchal world, since there is no way they can fulfill the totally contradictory expectations it places on them. At least Rousseau allows that a man can be either an individual or a citizen. He does not allow a woman to be either.

PART IV

MILL

9

John Stuart Mill,
Liberal Feminist

The practice of asserting general convictions about humanity and its rights and needs, and denying their applicability to a major segment of the human race, has been by no means confined to the ancients. As we have seen, Rousseau stated his most basic principles in universal terms, and then proceeded to exclude women from their scope. What is even more striking, however, is that, despite the individualist orientation of liberal thought, John Stuart Mill is the only major liberal political philosopher to have set out explicitly to apply the principles of liberalism to women. Before embarking on a discussion of John Stuart Mill's feminism, therefore, it will be illuminating to look briefly at the way some of the earlier liberal theorists disposed of the female half of the human race.[1] Hobbes, Locke, and James Mill will be our examples, although Kant or Hegel—except that the latter's claim to being called a liberal is somewhat dubious—would serve the purpose equally well.

Hobbes's entire political philosophy is founded on the argument that human beings are naturally equal, on account of the fact that they are equally able to kill one another. This is the reason that nature provides no basis for inequality of rights and privileges, and that all authority must be grounded in consent.[2] Explicitly, in his works up to and including *Leviathan*, Hobbes includes women in this argument for equality. Repudiating the claim that, in the state of nature, dominion over children belongs to the father, "as being of the more excellent Sex," he applies his own argument about the equal ability to kill: "There is not always that difference of strength, or prudence between the man and the woman, as that the right can be determined without War."[3] In the bulk of his works, moreover, Hobbes acknowledges that, since "the birth follows the belly," the mother is in fact the original "lord" of her children in the state of nature.[4] Faced with the need to justify the prevalent rule of fathers over their families within commonwealths, however, he explains it in terms of the contingency that "for the most part Commonwealths have been erected by the Fathers, not by the Mothers of families."[5]

There is clearly something lacking in Hobbes's reasoning, here, for his explanation does not answer the problematical question of *how* just half of a race of people, all of whom are equal in what is for Hobbes the most important sense, could come to be in a position to found a commonwealth in which they had dominion over all the members of the other half. In other words, if women are the original sovereigns over their children, how did men become patriarchs while still in the state of nature? In *De Cive* and *Leviathan*, after a certain amount of lip service has been paid to the idea that the mother or the father might logically be the family's sovereign, toward the end of the pertinent chapter of each of these works—though he has provided no reasonable foundation for it at all—Hobbes proceeds to present the family as a strictly and solely patriarchal institution. He says, in fact, that a family consists of "a man and his children; or of a man and his servants; or of a man, and his children, and servants together: wherein the Father or Master is the Sovereign."[6] From this point on, the patriarchal family is the primary social and political unit with which Hobbes is concerned. The mother, with her original sovereignty over both herself and her children, and with no good reason to relinquish either, has disappeared from the story. The only time we hear of her again from Hobbes is when she appears, briefly, in the *Dialogue on the Common Law.* Here, he asserts that not only the family, but the patriarchal family, is an essentially natural institution —that "the Father of the Family by the Law of Nature was absolute Lord of his Wife and Children."[7] This attempted solution to the dilemma, however, is consistent neither with his insistence that the issue of dominion between the sexes cannot be decided without the possibility of continual war, nor with the fundamental principle of his political theory— that authority is not natural but arises from consent.

The problem that leads to all this inconsistency arises from the fact that Hobbes was not prepared to decide the issue of the equality of the sexes one way or the other. If the basis of his individualism was to be firm, he needed to argue that individual women were equal with individual men, just as weaker men were with stronger ones. His assumptions about the necessity for male dominance in both the family and society at large, however, made him unable to let this argument proceed to its logical conclusions.

Having taken the fatal step of admitting women to that basic human equality upon which his system of politics is built, the only way in which Hobbes could justify their exclusion from political life, and their obvious inequality in contemporary society, was to substitute the male-headed family for the individual as his primary subject matter.[8] But this solution is paradoxical, to say the least, since the tradition of which Hobbes is the founder is supposedly defined by its founding of politics on the characteristics and rights of individual, atomistic, human beings, and its renunciation of natural hierarchies or groups as the fundamental entities with which politics has to deal. Worse than paradoxical, however, the supposed solution is in fact no solution. Given his initial premises of human equality and egoism, there was no way that Hobbes could logically arrive at the institution of the patriarchal family, on which his political structure is based, for this institution depends on the assumption of the radical inequality of women.

Locke's dilemma about women is similar, in that he, too, presents them as men's equals for some purposes, but ultimately goes back on this commitment. In order to argue against Filmer's case for patriarchal government, Locke claims that male and female parents have an "equal Title" to power over their children.[9] If he can undermine the familial basis of patriarchy, by stressing that both parents have an equal share in what Filmer attributes to the father alone, he has gone far toward demolishing the foundation for absolute monarchy. Locke in fact uses the mother's "equal Title" as a *reductio ad absurdum* to refute the derivation of political from parental authority. For if the father dies, the children naturally owe obedience only to their mother. "And will anyone say," Locke asks, "that the *Mother* hath a legislative power over her children?" When it contributes to his case against absolute government, then, Locke treats husbands and wives as equals.[10]

The logical extension of such reasoning might seem to involve both the repudiation of patriarchalism within the family, and the acknowledgment of women's political rights. But Locke is not renowned as an early feminist, and the reason is not obscure. Although he uses parental equality to combat absolutism in the political realm, Locke peremptorily concludes in other passages that there is "a Foundation in Nature" for the legal and customary subjection of women to their husbands. Though the natural rights of individuals render illegitimate absolutism in the governmental realm, so far as the governance of the family is concerned it is quite justified. Where "the things of their common Interest and Property" are concerned, Locke argues, since husband and wife may disagree, "the Rule . . . naturally falls to the Man's share, as the abler and the stronger."[11]

Thus, when it does not suit his case or the prejudices of his time to promote women's equality, Locke appeals to "nature" to legitimize their subordination to men. With the patriarchal family thus reinstated, the exclusion of women from political rights is implicitly justified by the assumption that, as the head of his family, the father alone can represent its interests in the wider society. Just as in the case of Hobbes, then, the fundamental subject matter of Locke's political philosophy is not, as it first appears, the adult human individual but the male-headed family.

James Mill's essay, "Government"—influential as a relatively readable version of the Benthamite case for extension of the suffrage—is based on premises at least as individualistic as those of Hobbes and Locke. Together with the utilitarian proposition that the purpose of government is to maximize the pleasures and minimize the pains which people derive from one another, the foundation of Mill's case for representative government is an assertion which he presents as a "grand governing law of human nature"— that all human beings desire to exercise power over their fellow creatures, and that if given the means to do so they will use it without compunction so as to increase their own pleasures.[12] He concludes from these two premises that "unless the Representative Body are chosen by a portion of the community the interests of which cannot be made to differ from that of the community, the interest of the community will infallibly be sacrificed to the interest of the rulers."[13]

Having stated his case, however, Mill sets out to see whether some limitation of the franchise would be possible or even advantageous, and argues as follows:

> One thing is pretty clear, that all those individuals whose interests are indisputably included in those of other individuals, may be struck off without inconvenience. In this light may be viewed all children up to a certain age, whose interests are involved in those of their parents. In this light also, women may be regarded, the interest of almost all of whom is involved either in that of their fathers or in that of their husbands.[14]

Thus, having based his entire case for representative government on man's inevitable concern for his own selfish interests, Mill completely ignores his egoistical hedonism in order to "involve the interests" of women conveniently in those of men.

Here, as with Hobbes and Locke, the individualist implications of liberalism are severely constrained by the assumption of the inevitable existence and the legitimacy of the patriarchal family. There is, thus, a fundamental ambiguity which pervades not only the writings of these three philosophers, but most liberal thought. Whereas the liberal tradition appears to be talking about individuals, as components of political systems, it is in fact talking about male-headed families. Whereas the interests of the male actors in the political realm are perceived as discrete, and often conflicting, the interests of the members of the family of each patriarch are perceived as entirely convergent with his own, and consequently women disappear from the subject of politics. As we shall see in the following chapter, John Stuart Mill did *not* subscribe to the previous liberal "solution" to this question of the interests and rights of women.

Though not nearly so abstract as Plato or Hegel, John Stuart Mill was a philosopher who was concerned with the broadest and most profound issues affecting the life of human beings in political society. Liberty, individuality, justice, and democracy were his values, and at the root of his whole philosophy was his conviction that the utilitarian goal, the greatest happiness of the greatest number, could not be achieved apart from the greatest possible moral and intellectual advancement of the human race. Thus, for Mill, unlike Bentham and James Mill, one of the principal purposes of societal and political institutions was to develop human potential to the highest possible stage. One of the most intriguing things about his feminist writings, then, is that they are clearly an application of his most dearly held principles to a specific case where he perceived that they were being most flagrantly ignored.[15] His feminism was certainly not a sideline; rather, it constitutes, for the student of Mill, a valuable opportunity to see how he applied his central ideas. The emancipation of women to a level of equality with men was not, for Mill, aimed solely at the increased happiness of women themselves, although this was an important part of it. It was also a very important prerequisite for the improvement of mankind.

Mill's opposition to the prejudices and beliefs which kept women in a subordinate position in all aspects of social and political life was based on convictions formed very early in his youth, which found expression in many of his works on political and ethical subjects. At the beginning of the work he devoted specifically to these issues, *The Subjection of Women*, he states: "That . . . the legal subordination of one sex to the other . . . is wrong in itself, and now one of the chief hindrances to human improvement . . . [is] an opinion which I have held from the very earliest period when I had formed any opinions at all on social or political matters, and which . . . has been constantly growing stronger by the progress of reflection and the experience of life."[16] Evidence for his continual concern with the position of women is offered by his various biographers and in his letters; he often judged peoples, philosophical systems and periods of history according to their attitudes toward women and their role in society.[17] It will not suffice to confine the following discussion to *The Subjection of Women* alone, since there is in some of his other published works and in his letters, a fuller treatment of some ideas that are rather summarily dealt with in that work. For example, both to guard his own and Harriet Taylor Mill's personal reputations, and in order to avoid endangering the respectability of the incipient movement for women's rights, he played down or omitted his radical ideas about divorce and birth control.[18] Where this occurs, I shall make reference to his more explicit discussions of these subjects, and I shall also point out instances in which Harriet Taylor's ideas, as expressed in her own writings on the subject of women, are significantly different from those Mill himself espoused.[19]

Alien though Mill's radical ideas about women were to the mid-nineteenth century climate of opinion in general, it is easy to find stimuli to the development of his feminist convictions amongst several of the groups of thinkers with whom he was in contact during his formative years. The Utilitarians, by whom he was educated, were certainly not unconcerned with the issue. Bentham, for instance, though he thought it would be premature to allow the issue of women's suffrage to distract attention from or endanger his broader purposes, did concede the crucial points that existing differences between the sexes had certainly not been shown to be innate or inevitable ones, and that according to the principle of utility women should have the vote on the same grounds as men.[20] As for his father, John Stuart Mill notes in his *Autobiography* that "he looked forward . . . to a considerable increase of freedom in the relations between the sexes, though without pretending to define exactly what would be, or ought to be, the precise conditions of that freedom."[21] On the subject of female suffrage, however, James Mill, in his *Essay on Government*, had greatly offended the other philosophical radicals by suggesting that women might well be excluded from voting without any bad consequences, since their interests are included in those of the men in their families. A violent controversy was produced in Utilitarian circles, by this single, most unacceptable sentence, from which the young Mill tells us that he and his associates, including Bentham, "most positively dissented."[22] It is clear from his use of the phrase in his subsequent writings about women that Mill was particularly struck by the somewhat exaggerated statement in Macaulay's critical attack on the *Government* essay, that the interests of women were no more identical with those of their husbands than were the interests of subjects with those of their kings.[23] The whole controversy must surely have stimulated John Stuart Mill's concern with feminism. In addition, the Utilitarian's mouthpiece, the *Westminster Review*, had established itself as an early champion of the cause of women's rights. As early as 1824, Mill himself had published in that periodical an article attacking the prevalent custom of regarding morality and personal characteristics in completely different lights with reference to the two sexes.[24]

Mill's feminism also derived inspiration from the early French and English Socialists. He mentions meeting William Thompson, an Owenite who had written a lengthy feminist work in the 1820s. He says that he considers it "the signal honour of Owenism and most other forms of Socialism that they assign [to women] equal rights, in all respects, with those of the hitherto dominant sex."[25] We know, also, from his letters, that he was very interested in the ideas of Enfantin and the other Saint-Simonian *missionaires* who came to London in the early 1830s.[26] Tempered though his admiration was by his subsequently justified suspicions of their fanaticism and charlatanry, he continued to recognize the debt owed them by the feminist cause. In his *Autobiography* he writes, "In proclaiming the perfect equality of men and women, and an entirely new order of things in regard to their relations with one another, the St. Simonians, in common with Owen and Fourier, have entitled themselves to the grateful remembrance of future generations."[27]

Another factor which must have tended to confirm Mill's already strongly held feminist convictions was his connection with W. J. Fox and the Unitarian periodical, the *Monthly Repository*. As early as 1823, when Harriet Martineau contributed on the subject of equal education for women, but especially in the 1820s, when Fox was editor, this magazine published articles advocating female suffrage, a more rational attitude toward divorce, and the correction of the countless other injustices in the treatment of women. In his history of the periodical, Francis Mineka says: "Altogether, the *Repository*'s record on the emancipation of women is a distinctly honorable one. For its day, it was far in advance of common opinion; no contemporary periodical so consistently advocated an enlightened policy."[28] Mill wrote for the *Repository* in the early and mid-1830s, and his frequent correspondence with Fox over these years shows that the latter was a distinct spur to his feminist principles.[29]

Finally, we cannot ignore the direct influence on Mill's ideas of the women he met in the intellectual circles in which he moved. Such talented and intelligent, educated and productive women as Harriet Martineau, Sarah Austin, Harriet Grote, Jane Carlyle, and Eliza and Sarah Flower cannot fail to have made their impression on his ideas about their sex and the way it was regarded by contemporary society. Most important of all in this respect, however, was Harriet Taylor.

There has been much dispute about the extent of Harriet Taylor's influence on Mill, and the originality of her contribution to his work.[30] This stems from the divergence between, on the one hand, Mill's enraptured statements about her limitless genius and his claims that a great deal of his later work was in fact based on ideas that were hers, so that she played Bentham to his Dumont,[31] and, on the other hand, the decidedly unfavorable impression she made on their contemporaries, and the hardly startling quality of her own extant writings. I am inclined to agree with H. O. Pappe, who concludes his examination of the evidence by saying that it is only Mill's distorted impression of her abilities that suggests that she was endowed with any qualities of genius. However, it is not necessary in the context of Mill's feminist ideas to go deeply into this controversy, for two reasons.

First, Mill has left us with a very clear statement about his wife's effect on his feminist beliefs. He stresses that she was not the source of his convictions about the need for the equality of men and women, and this statement is borne out by his many letters and several publications on the subject which date from before their first meeting. He says, in fact, that it may well have been his strong views on the subject that initially attracted her to him. However, he adds that, in the course of their long relationship and eventual marriage, she had played the part of transforming what had been "little more than an abstract principle" into a real appreciation of the practical, day-to-day effects of women's lack of rights and opportunities. She had also, he says, made him aware of "the mode in which the consequences of the inferior position of women intertwine themselves with all the evils of existing society and with all the difficulties of human improvement."[32] Thus, although there is no doubt that Mill was a convinced feminist independently of the influence of Harriet Taylor, both the existence and the difficult circumstances of their relationship must have increased the strength of his convictions, and of his determination to do what he could to have women's many disabilities remedied.

Secondly, it is impossible to tell which of the ideas that Mill and Harriet Taylor expressed on the subject of women originated in his mind, and which in hers, with the possible exception of those they expressed to each other in two short essays on marriage and divorce, very early in their relationship, and those that appear in the earlier essay, *The Enfranchisement of Women*, but not in *The Subjection of Women*, which Mill wrote after Harriet Taylor's death. From this evidence, one derives the distinct impression that her ideas were somewhat more radical than his. She proposes, for example, that once women have been given full civil and political rights, all marriage laws could be done away with, without harmful results. While Mill was in favor of considerable relaxation of the divorce laws, he never suggested that the contractual basis of marriage be abolished. On most issues, however, it seems that their ideas became very much enmeshed on this subject which was so important to them both. Many of the arguments included in *The Subjection of Women* appeared first in *The Enfranchisement of Women*, but this is not sufficient evidence that they were all originally her ideas, since although the pamphlet was published under her name, Mill refers to it at least once as written by himself. This may, however, have been in order to avoid the publisher's prejudices. Most probably they worked on it together, or at least were in constant touch about the ideas it contained. As Mill himself says, they came from "the fund of thought which had been made common to us both, by our innumerable conversations and discussions on a topic which filled so large a place in our minds."[33]

Thus, to feminist convictions which Mill held from very early in his life were added the influences of a number of groups of thinkers with whom he mixed or at least had considerable contact—the Utilitarians, the early Cooperative Socialists, Saint-Simonians and Fourierists, and the Unitarian radicals. He had come into contact with a number of women whose qualities strongly contradicted contemporary stereotypes of what women were and should be like, and he had a lengthy and intimate relationship with a woman who had directly suffered the effects of discrimination against her sex, particularly in the form of the marriage laws and the denial of educational opportunities. It is, then, not surprising that he should decide to apply his most basic principles to arguing for the emancipation of women.

In *On Liberty*, Mill eschews any appeal to "abstract right, as a thing independent of utility." In *The Subjection of Women*, too, he feels obliged to answer those who might accuse him of advocating "a social revolution in the name of an abstract right."[34] At times, however, in spite of this protestation, he does come very near to sounding like a natural rights theorist, rather than a simple utilitarian. He refers, for example, to the injustice of denying to women "the *equal moral right* of all human beings to choose their occupation (short of injury to others) according to their own preferences."[35] Despite a few un-utilitarian "lapses" such as this, however, the basic arguments of the work on women, as of *On Liberty*, are made in the name of utility— that is, in the name of John Stuart Mill's version of utility. The appeal of *The Subjection of Women*, too, is to "utility in the largest sense, grounded on the permanent interests of man as a progressive being."[36]

Mill vehemently rejects the narrow, Benthamite conception of human nature, explicitly in the essay on Bentham,[37] but also implicitly in all his other works. "Human nature," he says in *On Liberty*, "is not a machine to be built after a model . . . but a tree, which requires to grow and develop itself on all sides, according to the tendency of the inward forces which make it a living thing."[38] Whether Mill's totally unmechanistic conception of human nature means that he cannot be regarded as a real utilitarian is a much debated issue. It has been argued that the emphasis he places on the development of the human faculties, rather than simply the pleasures experienced by a given population, takes him so far away from "the greatest happiness of the greatest number" that he cannot be considered a utilitarian in the Benthamite sense. He certainly did not believe that "pushpin is as good as poetry." However, neither did he give up the greatest happiness principle. The basic reason for this is that Mill was convinced that the moral and intellectual advancement of mankind would result in greater happiness for everybody. Believing as he did that the higher pleasures of the intellect yielded far greater happiness than the lower pleasures of the senses,[39] and that consequently, "next to selfishness, the principal cause which makes life unsatisfactory is want of mental cultivation,"[40] he could only conclude that an essential means to the greatest happiness was the opening up to everybody of the joys of poetry and the other higher pleasures. The moral development of humanity, too, would lead to ever greater happiness, because to a moral being virtue was not just a means to good action, but a feeling which contributed to his or her own happiness;[41] and also because the decline of selfishness would mean that people would become united in aiming at the greatest happiness of all, rather than just pursuing their own individual pleasures. Thus, Mill's utilitarianism is certainly different from Bentham's, in that

Mill did not hope to find the answer to the question "Is the greatest happiness presently being experienced?" simply by asking everyone how they are feeling. As he made clear, particularly in the "Socrates and the pig" passage, he did not consider that people were at all capable of knowing how great and profound their happiness could be, if their full moral and intellectual potential were developed.

There is, undoubtedly, a strong current of intellectual elitism running through Mill's thought. While he had criticized Bentham for basing his concept of human nature on his own narrow and unimaginative person, Mill proceeded to reason in the same way. He assumed that the model for humanity was the intellectual and ascetic aesthete that he himself personified. However, once this bias is acknowledged, it cannot be maintained that he rejected the greatest happiness principle in favor of a "greatest human development" principle. The point is that he was quite convinced that only the cultivated could achieve the greatest happiness available to mankind.

The purpose of this digression from the specific subject of women has been to explore the importance for Mill's version of utilitarianism of his concept of man as a progressive, a morally and intellectually improvable being. In *The Subjection of Women* and in those parts of his other works in which he argues the need for women's emancipation, the theme of human advancement recurs frequently. This emphasis is most succinctly summarized in a passage in the *Principles of Political Economy*, where he says: "The ideas and institutions by which the accident of sex is made the groundwork of an inequality of legal rights, and a forced dissimilarity of social functions, must ere long be recognized as the greatest hindrance to moral, social, and even intellectual improvement."[42] There are two other principles that figure very prominently in *The Subjection of Women* and his other feminist statements—liberty, or the opportunity for self-determination, and justice, in the sense of equal consideration or impartiality. Both of these other concerns, however, are explicitly related to the moral and intellectual advancement of mankind, as well as to the happiness of women themselves.

As is clear from *On Liberty*, Mill was deeply concerned about the value of individual freedom, regarding it as such an important means to happiness and self-development that it could justifiably be sacrificed only to the extent that is absolutely necessary for the maintenance of security and social cooperation. "After the primary necessities of food and raiment," he asserts, "freedom is the first and strongest want of human nature,"[43] and he recalls the joys of emerging from the tutelage of childhood into the responsibilities of adulthood as indicative of the feeling of added vitality that self-determination can give. Thus, freedom is so essential a part of human well-being that Mill concludes "that the only purpose for which power can be rightfully exercised over any member of a civilized community, against his will, is to prevent harm to others."[44]

Unlike Rousseau, with his rigidly patriarchal conception of freedom, Mill had no doubts about there being ample scope to apply this strongly held value to the contemporary social and legal position of women. Liberty and self-determination are recurrent themes of Mill's arguments against the gross inequality of the marriage laws and the severe discrimination suffered by women in the areas of educational and occupational opportunity. He states that the most direct benefit he envisages resulting from the emancipation of women will be the added happiness of women themselves, resulting from the difference between "a life of subjection to the will of others, and a life of rational freedom."[45] Whereas a woman at the time he wrote had practically no opportunity of any occupation (outside of unskilled labor and a few of the menial service industries) except that of a wife, in a marital relationship in which she was legally bound to obey her husband and had no rights to own property, it was obvious to Mill that an inestimable increase in happiness would result from giving women a real choice of how to spend their lives. He was convinced that "if there is anything vitally important to the happiness of human beings, it is that they should relish their habitual pursuit";[46] thus it was essential that all the careers open to men should be made equally accessible to women. Only then would the choice of whether to marry or not be a meaningful one, rather than the only means of escape from the despised dependency of "old maidhood." It was also essential that those who chose to marry should be granted an equal share in the legal rights and responsibilities of the relationship. Although he did not express his most radical ideas on the subject of marriage in *The Subjection of Women*, he says elsewhere that it should be a free contract in the sense of being dissoluble at the wish of the contracting parties, provided that any children who had resulted from the marriage were well cared for. His dissent from the contemporary view of the binding nature of the marriage contract is summed up in his statement that "surely it is wrong, wrong in every way . . . that there should exist any motives to marriage except the happiness which two persons who love one another feel in associating their existence."[47] Any denial of liberty which was not for the sake of protecting some third party from harm was anathema to him.

It was not only, however, for the sake of the added happiness of women themselves that Mill advocates giving them more freedom of choice about how they should spend their lives, but also for the sake of the progress of society as a whole. As he states in *On Liberty*, "the only unfailing and permanent source of improvement is liberty, since by it there are as many possible permanent centres of improvement as there are individuals."[48] The extension of education and the opening up of careers to women, freeing them from the bondage of compulsory domesticity, should also have the beneficial effect of "doubling the mass of mental faculties available for the higher service of humanity."[49]

In addition to this vast increase in available talent, Mill

considered that freeing women to become educated and to work at a career would have most valuable effects on men. Both the stimulus of female competition and the companionship of equally educated partners would result in men's greater intellectual development as well. Mill was most impressed by the fact that, since men were becoming less bound up with outdoor pursuits and what were regarded as exclusively masculine activities, their domestic lives were becoming more important, and the influence of their wives was therefore continually increasing. Taking the rather pessimistic point of view that any society or individual which is not improving is deteriorating, he stresses the insidious effects that the constant companionship of an uneducated and frivolous wife can have on a man, even though he might previously have had serious intellectual interests. He asks how it could be considered anything but detrimental to a man's development to be confined for a large proportion of his life with a partner whose mind has been so studiously concentrated on trivia, who is utterly ignorant about matters which should be of the highest concern, and who is bound because of the narrowness of her education to consider the immediate and material interest of her family of greater importance than any public-spirited or intellectual aspirations that her husband might wish to pursue. "With such an influence in every house," Mill asks, "is it any wonder that people in general are kept down in that mediocrity of respectability which is becoming a marked characteristic of modern times?"[50] Rousseau's solution to what he perceived as the unfavorable influence of contemporary women—the segregation of the sexes in the wider world and even within the home—was, needless to say, quite repugnant to Mill. Though women in their current state of subjection and lack of opportunity were in Mill's view acting as a constant force against progress, he was convinced that liberating them would reverse this force.

Second only to freedom, in the arguments set out in *The*

Subjection of Women, is the principle of justice. Just treatment, no less than liberty, is regarded both as essential for the happiness of women themselves and as a necessary condition for the advancement of humanity. Mill's most comprehensive discussion of justice is found in the last chapter of *Utilitarianism.* Here, he deals with the fundamental concept of impartiality, or the requirement that like cases be treated alike, and then goes on to show that the reason different societies have had such different conceptions of what constitutes just treatment is that they have considered different qualities to be grounds for departing from impartiality. As discussed in Chapter 4 above, in Aristotle's theory of justice, citizens, women, artisans and slaves receive entirely different treatment according to what he perceived as their inherent characteristics and their functions in society. Whereas it is, Mill says, crucial to the idea of justice that "all persons are deemed to have a *right* to equality of treatment, except when some recognized social expediency requires the reverse,"[51] different conceptions of what constitutes social expediency have resulted in acceptance by societies of slavery, caste systems, and many other unequal arrangements now considered completely unjust, as thoroughly justified by the requirements of circumstances. Only when social inequalities have ceased to be considered expedient, have they come to be regarded as not only inexpedient, but also unjust. However, people tend to be "forgetful that they themselves perhaps tolerate other inequalities under an equally mistaken notion of expediency,"[52] and a paradigmatic case of this is the subjection of women. Rousseau, of course, is a perfect example of such thinking. Although the inequality of the sexes "is not felt to jar with modern civilization, any more than domestic slavery among the Greeks jarred with their notion of themselves as a free people,"[53] Mill perceived it as an isolated and anomalous instance of bondage in a world whose guiding principle was human equality. "Marriage," he asserts, "is the only actual bondage known to our law;

there remain no legal slaves, except the mistress of every house."[54]

Like entrenched inequalities in the past, however, the unequal position of women was regarded as "natural." "But was there ever any domination which did not appear natural to those who possessed it?" Mill asks.[55] The most cultivated intellects of the ancient world, including Aristotle, were sure that slavery was natural; theorists of absolute monarchy claimed that it was the only natural form of government, conquering races that the right of the stronger was natural, and the feudal nobility that their dominion over their serfs was natural. Since the subjection of women to men is a universal custom, it is not surprising that society feels so certain of its naturalness. Mill's awareness of the extent to which nature has been used to legitimize convention is striking. He comments: "So true is it that unnatural generally means only uncustomary, and that everything which is usual appears natural."[56] However, since he believed fervently that society in its most desirable form was the society of equals, it was essential for him to combat the prevalent claims for the naturalness of the glaring inequality of the sexes. He looked forward to the day when discrimination on the grounds of sex would follow that based on nobility of birth into disrepute and oblivion.

In order to build his case for female equality on what he regarded as the universally accepted principle of just treatment, Mill considered that he was obliged to demonstrate two things. First, he had to contend with the assumption that women are inherently inferior. "The objection with which we are now principally met," he states, "is that women are not fit for, or not capable of, this, that or the other mental achievement."[57] Consequently, he determined to show, against the strong force of contemporary opinion, that the reasons which had always been considered ample grounds for treating women differently from men—that they are naturally inferior, less rational, more emotional—

were not founded on good evidence, and were probably all false. Second, even when he had demonstrated this to the extent that anyone could at that time, Mill considered it essential, as a utilitarian, to show that doing away with the unequal treatment of women would be expedient in the sense of contributing to the general welfare of society.

In arguing the first of these two claims, Mill had to contend not only with popular prejudice, but also with the violent reaction which many intellectuals of the mid-nineteenth century were expressing against eighteenth-century environmentalism. Many of Mill's contemporaries considered that French educational theorists of the Enlightenment, such as Helvétius and Holbach, had attributed excessive importance to environmental factors in the formation of human character and intellectual capacity. Mill, by contrast, claimed that certainly most, and probably all, of the existing differences of character and intellect between men and women were due to the very different attitudes of society toward members of the two sexes from their earliest infancy, and the vastly different types and qualities of education afforded them. In his fragment on marriage, written about 1832, Mill had vehemently denied any innate inequality between the sexes apart from that of physical strength—and even this, he said, could be doubted.[58] He was, however, so opposed to dogmatism on any issue that he later modified his position to the claim that none of the alleged differences between the mental or moral capacities of the sexes had been proved to be the inevitable consequences of innate factors, though some of them might possibly be.[59] His only dogmatic assertion was that nothing was yet certainly known on the subject: "If it be said that the doctrine of the equality of the sexes rests only on theory, it must be remembered that the contrary doctrine has only theory to rest upon."[60]

What "the contrary doctrine" had rested on for millenia, in fact, was a series of assertions about the nature, and natural qualities, of women. Mill points out that these con-

ceptions of the natural woman often differ entirely from
one culture to another. In the Orient, women are "by
nature" voluptuous, in England, "by nature" cold; in
France, they are "naturally" fickle, but in England constant. This in itself is enough to make one question such
dogmas. Clearly, women have been assigned different versions of the female role in these different cultures, and
their "nature" has been defined accordingly. Thus, Mill
argues, it does not get one anywhere in a rational argument
to say "that the *nature* of the two sexes adapts them to their
present functions and position, and renders these appropriate to them."[61] He asserts emphatically:

> I deny that any one knows or can know, the nature of
> the two sexes, as long as they have only been seen in
> their present relation to one another. If men had ever
> been found in society without women, or women with-
> out men, or if there had ever been a society of men
> and women in which the women were not under the
> control of the men, something might have been posi-
> tively known about the mental and moral differences
> which may be inherent in the nature of each.[62]

Until conditions of equality exist, no one can possibly assess the natural differences between women, distorted as
they have been, and men. What is natural to the two sexes
can only be found out by allowing both to develop and
use their faculties freely. Thus Mill radically dissents from
the functionalist definition of women's nature that we have
seen prevailing in the works of Aristotle and Rousseau.

In order to analyze the environmental influences on
women in contemporary society, Mill returns to his metaphor of human nature as "a tree, which requires to grow
and develop itself on all sides." What has been called "the
nature of women" is so far from being the result of free
development and growth that he likens it to a tree that
has been reared with one half in a vapor bath and the
other in the snow. It is not natural growth, but "forced

repression in some directions, unnatural stimulation in others,"[63] with the aim of pleasing and benefiting men, that have made women into the half-stunted, half-overdeveloped human beings that they are. In Mill's view, anyone who took the trouble to consider the very different ways in which contemporary boys and girls were educated, and their very different assigned tasks in adult life, could readily explain a great many of the intellectual incapacities and special moral qualities attributed to women as natural characteristics of their sex. Those, such as Rousseau, who summarily assessed them as "naturally" practical and intuitive, capable in small, day-to-day affairs but lacking in any capacity for rational thought, had only to look at the way girls were trained to cope with domestic trivia, while boys were educated in the classics and the sciences. A woman's mistakes were therefore like those of a self-educated man, who would grasp the common-sense factors of a situation, some of which might elude the theorist, but who was likely to suffer from a lack of knowledge of general principles and of ability to grasp the abstract, conceptual aspect of the problem.[64] One did not need to look further than the vastly different environments of the sexes to explain what were almost invariably assumed to be innate differences in their abilities to reason.

Mill was no more prepared to accept as innate the distinctions drawn in favor of the female character than to accept its allegedly natural inferiorities. He considered the prevalent nineteenth-century claim that women are naturally morally superior to men to be just as absurd as the allegation that they are mentally inferior.[65] Women, like negro slaves, he says, have had scarcely any opportunity to commit crimes, so it is not remarkable nor particularly laudable that they have not often been criminals. Since he believed moral excellence to be "always the fruit of education and cultivation," to which both sexes were equally susceptible, he considered that all such "feminine" qualities as unselfishness and moral restraint could be explained in terms of women's particular circumstances of dependence on and accountability to others. He concludes:

> I do not know a more signal instance of the blindness with which the world, including the herd of studious men, ignore and pass over all the influences of social circumstances, than their silly depreciation of the intellectual, and silly panegyrics on the moral, nature of women.[66]

Mill also reacted against the prevailing wisdom, which we have seen in the writings of Aristotle and Rousseau, that the moral qualities required in women should be different from those required in men. The piece he had written at the age of eighteen for the *Westminster Review* had attacked the application of moral standards according to the sex of the person being judged. It is in order to have their wives entirely dependent and uncritically devoted to them, he argues, that men have set up an entirely different set of values for them. Thus:

> It is considered meritorious in a man to be independent: to be sufficient to himself; not to be in a constant state of pupillage. In a woman, helplessness, both of mind and of body, is the most admired of attributes. A man is despised, if he be not courageous. In a woman, it is esteemed amiable to be a coward. To be entirely dependent on her husband for every pleasure, and for exemption from every pain; to feel secure, only when under his protection; to be incapable of forming any opinion, or of taking any resolution without his advice and aid; this is amiable, this is delicate, this is feminine: while all who infringe on any of the prerogatives which man thinks proper to reserve to himself; all who can or will be of any use, either to themselves or to the world, otherwise than as the slaves and drudges of their husbands, are called masculine, and other names intended to convey disapprobation.[67]

In contrast to this virtually universal notion of the qualities proper to men and to women, Mill argues in a letter to Thomas Carlyle that in his experience the best people of both sexes have combined the highest so-called "masculine" qualities with the highest of those considered "feminine." He asks, "*Is* there really any distinction between the highest masculine and highest feminine character?"[68] It may not seem remarkable that Mill's conception of morality and excellence was uniform for the two sexes—until one realizes how vast a weight of historical opinion had asserted the opposite. Mill was the first major philosopher since Plato to have argued that goodness was the same in a woman as in a man.

In his attempt to refute the prevailing doctrine that women were innately and irremediably inferior in ability to men, Mill felt greatly hampered by the backward state of psychology. The contemporary preoccupation was with the biological sciences, and there was, he thought, a deplorable lack of attention paid to the influence of environment on the formation of the human character.[69] This had led to far too great a reversal of the Helvétian claim, "l'éducation peut tout," to the point where organic characteristics were now supposed capable of explaining everything. Mill's chief adversary, in his battle to win recognition for the importance of environmental factors in the character-formation of women, was Auguste Comte. The substantial correspondence carried on between the two during 1843 contains an important part of Mill's thinking about this aspect of his case for the emancipation of women.[70]

Comte's view was a clear reflection of the confident conviction that the physical sciences were not just potentially capable of solving all human problems, once their findings were applied by the social sciences, but that they had found practically all the important answers already. Thus Comte was sure that biology was already "able to establish the hierarchy of the sexes, by demonstrating both anatomically and physiologically that, in almost the entire animal kingdom, and especially in our species, the female sex is formed for a state of essential childhood, which renders it necessarily inferior to the corresponding male organism."[71] With a pre-Darwinian confidence in the uniqueness of the human species, he asserts that "the organic condition must certainly prevail, since it is the organism and not the environment that makes us men rather than monkeys or dogs, and which even determines our special type of humanity, to a degree much more circumscribed than has often been believed."[72] Thus, it is not simply for the sake of social expediency that women should be subordinate to men; any other arrangement would be biologically absurd. The causes of all mental characteristics were to be found in the physical organism, the brain, and women, with their physically weaker constitution, must therefore be intellectually inferior to men. Comte granted generously, however, that they were compensated to some extent by being endowed by nature with greater delicacy of feeling and sympathy. They were to be pampered, worshiped, even prayed to, in the society Comte envisaged for the future, but to expect them to be capable of any sort of decision-making or political participation that required reasonable or objective thought, was to go against nature in a way that could only be disastrous both for women and for society as a whole.

Mill, who initially acknowledged the gaps in his knowledge of biology which he was vainly attempting to remedy, adopted a tone that seems extremely humble and conciliatory in contrast to Comte's arrogant confidence in his own convictions.[73] He was simply not prepared to accept, however, the claim that biology had produced any conclusive findings on the subject. He admitted the possibility that it might one day be proved that there are certain physiological differences between the brains of the two sexes, but he stressed in answering Comte that there was, as yet, no definite knowledge of the precise relationship between the physical characteristics of a brain and the intellectual powers of its owner. To rely on such an oversimplification as the contention that men, being bigger than women, have bigger brains and therefore greater mental powers, was to lay oneself open to the charge that big men are more intelligent than little ones, and whales and elephants more intelligent than either.[74]

Mill was convinced that the sort of reasoning that Comte was engaged in was likely to produce no sound conclusions about the differences between the sexes, as long as the study of the environmental influences on personal development, or ethology, remained so neglected. In *The Subjection of Women* he speaks urgently of the need for the advancement of this science, saying that "of all the difficulties which impede the progress of thought, and the formation of well-grounded opinions on life and social arrangements, the greatest is now the unspeakable ignorance of mankind in respect to the influences which form human character."[75] He was not under any illusions about the difficulty of carrying out such a study, with its problems of isolating causal factors in a sphere in which experimental laboratory conditions are impossible. Despite the difficulties, however, he was convinced that this area of science must not continue to be so neglected, and in the *Logic*, he set out some preliminary ideas for such a science, though he went no further in carrying it into operation.[76] Meanwhile, until that science was well advanced, he argued that none of the intellectual and moral differences between the sexes could reasonably be said to be caused by innate, physiological factors. "No one," he writes bluntly in *The Subjection of Women*, "is thus far entitled to any positive opinion on the subject."[77]

Thus, with knowledge in its limited state, it could certainly not be demonstrated that women were incapable of the same levels of intellectual achievement as men. Such a belief could in no way be regarded as just grounds for keeping them subordinate in society, and denying them all opportunity to show what they could in fact achieve. Further, Mill argues, in many fields women had already achieved a considerable measure of success, despite the weight of circumstance, lack of education, and force of prejudice which worked against them. Though this was to rest the case on very humble grounds, "when we consider how sedulously they are all trained away from, instead of being trained towards, any of the occupations or objects reserved for men,"[78] he cites the achievements of women such as Mme. de Staël and George Sand in the field of literature, and applied his argument most forcefully to the case of politics, in which women had proved their competence at the top executive level. Here one was not confined to speculation about what women might be capable of if suitably educated; what women had achieved in the political sphere was in itself most persuasive evidence of what they could do. At the top political level, Mill points out, which is practically the only sphere of public affairs to which they have ever been admitted, the great qualities of a proportionately larger number of queens than kings has demonstrated that "exactly where and in proportion as women's capacities for government have been tried, in that proportion have they been found adequate."[79] Citing such examples as Deborah, Joan of Arc, Elizabeth, and Margaret of Austria, he argues that these and other women who have been expert governors or leaders make it quite ridiculous to regard their sex as unfit to participate on all other levels of political life. For their potential in the field has already been demonstrated to be at least equal to that of men.

Of all the spheres of human endeavor, Mill asserts that there are very few in which, however little opportunity they have had to prove themselves, some women at least have not reached a very high level of accomplishment. The fact that they have not, so far, achieved first-class works of genius and originality can, he says, be explained by their lack of the thorough education which is prerequisite to reaching original conclusions once all the first principles in a field are established, by the fact that women are traditionally expected to be always available to minister to the needs of men and children, and therefore seldom have sustained periods in which to concentrate, and by the circumstances of their coming, like the Romans after the Greeks, second to men chronologically in all fields of study and art. For these reasons, he regards what women have achieved as conclusive proof of what they can do, but refuses to treat what they have not so far achieved as conclusive proof of anything at all.

Mill does not consider that he has closed the case for female equality by showing his contemporaries that their grounds for discriminating against women are scientifically undemonstrable, and in many cases contradicted by the facts of history. For, as he points out in the last chapter of *Utilitarianism*, people in general have showed themselves consistently unwilling to admit to the injustice of any social discrimination, until they are convinced that it is also inexpedient. Thus, Mill feels obliged to argue not only that the discriminatory treatment of women has no rational basis in the natures of the sexes, but that it is socially harmful as well, and that to treat women as equals would be beneficial for the happiness and advancement of all. Justice, then, like liberty, is linked in Mill's feminist arguments with the constant theme of the improvement of mankind.

The unjust treatment of women has, Mill argues in *The Subjection of Women*, the detrimental effect that they attempt to gain influence in subversive ways, and to use it for selfish purposes, as happens in other cases in which legitimate access to power is denied.[80] Under existing conditions within the family, he argues, women are forced to resort to cunning and underhand tactics in order to have their wishes fulfilled, when they and their husbands disagree. There exists no motivation to discuss such issues openly and rationally, since the husband is legally constituted as the family's decision-maker. As far as women's political influence is concerned, Mill is sure that the indirect influence they exert, through their pressure on their enfranchised husbands, is bound to be unconcerned with the welfare of anyone beyond their own immediate families. Thus he, unlike Rousseau, recognizes that the outside world has no hope of winning over the family in the conflict of loyalties that unenfranchised women face. For "their social position allows them no scope for any feelings beyond the family except personal likings & dislikes, & it is assumed that they would be governed entirely by these in their judgment & feeling in political matters."[81] But if they were themselves enfranchised, and thereby given their own legitimate means of influencing the political process, Mill argues, they would in the course of time become far more likely to use these means responsibly and in a more humanitarian spirit. "It is precisely by creating in their minds a concern for the interests which are common to all, those of their country and of human improvement, that the tendency to look upon all questions as personal questions would most effectively be corrected."[82] Convinced by de Tocqueville's impressions of the educative effects of political participation, he is sure that women who were to exercise their political rights would "receive that stimulus to their faculties, and that widening and liberalizing influence over their feelings and sympathies, which the suffrage seldom fails to produce on those who are admitted to it."[83] Thus, by granting women the vote, society would benefit doubly. It would minimize the selfish and narrow influences that many of them already exerted, via their husbands, and it would increase the selflessness and responsibility of the electorate as a whole.

Mill argues, too, that the abolition of the legal inequality of husband and wife would have immeasurable effects on the value of the family as an educative institution. Since he believes that "society in equality is its normal state," and moreover that "the only school of genuine moral sentiment is society between equals,"[84] he considers that the everyday assumption by men of their superiority over women constantly detracts from the value of their own lives as well as those of their wives, and has very harmful effects on their children. There can be nothing approaching the highest potential of human companionship between two human beings, one of whom is convinced a priori of his greater capacities and value, and of the justice of his always taking precedence over the other. What hope, Mill asks, is there for the moral advancement of society, so long as the domestic atmosphere in which all its members receive their earliest moral education is based on such an unjust distribution of rights and powers? Only when marriage were to become recognized by law and society as a cooperative partnership between equals, might the family at last become, for the children, "a school of sympathy in equality, of living together in love, without power on one side and obedience on the other." Only then could children be prepared for what he regards as the "true virtue of human beings," that is, "fitness to live together as equals."[85]

In spite of these protestations about equality within the family, however, it is in fact because of John Stuart Mill's assumptions and convictions about the family and its traditional roles that his feminism falls short of advocating true equality and freedom for married women. Mill's feminist writings are, implicitly, concerned only with middle- and upper-class women, and it is the bourgeois family that is his model.[86] Though he rejects the legalized inequalities of its patriarchal form, he regards the family itself as "essential for humanity,"[87] and is concerned to reassure his readers that family life has nothing to fear, but rather much to gain, from the complete political and civil equality of the sexes. Though presently "a school of despotism," once justly constituted, it would be "the real school of the virtues of freedom."[88]

Moreover, Mill argues in favor of the traditional division of labor within the family. While he asserts that women should have a real choice of a career or marriage, he assumes that the majority of women are likely to continue to prefer marriage, and that this choice is equivalent to choosing a career. He states:

Like a man when he chooses a profession, so, when a woman marries, it may in general be understood that she makes choice of the management of a household, and the bringing up of a family, as the first call upon her exertions, during as many years of her life as may be required for the purpose; and that she renounces, not all other objects and occupations, but all which are not consistent with the requirements of this.[89]

In keeping with this mode of thinking, Mill asserts that there is an "infinitely closer relationship of a child to its mother than to its father,"[90] and that "nothing can replace the mother for the education of children."[91] He does not pause to reflect that the qualities of motherhood, just as much as any of the other existing differences between the sexes, might be at least partly due to environmental factors, most particularly to the conditioning that resulted from customary modes of socialization. Again, in spite of his general rejection of the pressures of opinion, he calmly accepts that the sexual division of duties within the family is "already made by consent, or at all events not by law, but by general custom," and he defends it as "the most suitable division of labour between the two persons."[92]

In Mill's early essay on marriage and divorce, this position is put much more dogmatically than later, and in terms which he could not consistently use in *The Subjection of Women*. This, then, is one area in which it seems highly likely that the way he stated his views (though not their substance) was modified by the divergent ideas of Harriet Taylor. For in 1832, having just asserted that "there is no natural inequality between the sexes," he goes on to say that, in a home where there are no servants, it is "good and will *naturally* take place . . . that the mistress of a family shall herself do the work of servants," and "the mother is the *natural* teacher." He concludes, with little attention to their own preferences, that "the great occupation of women should be to beautify life . . . and to diffuse beauty, elegance and grace everywhere," since women are *"naturally"* endowed with greater elegance and taste.[93]

By the time he wrote *The Subjection of Women*, Mill could no longer assert that women's domestic role is natural, in so many words, since in that work he clearly recognizes the invalidity and fraudulence of identifying the natural with the conventional and then using appeals to woman's "nature" in order to justify her conventional functions. Despite changes in terminology, however, with "most suitable" and "desirable custom" replacing the appeals to nature, the substance of Mill's ideas remained unchanged. In those days of primitive contraceptive techniques, a high rate of infant mortality, and onerous household chores, it would have been far harder for Mill than it is for us to conceive of the sharing of child rearing and domestic duties. However, it is striking that Mill chose not to question the family and the way it had developed, in any way, or to consider the relationship between the institution of the bourgeois family itself and the contemporary position of women in society. For, clearly, it was no dictate of nature that had led to the formation of the isolated private household, with its "woman's work," and the professional and industrial world of "man's work" outside, and to the vast separation between these two spheres. Mill's assumption of the immutability of the existing family structure, and his failure to discuss its repercussions for the lives of women, constitutes a gap in his feminist thought which the current feminist movement is attempting to remedy.

Mill's acceptance of traditional sex roles within the family places serious limitations on the extent to which he can apply the principles of freedom and equality to married women. First, though he argues in favor of equal property *rights* for married women, these are rights to property inherited or earned by the woman herself, not rights to equal shares in the family income. "The rule," Mill says, "is simple: whatever would be the husband's or wife's if they were not married, should be under their exclusive control during marriage."[94] Clearly, then, the income of the male earner is his, as much after marriage as before, and Mill does not recognize the anomaly that women's work in the home is unpaid labor. Only in *The Enfranchisement of Women* do we find the assertion that it is not only necessary for married women to be able to earn their own subsistence, but that their position in the family would improve significantly "if women both earned, and had the right to possess, a part of the income of the family."[95] Although in *The Subjection of Women* Mill agrees that married women must be able to support themselves, he explicitly rejects the idea that they should actually do so, regarding such a practice as liable to lead to the neglect of the household and children. It seems, therefore, highly likely that the idea stated in the earlier work is Harriet Taylor's, and it is an example where her thought is considerably more in tune than Mill's with present day feminism. She recognizes, as he does not, the importance to women of continuous economic independence, both within the marital relationship, and in case of its disintegration.

Second, Mill's defense of traditional sex roles within the family amounts to a denial of freedom of opportunity and individual expression of talents to that majority of women whom he assumes would always choose to marry. Though he is so much aware that the care of a household is an incessantly preoccupying duty that he cites it as a major reason for women's comparative lack of achievement in many artistic fields, he in fact condones the continuance of this barrier for most women.[96] His refusal to concede that the tiresome details of domestic life should be shared by both sexes, and his failure to question the social institutions that made such sharing practically impossible are striking in the light of the fact that he recognizes that the principal means by which women would come to be recognized as equals was via success in fields formerly monopolized by men. As he writes to Harriet Taylor, the only way of dispelling most people's prejudicial beliefs about women's inferiority is by showing them "more and greater proofs by example of what women can do."[97] If the great majority of women are to remain practically if not legally barred from such achievements, how might these deep-rooted prejudices ever be expected to change?

Here again, *The Enfranchisement of Women* is a more radical document than the work written after Harriet Taylor's death. This essay written in collaboration speaks out more strongly than Mill alone ever did in favor of the married woman's need to have a life and a career of her own, so as not to be "a mere appendage to a man," attached to him "for the purpose of bringing up *his* children, and making *his* home pleasant to him."[98] These were probably aspects of his wife's thought with which Mill did not feel at all comfortable.

John Stuart Mill tried fervently to apply the principles of liberalism to women. He eschewed patriarchy within the family, and the legal and political subordination of women, as anachronisms in the modern age and as gross violations of liberty and justice. However, although a very forward-looking feminist in many respects, he in no way perceived the injustice involved in institutions and practices which allowed a man to have a career and economic independence, *and* a home life and children, but which forced a woman to choose between the two. His refusal to question the traditional family and its demands on women set the limits of his liberal feminism.

PART V

FUNCTIONALISM, FEMINISM
AND THE FAMILY

10

Women and Functionalism, Past and Present

Alfred North Whitehead once said that "the safest general characterization of the European philosophical tradition is that it consists in a series of footnotes to Plato."[1] We have seen that as far as the philosophical treatment of women is concerned, Whitehead's statement is clearly untenable. The legacy of Aristotelian thought, while repudiated in many other areas, has continued in modern times to pervade discussions of the subject of women, their nature, and their proper position and rights in society. The predominant mode of thought about women has been a functionalist one, based on the assumption of the necessity of the male-headed nuclear family, and of women's role within it. Now, after reviewing the course of the argument so far, we shall see how the mode of perceiving women that has been so predominant throughout the history of ideas persists in the writings of influential thinkers of our own time.

Socrates and Plato, having broken away from the prevailing Greek multiple standard of values, were predisposed to view women from a different perspective from their predecessors. In the *Republic*, moreover, Plato's abolition of the family necessitated his taking a radically new look at the subject of women and their nature. Since they were no longer to be "private wives," or to be defined by the functions of motherhood and housekeeping, he was obliged, despite his generally deprecating attitude toward the female sex, to consider their potential as individual citizens—as persons without a preordained and all-encompassing func-

tion in life. Book v of the *Republic* contains a more remarkable discussion of the socially and politically relevant
differences between the sexes than was to appear for more
than two thousand years thereafter. As a consequence of the
conclusions he came to, Plato dispensed, in an extremely
hierarchical society, with the usual hierarchy of the sexes.
He argued for the total equality, in education and role, of
the female guardians.

Having once thought about the potential of women, and
concluded that societies which confined them all indiscriminately to domestic seclusion were being extremely wasteful
of human resources, Plato found himself in a difficult position when, in the *Laws*, he reinstated the family, together
with other forms of private property. Whereas the theoretical argument for the equal potential, and therefore the
equal education and employment of the two sexes, was
carried further here than in the *Republic*, when it comes
to applying these precepts, Plato backed away. Clearly the
reason is that private wives could not be permitted to lead
the same kind of public lives as the female guardians and
philosophers of the ideal city. Consequently, women are
relegated to their traditional domestic functions and status.
They are conspicuously absent from the activities of citizenship. Moreover, in spite of having argued in the *Republic*
that men's and women's natures are the same apart from
their respective roles in procreation, Plato asserted in the
Laws that women must be sedate and pure in their natures,
whereas their husbands are to be noble and courageous.
Thus the nature of women, no less than their role, is prescribed by the presence or absence of the family.

Plato's treatment of women in the *Republic* is clearly
unparalleled in the history of Western thought. The essential difference between his discussion of women in the
Laws, moreover, and the later philosophical treatment of
them, is that Plato was aware of what he was doing to the
female sex, whereas subsequent philosophers give no indication of being so aware. Since Plato explicitly held that the

innate qualities of women could not be known, so long as the socialization and education of the sexes was so different, the "nature" he gave to women in the *Laws* is unambiguously prescriptive, rather than descriptive. It is the way women must be socialized, in order to perform their prescribed functions within the patriarchal and traditional structure of his proposed society.

What Plato did, consciously, to women and their "nature" in the *Laws*, has been done unconsciously by many of those political philosophers since Plato who have concerned themselves with the subject. To the extent that Plato advanced the rational discussion of women and their potential, Aristotle set it back again, and the history of political thought about women has unfortunately up to the present time consisted predominantly of footnotes to this Aristotelian legacy. In contrast to Plato, philosophers who have regarded the family as beyond question—a natural and indispensable part of the human order—have tended to view women entirely in terms of their sexual and procreative functions. Women's interests are not perceived as discrete, but as subsumed within those of the family; women's purpose is seen to be the reproduction and rearing of men, and their nature is prescriptively defined in terms of the optimal characteristics for the performance of these functions.

In the case of Aristotle himself, the treatment of women is consistent with the entire structure of his political philosophy. Because of his fundamental teleology and functionalist treatment of the world as a whole, he relegated the vast majority of people, both male and female, to the status of means, whose purpose was to enable the few to pursue their truly human ends.

In the case of Rousseau, however, the prescriptive, functionalist treatment of women stands out as a curious anomaly, in the context of a philosophy based on the ideals of human equality and freedom. Ignoring in this instance his own speculations about the original state of nature, Rousseau proceeded on the assumption that the patriarchal family was natural and necessary, and that woman's nature must therefore be defined according to its needs. Setting aside the entire environmentalist account of human development which he applied to men, he argued that women are naturally passive, subservient and chaste. They must be educated in such a way as to reinforce these natural qualities, for only thus can they be happy in a world in which they exist in order to please men. Strongly opposed though he was to Aristotle's conclusion that some men are by nature slaves and intended to serve others, Rousseau failed to perceive the applicability of his objections to his own arguments about the female sex. In spite of his preoccupation with the male individual and his rights and freedom, Rousseau continued to apply Aristotelian arguments about the nature and purpose of women. Her role in the bourgeois family was thereby rationalized: that she should propagate and nurture undisputed heirs to the family property, that she should provide for her husband a pleasant solace from the harsh realities of the competitive world outside, that she should obey him without question, be totally dependent on him and value her chaste reputation as her most prized possession—all these were merely the dictates of nature. While his ultimate prognosis for men is that they can be educated to be either individuals or citizens, but not both, his tragic conclusion for women is that they can be neither.

John Stuart Mill tried to integrate women as persons in their own right into his liberal political philosophy. He came to recognize the absurdity of claiming that the contemporary characteristics of that sex which had always been subordinated to the other, constituted female "nature." No one could presume to know the nature of women until women were free to develop it. Mill's conviction of the importance for human happiness of individual freedom and just treatment became the basis of his case for the emancipation of women. However, to the extent that his vision of the liberated woman falls short of complete equality of opportunity or of power, it bears witness to the thesis that it is the philosophers' attitude to the family, above all else, which has determined their conclusions about the rights and the social role of women.

On the one hand, Mill certainly rejected many of the legal and customary inequalities of the patriarchal family. He did not assume, as have so many others, that the best interests of all the members of the family are included in those of its male head. Thus he concluded that women must have equal civil and political rights, and the same education and opportunities to earn their own livings as men. On the other hand, however, Mill never questioned or objected to the maintenance of traditional sex roles within the family, but expressly considered them to be suitable and desirable. In spite of his explicit recognition of the extent to which domestic preoccupations hamper women's progress in other areas of life, he gave no consideration to even the eventual possibility of the sharing of domestic and child-rearing tasks between the sexes. The assumption that married women should not earn their own livings or pursue careers, except insofar as the onerous obligations of the household leaves them free to do so, means that Mill's feminism is severely constrained. He in effect condoned the continuation of considerable differences in power and in opportunity, for men and married women. Thus, though he argued that women must be admitted to citizenship, there is no way that the realities of the lives he envisaged for them could allow them to be equal citizens. While Mill, exceptionally among political philosophers, tried to treat women as individuals whose happiness and freedom were as important as those of men, his reluctance to question traditional family structure and its intrinsic sex roles prevented him from fully succeeding in his aim.

The importance of the preceding analysis is heightened by the fact that the functionalist mode of thinking about women, their rights and needs and their position in society, is by no means dead. Functionalism as a whole has undergone a considerable revival in recent decades, especially in the fields of social psychology and sociology. Two examples —the works of psychoanalyst Erik Erikson and of sociologist Talcott Parsons—will suffice to demonstrate current lines of argument on the subjects of women and the family that parallel those of Rousseau and Aristotle. It is important to understand how this type of thought, as applied to women and the family, retains such appeal.

Freud posed the curious question "What does a woman want?"[2] A number of well-respected psychologists and psychiatrists have not hesitated to provide answers which support the ancient idea that woman and her wants and needs are determined by her sexual and reproductive characteristics.[3] Bruno Bettelheim, for example, addressing the subject of women in the scientific professions, asserts:

> We must start with the realization that, as much as women want to be good scientists or engineers, they want first and foremost to be womanly companions of men and to be mothers.[4]

Some male scholars have felt in no way impelled to disguise the fact that they are defining women functionally in relation to society's needs. Psychiatrist Joseph Rheingold, for example, writes:

> Woman is nurturance . . . anatomy decrees the life of a woman. . . . When women grow up without dread of their biological functions and without subversion by feminist doctrine, and therefore enter upon motherhood with a sense of fulfillment and altruistic sentiment, we shall attain the goal of a good life and a secure world in which to live it.[5]

It is only, apparently, when women are successfully socialized into believing that their anatomy is their destiny, that "we" (who?) shall be able to live the good life.

None of this, of course, is very far removed from the ideas about women expressed by Rousseau. However, the modern archetype of his mode of thought is Erik Erikson. In an attempt to revise the negative Freudian concept that the development of the female personality derives largely from the little girl's inevitable penis envy, Erikson instead structures that development around the possession of an "inner space" with great potential—the womb.[6] Woman's capacity to bear and nurse children is therefore not just one aspect of her nature; her entire identity and the life she lives must revolve around her "inner space" and its desire to be filled. Erikson tells us that "emptiness is the female form of perdition . . . standard experience for all women,"[7] and that whatever sphere of life a woman enters into, she must take her peculiarly feminine personality— defined by its "inner space"—with her. In the political sphere, for example, Erikson says, "the influence of women will not be fully actualized until it reflects without apology the facts of the 'inner space' and the potentialities and needs of the feminine psyche."[8] Thus, women will always perform a different type of role in life from men; whatever they do, they can never forget the unique "groundplan" of their bodies. "Since a woman is never not-a-woman," Erikson concludes, "she can see her long-range goals only in those modes of activity which include and integrate her natural dispositions."[9]

Thus Erikson claims, no less positively than Rousseau, that he knows what women are really, and naturally, like. The reasoning he employs on the subject, however, is no more conclusive or convincing than Rousseau's. His demonstration that women are essentially conscious of their "inner space" is the outcome of an experiment in which boys and girls in their early teens were asked to construct scenes from a number of given toys.[10] Erikson uses the differences between the scenes created by the two sexes as evidence that their respective personalities are greatly affected by the differences in their genitalia and reproductive organs. Reminiscent of Rousseau's neglect, in his discovery of the "natural" differences between the sexes, of environmental influences up to the age of six, Erikson dismisses "the purely 'social' interpretation" quite peremptorily, on account of the fact that it cannot explain *all* the differences that were observed. He refuses to consider as significant the influences on the scenes constructed by the girls and boys of either their total play experience in a culture in which many toys and activities are considered strictly sex related, or their identification with the socially conditioned behavior and aspirations of the parent and other adults of their own sex.

Later in the essay, Erikson argues that it is the biological necessities of human life which make child-rearing "woman's unique job," and that it is therefore biology which explains many of the observable differences in a little girl. Not only does she react to things with greater compassion than a little boy, but she "learns to be more easily content within a limited circle of activities and shows less resistance to control and less impulsivity of the kind that later leads boys and men to 'delinquency.' "[11] In the absence of any consideration of the socialization of the two sexes or the expectations placed on them by society, how can we be supposed to believe that such differences are the result of biology? Rousseau's similar conclusions are not founded on much worse evidence.

Altogether, Erikson's essay demonstrates well the extraordinary degree of muddled thinking that continues to impede rational discussion of the differences between the sexes. Just as in Rousseau's treatment of the subject, descriptive and prescriptive statements are confusingly interwoven. Erikson tells us, for example, in a statement that is crucial to his argument, that women have "a biological, psychological, and ethical commitment to take care of human infancy."[12] It is difficult to see what could be meant by "a biological commitment"—a commitment, surely, is something that is undertaken by the person involved. That women have the ability to bear children is indisputable, but to call this, let alone the total care of the infant, her biological commitment, is meaningless. As for women's psychological and ethical commitments to raise children, these are both, at least to a very large extent, culture related, and the first is to an unknown degree the result of sex-role conditioning. Erickson's fusing together of a universal biological fact with culturally prescribed factors is a shrewd way of deriving his unwarranted conclusion that child-rearing is necessarily a task in which "years of specialized *womanhours* of work are involved."[13]

The importance of Erikson's work for the defense of the status quo is that it claims to give the sanction of twentieth-century science to an age-old myth. This myth claims that existing sex-role differentiation and the aspiration of girls and boys to very different future roles are due not to environmental influences or social sanctions, but to physical sexual differences. Thus the confinement of the vast majority of women to the home or to low-status positions in the sphere of employment is claimed to be in no way an anomaly in the modern world, or a state of affairs which any normal woman would find cause to challenge. This is, Erikson assures us, because their very biology ensures that women—in contrast to men, who have conquered space and disseminated ideas—"have found their identities in the care suggested in their bodies and in the needs of their issue, and seem to have taken it for granted that the outer world space belongs to the men."[14]

The task embarked on by psychologists is completed in the works of sociologists, particularly those of the "structural-functionalist" school. Talcott Parsons and colleagues, in *Family, Socialization and Interaction Process*, and in a number of articles, undertake to demonstrate that it is the essential functions which the nuclear family performs for society that necessitate the conventional differentiation between male and female sex roles. If Erikson, with respect to his treatment of women, is this century's Rousseau, Talcott Parsons's functionalist analysis of the family and woman's role within it reveals him to be the modern Aristotle.

Parsons, unlike Erikson, does not appear to believe that

the conventional roles of the sexes are a biologically determined extension of their distinct roles in procreation. Rather, the fact that pregnancy and lactation become the basis of an entirely different role and life style for women has to be explained by the mediating factor of the family. "Indeed," Parsons writes, "we argue that probably the importance of the family and its functions for society constitutes the primary set of reasons why there is a *social*, as distinguished from purely reproductive, differentiation of sex roles."[15] Thus it is the indispensable functions of the modern nuclear family that necessitate "woman's place."

Parsons's work has been criticized by recent feminist sociologists.[16] However, there are several issues that warrant discussion in the present context. First, like Aristotle with regard to the *polis* and the Greek household, Parsons takes American society of the 1940s and 1950s and its conventional nuclear family as the basis of his theory. He takes it as given that the adult members of a "normal" family consist of a man who has a job and a woman who either stays home or if employed tends to have a job which does not compete for status with that of her husband.[17] He defines the status of married women as the status derived from their husbands' levels of employment. On the issue of the status of women as compared with that of men, however, he acknowledges the inequalities due to the "assymetrical relation of the sexes to the occupational structure."[18]

Parsons is not unaware that there are problems, especially for women, which result from the sex-role structure of the nuclear family he takes as a given. The rigid modern separation of the outside world of "work" from the household, he says, "deprives the wife of her role as a partner in a common enterprise." She is left with "a set of utilitarian functions in the management of the household which may be considered a kind of 'pseudo'-occupation."[19] He points out that, in spite of American high tolerance for drudgery, middle class women tend to employ domestic servants whenever financially able, to dissociate themselves as persons from the performance of household tasks, and to take on roles in community activity in order to avoid "the stigma of being 'just a housewife.' "[20] He also acknowledges that problems arise from the fact that women's child-rearing role is usually ending just as their husbands are at the height of their careers. The confined nature of women's life in the home and the narrow specialization of men's lives at work are not entirely good for either sex, he admits. But whereas the man is likely to be compensated by the achievement and responsibility of his job, it is for the woman, Parsons acknowledges, that the rigid sex-role differentiation of our society is most damaging. "It is quite clear," he writes, "that in the adult feminine role there is quite sufficient strain and insecurity so that widespread manifestations are to be expected in the form of neurotic behavior."[21]

It is particularly striking, given this perception of some of the effects of the conventional structuring of sex roles, that Parsons refuses to consider the possibilities of change. He asserts without comment that sex roles are becoming more rather than less well defined. (He was writing, of course, before the beginning of the current women's movement.) The general movement of women into the "masculine" pattern of behavior, he believes, "would only be possible with profound alterations in the structure of the family," and he regards the traditional structure of the family as more essential than ever before in terms of its vital social functions.[22] The implication is that such profound alteration, whatever its repercussions for the mental health of half of the population, is not an open issue.

From an analysis which takes the contemporary social structure as given, Parsons slides very easily into the role of predicting, or rather prescribing, the future. His tendency to start from the basis of the American family of his time, and then to claim that the conclusions he reaches are not "culture bound" is extremely reminiscent of Aristotle's sanctifying the status quo by proving it to be the natural order of things. Having justified male dominance within

the family as a result of the husband's standing in the occupational realm, Parsons goes on to assert:

> Even if, as seems possible, it should come to pass that
> the average woman had some kind of a job, it seems
> most unlikely that this relative balance would be up-
> set; that either the roles would be reversed, or their
> qualitative differentiation in these respects completely
> erased.[23]

As confirmation of this view, Parsons cites the existing distribution of women in the labor force—the fact that they
hold predominantly "expressive" roles, " 'supportive' to
masculine roles . . . analogous to the wife-mother role in the
family." While he recognizes, then, that there is a connection between the supportive and subordinate roles that
women are assigned both inside and outside the family,
Parsons is not at all disposed to consider that there may be
little rational basis for this role assignment in either case.
The fact that *even* in the world of work women play nurturing roles supposedly reinforces the conviction that this
is their proper role within the home.

The two basic points in Parsons's argument about the
importance of sex-role differentiation are that the family,
like any small group, must have an "expressive" leader and
an "instrumental" leader, and that the mother must assume
the first of these roles and the father the second. The first
claim has been well criticized by Ann Oakley, who points
out that all the subjects of the experiment that Parsons
relies upon were the products of socialization within nuclear families of the type he aims to draw conclusions about.
The small groups they formed, then, were highly likely to
take on the structure of the conventional family, and Parsons's conclusion that the characteristics observed are those
of "small groups everywhere" is unfounded.[24]

However, let us accept for the moment these conclusions
about the leadership roles of the small group, and therefore
the family. Why must the mother be assigned the "expres-

sive" and the father the "instrumental" leadership of the family? Parsons argues that the mother's expressive role derives from the two facts of pregnancy and lactation. It is by default that the father, since he cannot perform these functions, must go out to work and become the instrumental leader.[25] However, since Parsons denies that the fetal stage has any relevance for the child's socialization, and he was writing at a time when bottle feeding was at its height and nursing actively discouraged by the medical profession, there appears to be very little foundation to his assignment of life-long roles based on sex. Parsons seems to have been to some extent aware of this problem. Though in general he writes in terms of the "mother-child relationship" and calls the child-rearer the "mother," during his discussion of the crucial stage of oral dependency he says that what is essential for the development of the child's ego is " 'attachment' to one or a class of 'social objects' of which the mother is the prototype." He is careful to note that " 'agent of care' is the essential concept and that it need not be confined to one specific person; it is the function which is essential."[26] Each time, however, he immediately reverts to calling his agent of care "mother," giving the reader the misleading general impression that it has been demonstrated to be necessarily a female role.

It is clearly during the oedipal stage that Parsons thinks the clear differentiation of the sex roles of parents is most essential for the child's socialization. The reason it is essential, however, is that it is at this stage that the child, largely through identification with the parent of his or her own sex, must be directed successfully into the appropriate sex role. This is a crucial part of the child's absorption of "the institutionalized patterns of the society."[27] In order for the daughter to become a "willing and 'accommodating' person" and the son to become an "adequate technical performer,"[28] they must be socialized in a nuclear family in which this sex-role differentiation is clearly observed. But surely there is something rather circular about such reasoning. A large part of the explanation for the necessity of sex roles rests on the need to socialize the next generation into sex roles, so that they in turn will be able to socialize their children into sex roles, ad infinitum. Especially since Parsons was aware of some of the unhealthy consequences of conventional sex roles, one wonders why he was so concerned to preserve them.

Parsons, as a sociologist, is perfectly entitled to perform a theoretical analysis of the institutions of a sexist culture. However, he is no more justified than Aristotle in presenting a theory about a particular historical set of institutions as a dictum for human behavior throughout eternity. The supposedly neutral and academic nature of his study belies his reactionary conclusions about the necessity of maintaining strict sex roles in order to preserve a healthily functioning society.

Thus, in recent times, strong sanctions have been given to sexist mythology by scholars influential in the mainstream of their respective disciplines. Rousseauian reasoning about the nature of women presented by such thinkers as are exemplified here by Erik Erikson, and Aristotelian assumptions about the sacred immutability of the existing family structure such as are evident in the Parsonian school of sociology, have reinforced justification of the differential treatment of the sexes. Until the beginning of the women's movement in the late 1960s began to break the monopoly, moreover, both men and women were fed throughout their socialization on the fallout from such views. Through textbooks, advertising, child-rearing manuals, and countless other channels, the prescriptive "nature" which was imposed on women by their reproductive biology, in combination with the assumption of the conventional family structure, was virtually unopposed by any alternative views.

11

Persons, Women, and the Law

We turn now to a body of thought which has had, and continues to have, a similarly direct influence on the conditions in which women in this country have lived their lives—the law, particularly as it has been subjected to judicial review by the highest courts of the land. Here it will become obvious that it is not only in the history of political thought and the ivory towers of academia that functionalist modes of thought have served to rationalize the unequal treatment of women. The courts, too, have in the past and up to the present utilized arguments based on the conventional role of women within the family, sanctified as inevitable and natural, in making many important sexually discriminatory decisions.

The equality of individuals before the law is clearly established by the Constitution of the United States. The Fourteenth Amendment prescribes that:

> No State shall make or enforce any law which shall abridge the privileges or immunities of citizens of the United States; nor shall any State deprive any person of life, liberty, or property, without due process of law; nor deny to any person within its jurisdiction the equal protection of the laws.

In the light of such provisions, combined with the Due Process Clause of the Fifth Amendment, it may seem on first consideration odd that the Equal Rights Amendment, specifically disallowing the denial or abridgement of rights on account of sex, should be necessary. For although the Fourteenth Amendment was specifically intended to ensure legal equality for the newly freed slaves,[1] the clauses quoted above refer to "persons." However, lest we jump too quickly to the conclusion that "persons" automatically includes women, it is important to remember that the second section of the same amendment, in reference to the apportionment of representatives, introduced the word "male" into the Constitution for the first time. As Constitutional lawyer Ruth Ginsburg has noted, this "caused concern that the grand phrases of the first section of the fourteenth amendment would have, at best, qualified application to women."[2] Indeed, the history of the courts' arguments and decisions in sex-discrimination cases throughout the past century proves that it is only in a qualified sense that women have been adjudged to be persons. While a 1972 study revealed over eight hundred sections of the U.S. Code which contained explicit references to sex, and there are many thousands of similar state laws, judicial reasoning has been such that it was not until 1971 that the U.S. Supreme Court held a sex-based classification to be unconstitutional. In this chapter, we will analyze the ideas and arguments concerning women that have supported the discriminatory aspects of the law, and demonstrate the extent to which the modes of thinking about women and their position in society that pervade Western political thought have persisted in the reasoning of the modern American judiciary.

Just as we have found with reference to the reasoning of the philosophers, the principal clue to understanding legal reasoning on the subject of women is the family and assumptions with regard to woman's role therein. There is no doubt that the male-headed family has been regarded by both legislators and the courts as the fundamental basis of U.S. society. "Our whole society," said a judge in a 1949 case, in which he denied a woman custody of her two daughters because of her adultery, "is based on the absolutely fundamental proposition that: 'Marriage, as creating the most important relation in life,' has 'more to do with the morals and civilization of a people than any other institution.' "[3] And in a 1953 case, it was held that denial of the husband's right to choose the family's place of residence "tends to sacrifice the family unity, the entity upon which our civilization is built."[4] If the family is such a basic unit of society, it seems strange that the Constitution, and particularly the Bill of Rights, never mentions it, but is entirely worded in terms of individual persons. This is odd, however, only until one realizes that these "persons" of the Constitution, like the consenters to the original contracts of Hobbes, Locke and Rousseau, did not include every adult individual, but only the male heads of families, each of whom was understood to represent the interests of those who constituted his patriarchal entourage. Clearly indicating that the Founders in their wildest dreams did not intend "persons" in the Constitution to be read otherwise than this, Thomas Jefferson asserted: "Were our state a pure democracy there would still be excluded from our deliberations women, who, to prevent deprivation of morals and ambiguity of issues, should not mix promiscuously in gatherings of men."[5] The state and federal constitutions, we must recognize, were written with the understanding that in many important respects, women were not, legally, persons, but subordinate members of patriarchal households.

The exclusion of women, particularly after marriage, from legal personhood had a firm foundation in the common law fiction of coverture. As Blackstone explained in *Commentaries of the Laws of England*:

> By marriage, the husband and wife are one person in law: that is, the very being or legal existence of the woman is suspended during the marriage, or at least is incorporated and consolidated into that of the husband: under whose wing, protection, and *cover*, she performs everything: . . .
>
> . . . But, though our law in general considers man and wife as one person, yet there are some instances in which she is separately considered; as inferior to him,

and acting by his compulsion. And, therefore, all deeds executed and acts done, by her, during her coverture, are void. . . .[6]

Thus a married woman is either not a person at all, or she is such a subordinate person that she must be understood as coerced by her husband into all actions for which she might otherwise be held legally liable. Blackstone viewed this as preferential treatment for women, and he concludes his discussion of the issue by noting that "even the disabilities, which the wife lies under, are for the most part intended for her protection and benefit. So great a favourite is the female sex of the laws of England."[7]

While coverture applies, formally, only to married women, its implications have extended, in practice, to all members of the female sex. First, the great majority of women are married for a substantial portion of their adult lives. Second, the law and the courts have generally based their discrimination between the sexes on the assumption that women are wives, and not only wives but mothers.[8] Although the Married Women's Property Acts abolished many of the disabilities wives suffered under the doctrine of coverture, and some of the more absurd remaining aspects have been overridden in recent years, there are still many remnants of it in existence, one of the most obvious being the requirement that a woman take her husband's name and domicile as her own. It is not because of lack of opportunity to review or change them that these laws remain on the books. In 1971, the U.S. Supreme Court affirmed without opinion the constitutionality of Alabama's requirement that a woman take her husband's name unless she changes back legally to her own.[9] In December of 1976, the Court refused to hear a challenge to a Kentucky requirement that a married woman use her husband's name when applying for a driver's license. According to the state court, this classification is based not on sex but on marital status, and is therefore nondiscriminatory. Seven members of the Supreme Court apparently found this argument reasonable.

The doctrine of coverture has been applied, in some cases involving women's constitutional rights, in its most extreme form—the explicit denial of personhood to women. Just as philosophers such as Aristotle or Rousseau saw no inconsistency in making general statements about "human beings" or "mankind," and then excluding all women from their scope, several critical instances of judicial reasoning explicitly demonstrate this same tendency. One case, brought before the U.S. Supreme Court in the 1890s, concerned Virginia's exclusion of a woman from the practice of law, although the pertinent statute was worded in terms of "persons." The Court argued that it was indeed up to the state's Supreme Court "to determine whether the word 'person' as used (in the Statute) is confined to males, and whether women are admitted to practice law in that Commonwealth."[10] The issue of whether women must be understood as included by the word "persons" continued even into the twentieth century, and much the same attitude of doubt about the matter is apparent in a Massachusetts case in 1931. Here, women were denied eligibility for jury service, although the statute stated that every "person qualified to vote" was so eligible. The Massachusetts Supreme Court asserted: "No intention to include women can be deduced from the omission of the word male."[11] For legal purposes as well as in political philosophy, it appears, women have by no means always been considered to be persons.

While the courts have had occasional recourse to the notion that women are not necessarily persons, this has not been the primary mode of upholding the constitutionality of legal differentiation between the sexes. As we shall see, justices from the nineteenth century to the present, when justifying legal differentiation between the sexes, have relied upon that same functionalist mode of reasoning about women and their "nature" that we have found so prevalent in political thought. An early example is the case of Myra Bradwell, who in 1872 was denied a license to practice law in the State of Illinois. Appealing to the U.S. Supreme Court on the basis of her Fourteenth Amendment privileges and immunities, Bradwell was decided against, and moreover, was presented, in the concurring opinion of three justices, with the following argument:

> It certainly cannot be affirmed, as an historical fact, that (the right to engage in any and every profession, occupation, or employment in civil life) has ever been established as one of the fundamental privileges and immunities of the sex. On the contrary, the civil law, as well as nature herself, has always recognised a wide difference in the respective spheres and destinies of man and woman. . . . The natural and proper timidity and delicacy which belongs to the female sex evidently unfits it for many of the occupations of civil life. The constitution of the family organization, which is founded in the divine ordinance, as well as in the nature of things, indicates the domestic sphere as that which properly belongs to the domain and functions of womanhood. The harmony, not to say identity, of interests and views which belong, or should belong, to the family institution is repugnant to the idea of a woman adopting a distinct and independent career from that of her husband.[12]

Judicial appeals to the authority of the "divine ordinance" on the nature of the family or of women are more a nineteenth- than a twentieth-century phenomenon, though they have not completely disappeared.[13] There are two other outstanding features of this argument, however, which can be seen appearing and reappearing in judicial opinions up to the present. They are the same two ways of thinking about women, moreover, which we have shown to predominate through much of the history of our culture. First, it is the male-headed family, naturally if not divinely ordained, which has been held to define woman's proper function and sphere—that of domesticity. The family's unity must prevail over the potential rights of the individual woman and demands that she not have a separate career or existence outside the private sphere. Second, here as with Aristotle and Rousseau, there is an identity presumed between woman's so-defined sphere or function, and her nature. It is woman's peculiar "sphere and destiny" which dictates "the natural and proper timidity and delicacy" which supposedly disable her from doing anything outside of that sphere. And lest we ask, but what of the woman who chooses not to marry, Justice Bradley, the author of the opinion, responds not only that she is an exception, but that women *should* be married: "The paramount destiny and mission of woman are to fulfill the noble and benign offices of wife and mother. This is the law of the Creator."[14] Thus the Creator and nature have foreordained the family, and the family's needs dictate not only every woman's role, but her nature as well.

With a few exceptions, such as the Massachusetts case noted above, it has not been argued in this century that there is any doubt about whether the word "persons" includes women, or that the Fifth and Fourteenth Amendments are in principle not applicable to the female sex. What *has* happened, however, is that a far less strict standard of judicial review has been applied to discrimination on the basis of sex than that which has been applied for a number of decades to discrimination on other grounds such as race, alienage, or national origin. Although the purpose of the Fourteenth Amendment is clearly to prevent the arbitrary imposition onto some people—originally blacks—of laws from which others are exempt, the Supreme Court has stated that "the Constitution does not require things which are different in fact or opinion to be treated in law as though they were the same."[15] However, in a field as controversial as the differences between men and women, and the justifiable legal differentiation between them, this general maxim is of little use. As Justice Bradley's and many subsequent opinions demonstrate, the "facts" or opinions of some male justices about the differences between the sexes have been such as to allow virtually any degree of legislative discrimination between them.

Two distinct standards of judicial review have developed by which it is decided whether laws differentiating between classes of persons are in violation of the Due Process or Equal Protection Clauses of the Constitution.[16] The far stricter test (first made explicit in a 1944 case, *Korematsu v. U.S.*), in which the legislation is subjected to "the most rigid scrutiny," is applied in cases where either a "fundamental right" (such as freedom of religion or association, or the rights to travel, vote, have children, work) is involved, or the classification made by the challenged statute is considered to be "inherently suspect" (originally race, more recently alienage, national origin, or poverty). In such cases, the defenders of the law under review bear "a heavy burden of justification." They must show the most "compelling" reasons for the discrimination, which will be held constitutional "only if it is necessary, not merely rationally related, to the accomplishment of a permissible state policy." In all other cases where statutes are challenged on the basis that they violate due process or equal protection rights, the test of "reasonable classification" is applied. The burden in such cases is on the challenger of the statute to show that the challenged classification is arbitrary and not reasonably related to the purpose of the statute. Only "invidious discrimination" or classification which is "patently arbitrary (and) utterly lacking in rational justification" is declared unconstitutional. Under this less strict test, a discriminatory provision of a state law "will not be set aside if any state of facts reasonably may be conceived to justify it."

It has been this second standard of review which has consistently, until the 1970s, been applied to cases involving sex-based discrimination. Since sex was not held to be a "suspect" classification, the burden has been on the challenger to show that each legal differentiation between men and women was invidious and patently arbitrary. In fact, no case had been won on such grounds in the U.S. Supreme Court until 1971. Moreover, when we turn to the legal disabilities and protections that the Court has found to be "reasonably related" to the difference between the sexes, we find, though generally more subtly presented, the same basic themes and prejudices that were expressed in the Bradley opinion of 1872, and which we have seen in the course of this study to have been expressed by some of the greatest philosophic minds of Western civilization. Thus, in cases where the physical differences between the sexes were totally irrelevant, the judgments of the Supreme Court have declared due process and equal protection requirements to be satisfied by the rationality of treating the sexes differently on account of woman's special function within the family, and her corresponding "nature." Moreover, even in cases involving rights and obligations that the courts have acknowledged to be basic or fundamental, such as jury service, procreation and work,[17] the less strict standard of scrutiny has been applied, and legal discrimination between the sexes has been upheld.

One of the first cases to consider at length the constitutional position of women was *Muller v. Oregon*,[18] which in 1908 established the constitutionality of legislation to protect female workers, at a time when similar legislation applying to male workers was held to be unconstitutional. Thus in spite of its ruling three years previously that protective labor legislation for men violated the constitutional right of freedom of contract,[19] the Court in *Muller*, greatly influenced by the famous Brandeis brief, decided that it was not arbitrary or unreasonable to allow maximum hours to be legislated for women. The brief, and the Court's opinion in this case, were to be extremely important for the future struggle for women's equal rights before the law. As Leo Kanowitz has said:

The Court in *Muller* simply could not resist giving
expression to some old-fashioned male supremacist notions. While rising to a greater level of sophistication
than Mr. Justice Bradley's observations in the *Bradwell* case, the words of Mr. Justice Brewer in *Muller
v. Oregon* have continued to plague later constitutional
litigation over a broad range of sex-based discriminatory laws.[20]

The *Muller v. Oregon* decision was eventually to be of
great, positive significance in the labor movement's struggle for rights. However, while in retrospect it seems obvious
that male workers were and are in a fairly similar position
of inequality in relation to their employers as are female
workers, and that the legal regulation of working hours and
conditions of both sexes is therefore by no means an unacceptable limitation of freedom of contract, the Supreme
Court did not recognize this wider principle until 1937. In
1908, then, the argument for protective legislation for
women had to rest on the claim that the differences between
the sexes made it reasonable in the case of women, while
a violation of freedom in the case of men. Brandeis, after
presenting a great amount of evidence on female working
conditions and their regulation in other countries, argues
that " (a) the physical organization of woman, (b) her maternal functions, (c) the rearing and education of the children, (d) the maintenance of the home—are all so important that the need for such reduction [of working hours]
need hardly be discussed."[21] Here we can see immediately
the intermingling of the physical differences between the
sexes with their conventional roles, based on the assumption not only that all women are wives and mothers, but
that their proper and predominant role in life is that of
child-rearer and housekeeper. In one sense, of course, this
is a perfectly reasonable representation of what most women
did, much of the time, and of how they thought of themselves. However, if Brandeis[22] really considered this role of

women to be essential to the well-being of society, it seems odd that he did not question why some women were forced by necessity into working the ten-hour day in laundries that *was* allowed by the decision. Clearly, the argument about woman's maternal and domestic role is not taken to its logical conclusions. To do so would have been to deprive employers of a growing source of cheap labor. But how could that sex considered too timid and delicate for the practice of law be imagined capable of a ten-hour workday in a commercial laundry?

In the Court's opinion, as in the brief, woman's physical differences from men are conflated with her "proper functions": "That woman's physical structure and the performance of maternal functions place her at a disadvantage in the struggle for subsistence is obvious."[23] Here, the Court purports to be reasoning in a totally ahistorical way, and makes no reference to the fact that it is not a dictate of nature, but particular socio-economic conditions that determine whether child-rearing and housework are to place those who do them at a disadvantage, or whether they are to be considered valuable aspects of social production and rewarded accordingly. Moreover, it is not for the sake of women themselves, but because "healthy mothers are essential to vigorous offspring," that "the physical well-being of woman becomes an object of public interest and care in order to preserve the strength and vigor of the race."[24] Throughout the opinion, it is the combination of the "inherent difference between the sexes" with "the different functions in life which they perform" that leads to the Court's conclusion—of critical importance for future litigation—that woman is "properly placed in a class by herself" and that sex is therefore a reasonable and justifiable basis for legislative classification. The Court is manifestly not confining itself to the question "What are women like?" It is asking, rather, just as Aristotle and Rousseau did, "What are women *for*?"

In addition, the Court makes the rather large assump-

FUNCTIONALISM, FEMINISM AND THE FAMILY

tion that, even if women were granted completely equal rights, they would remain dependent on men and their protection, for

> history discloses the fact that woman has always been dependent upon man. He established his control at the outset by superior physical strength, and this control in various forms, with diminishing intensity, has continued to the present. . . . Though limitations upon personal and contractual rights may be removed by legislation, there is that in her disposition and habits of life which will operate against a full assertion of those rights. She will still be where (sic) some legislation to protect her seems necessary to secure a full equality of right. Doubtless there are individual exceptions, and there are many respects in which she has an advantage over him; but looking at it from the viewpoint of the effort to maintain an independent position in life, she is not upon an equality. Differentiated by these matters from the other sex, she is properly placed in a class by herself. . . .[25]

First, the reliance on man's superior physique as a truth of universal and fixed importance ignores the fact that, by the early twentieth century, the importance of physical strength for subsistence had diminished vastly on account of the advancement of technology. Second, the argument involves the assumption that not only woman's physical inferiority, but also her "disposition and habits of life" are fixed characteristics, independent of the male-dominated institutions in which she is socialized and lives her life. While "history," man's superior physical strength and woman's "disposition and habits of life" replace explicit appeal to the "law of nature," the reasoning here is essentially Rousseau's. The economic dependence of women on men is perceived as an inevitability unrelated to the values and norms of particular social and economic structures. The result is that the socio-economic disadvantages suffered by women are seen as the same *type* of disadvantages, or as naturally concomitant upon, their physical differences from men, instead of being recognized as the effects of a patriarchal and exploitative society.

While there is no doubt that protective labor legislation for *both* sexes is necessary, and was particularly warranted by early twentieth-century working conditions, protective legislation of any kind restricted just to women has had the effect of perpetuating the myth that women are not really members of the labor force in the same serious sense that men are. It has perpetuated a social and economic hierarchy in which women are prejudicially placed. Significantly, the U.S. Supreme Court itself in recent years has recognized its dual effects. "Statutory distinctions between the sexes," a Supreme Court opinion asserted in 1973, "often have the effect of invidiously relegating the entire class of females to inferior legal status without regard to the actual capabilities of its individual members." Discrimination between the sexes, the opinion acknowledges, "was rationalized by an attitude of 'romantic paternalism' which, in practical effect, put women, not on a pedestal, but in a cage."[26]

This enlightenment is very recent and partial, however, and for a long period, the *Muller* opinion was of overwhelming importance as a precedent. In fact, as Kanowitz states, "The subsequent reliance in judicial decisions upon the *Muller* language is a classic example of the misuse of precedent, of later courts being mesmerized by what an earlier court had *said* rather than what it had *done*."[27] The finding that sex is a reasonable basis of classification has been used, in equal protection as well as due process contexts, in cases where sex is a far less reasonable basis for classification than it was in *Muller*. It has been used, for example, to exclude women from juries, from occupations where physical strength is not necessary, and from state-supported colleges.[28] Even in the sixties and seventies, the U.S. Supreme Court and other high courts have held discrimination by sex to be "rationally justified" in cases which clearly did not involve the physical differences between the sexes.

A good example of the abuse of the presumption that classification by sex is reasonable is a 1948 case in which the U.S. Supreme Court was asked to decide on the constitutionality of a Michigan statute which prohibited women in general from being barmaids while at the same time excepting the wives and daughters of the owners of liquor establishments.[29] In *Goesaert v. Cleary*, the claim for women's rights was at last raised directly under the Equal Protection Clause of the Fourteenth Amendment. What is important to notice here is that even in a case involving what the Court had previously held to be an essential Fourteenth Amendment right—the right to work, it was the "reasonable classification" rather than the "strict scrutiny" test that was used, and the plaintiff was left with the burden of proof that the discrimination was arbitrary. The Court found that it was not arbitrary. They decided that it was not unconstitutional for the states to draw "a sharp line between the sexes," that they could therefore if they chose exclude all women from working behind bars, but that it was not unreasonable for the Michigan legislation to make the exception it did, since the presence of a barmaid's father or husband minimized the "hazards" that might confront her otherwise.[30] Moreover, the Court specifically stated, in direct contrast to its reasoning in *Brown v. Board of Education* only six years later, that "the Constitution does not require legislatures to reflect sociological insight, or shifting social standards, any more than it requires them to keep abreast of the latest scientific standards."[31] Twenty-five years later, this approach to women's role and women's rights is finally in the process of being rendered obsolete.

The "sharp line between the sexes" that legislators have, until very recently, been permitted to draw has played a significant part in maintaining women's second-class socioeconomic status. In addition, moreover, it has directly af-

fected the seriousness with which women have been regarded as citizens, as a brief examination of judicial review
of laws relating to women's jury service will make clear.
Here too, in case after case, we can see that defining women
in accordance with their function within the family has
circumscribed their lives and severely limited the extent to
which they have been able to be full participants in the
political realm.

As a Federal District Court asserted in 1966, "Jury service on the part of the citizens of the United States is considered under our law in this country as one of the basic
rights and obligations of citizenship."[32] Moreover, the idea
that exclusion from jury service is a mark of inferiority
goes back at least as far as 1879, when the Supreme Court
stated:

> The very fact that colored people are singled out and
> expressly denied by a statute all right to participate in
> the administration of the laws, as jurors, because of
> their color, though they are citizens, and may be in
> other respects fully qualified, is practically a brand
> upon them, affixed by the law, an assertion of their in-
> feriority, and a stimulant to that race prejudice which
> is an impediment to securing to individuals of the race
> that equal justice which the law aims to secure to all
> others.[33]

Ironically, it was in this very opinion that the Court expressly confirmed the states' right to confine jury service to
males. It apparently did not strike them as important, if
indeed it struck them at all, that the stigma and prejudice
associated with the denial of such a basic right was suffered
by all women, as well as by black men.

It is only in the twentieth century, and in many cases
long after they received the suffrage, that women have been
admitted at all to serve on juries, and in many jurisdictions
they still do not serve on the same terms as men. The last
state to repeal its statutory exclusion of women from jury

service was Mississippi, in 1968. Two years previously, the perennial excuses—women's special delicacy and domestic functions—were cited to demonstrate the rationality of excluding them from this right of citizenship. The Mississippi Supreme Court decided that "the legislature has the right to exclude women so they may continue their service as mothers, wives and homemakers, and also to protect them (in some ways they are still upon a pedestal) from the filth, obscenity, and noxious atmosphere that so often pervades a courtroom during a jury trial."[34] However, the climate of opinion was changing, and in the same year a Federal District Court ruled unconstitutional a similar Alabama statute, stating that it was "arbitrary in view of modern political, social and economic conditions,"[35] and consequently a violation of the Equal Protection Clause.

It is not until more recently, however, that *exemptions* of women solely on account of their sex have been declared unconstitutional. In this context it must be kept in mind that for a class of persons to be automatically exempted from jury service amounts in practice to their virtual exclusion.[36] On the issue of women's automatic exemption, there have been two Supreme Court decisions, in 1961 and 1975, which are indicative of the radical change that has begun to occur in the Court's view of women. This change amounts to at least a partial abdication of the idea that women can be functionally defined by their role within the family, and legally discriminated against, accordingly. In 1961, in *Hoyt v. Florida*, the Court upheld unanimously a Florida statute which granted women absolute exemption from jury service, unless they expressly volunteered. "We of course recognize," the opinion states, "that the Fourteenth Amendment reaches not only arbitrary class exclusions from jury service based on race or color, but also all other exclusions which 'single out' any class of persons for different treatment not based on some reasonable classification.' "[37] However, it is then argued that the statutory exemption of women did not violate the Fourteenth

Amendment rights of the female appellant (who had been convicted of the second-degree murder of her husband, by an all-male jury), because it was indeed "based on (a) reasonable classification." The crux of the Court's opinion is the statement that:

Despite the enlightened emancipation of women from the restrictions and protections of bygone years, and their entry into many parts of community life formerly considered to be reserved to men, woman is still regarded as the center of the home and family life. We cannot say that it is constitutionally impermissible for a State, acting in pursuit of the general welfare, to conclude that a woman should be relieved from the civic duty of jury service unless she herself determines that such service is consistent with her own special responsibilities.[38]

Clearly, the Supreme Court in 1961 still perceived women's special family duties as taking priority over their basic duties as citizens.

As recently as 1970, a federal district court upheld the exemption of women on the basis of their sex alone as constitutional, on the grounds that such a distinction between the sexes had "sound and reasonable basis." The court argued, much as the Supreme Court had eight years earlier:

Granted that some women pursue business careers, the great majority constitute the heart of the home, where they are busily engaged in the twenty-four hour day task of producing and rearing children, providing a home for the entire family, and performing the daily household work, all of which demands their full energies. Although some women now question this arrangement, the state legislature has permitted the exemption in order not to risk disruption of this basic family unit. Its action was far from arbitrary.[39]

The demand that wife and mother be always available to nurture both men and children is right out in the open in this passage. The clear message is that women are indispensable at home, where no alternative arrangements for the family's health and comfort can be conceived of, even temporarily, but that they are dispensable in the courtroom, where justice is not impaired nor rights violated by the continued domination of men in their traditional spheres of activity.

Attitudes toward women were changing rapidly, however, in the late sixties and early seventies, and the Supreme Court was ultimately to reflect this change. By the early 1970s only one state, Louisiana, retained legislation by which women were automatically exempted from jury service unless they expressly volunteered. In 1975 the U.S. Supreme Court reviewed the issue, and, with one dissenter, handed down a decision which in effect reversed its ruling of fourteen years before. In *Taylor v. Louisiana*, the Court held that provisions exempting and in effect excluding women from jury service are unconstitutional, since they violate the requirements of the Sixth Amendment that juries should comprise a fair cross section of the community. "If the shoe were on the other foot," asks the opinion, "who would claim that a jury was representative of the community if all men were intentionally and systematically excluded from the panel?"[40] Although the Court regards the plaintiff's right to a proper jury as a basic right which "cannot be overcome on merely rational grounds," the opinion does consider the reasonableness of exempting women, as allowed in *Hoyt*, and rejects it: "It is untenable to suggest these days," the Court reasons, "that it would be a special hardship for each and every woman to perform jury service or that society cannot spare *any* women from their present duties."[41] Specifically citing the appeal in the *Hoyt* opinion to woman's function as the "center of the home and family life," the Court in *Taylor* draws attention to the fact that a majority of women between the ages of eighteen and sixty-four are in the labor force, and asserts that "these statistics . . . certainly put to rest the suggestion that all women should be exempt from jury service based solely on their sex and the presumed role in the home."[42] Thus the Court's ruling, reversing that of *Hoyt*, is that

> it is no longer tenable to hold that women as a class may be excluded or given automatic exemptions based solely on sex if the consequence is that criminal jury venires are almost totally male. . . . If it was ever the case that women were unqualified to sit on juries or were so situated that none of them should be required to perform jury service, that time has long since passed.[43]

The positive significance of the *Taylor* decision is that it demolishes the idea that women as a class are indispensable from their domestic responsibilities, and that their role as citizens must always give precedence to their role as wives and mothers. Its limitation is that, based as it is on the Sixth Amendment rights of the plaintiff, it may not be held applicable in cases where the differential treatment of women does not lead to their being significantly underrepresented on jury venires. Yet even in such circumstances, the mere exemption of women on grounds other than those for men, quite apart from its consequences, amounts to pronouncing them as of lesser importance in the civic sphere. As the Supreme Court acknowledged a hundred years ago, the exclusion of a class of citizens from jury service is indeed "an assertion of . . . inferiority." The exemption of a class surely has some of the same serious implications.

From this account of the litigation over women's jury duties alone, it is clear that significant changes in judicial attitudes have occurred—but only since the early 1970s. As recently as 1971, Johnston and Knapp, two New York University law professors, reviewing the field of sex-discriminatory legislation, could still justly assert:

By and large, the performance of American judges in the area of sex discrimination can be succinctly described as ranging from poor to abominable. With some notable exceptions, they have failed to bring to sex discrimination cases those judicial virtues of detachment, reflection and critical analysis which have served them so well with respect to other sensitive social issues. . . . "Sexism"—the making of unjustified (or at least unsupported) assumptions about individual capabilities, interests, goals and social roles solely on the basis of sex differences—is as easily discernible in contemporary judicial opinion as racism ever was.[44]

In another 1971 law review article, the authors, arguing the need for the Equal Rights Amendment, pointed out that by that date the Supreme Court showed no indication of applying strict standards when deciding sex discrimination cases.[45] Noting that most of the language used in the decisions "follows the . . . nineteenth-century view of women's status and function in society," they conclude that, given the very limited application of the Fifth and Fourteenth Amendments to women, the only way to assure the end of legal sex discrimination was via an Amendment explicitly prohibiting it.

Since these articles were written, however, there has been an accelerated change in the judicial view of women's legal status, no doubt catalyzed by the renewed feminist movement and the passage through Congress of the Equal Rights Amendment. In 1971, in a landmark decision, the Supreme Court finally found a statutory distinction between the sexes to be in violation of the Equal Protection Clause of the Fourteenth Amendment. In *Reed v. Reed*, the Court unanimously struck down an Idaho statute which automatically preferred a male to a female as administrator of an estate, in circumstances where the two were identically related to the deceased.[46] Whereas the Idaho Court had claimed that "nature itself has established the distinction [between the sexes] and this statute is not designed to discriminate, but is only designed to alleviate the problem of holding hearings,"[47] the Supreme Court decided that the discriminatory statute did not satisfy even the less strict equal protection standard. The opinion states:

> To give a mandatory preference to members of either sex over members of the other, merely to accomplish the elimination of hearings on the merits, is to make the very kind of arbitrary legislative choice forbidden by the Equal Protection Clause of the Fourteenth Amendment; and whatever may be said as to the positive values of avoiding intrafamilial controversy, the choice in this context may not lawfully be mandated solely on the basis of sex.[48]

While the decision in this case shows that the Court was no longer prepared to assume that any interest of the family automatically took priority over the woman's rights, and was prepared to impose a stricter test of "rational relationship" than in the past, the burden was still left on a plaintiff to prove the discrimination made by the statute unreasonable.

The most important conceptual breakthrough of the seventies, in this area, has been the recognition by some high-court judges that sex, like race, alienage and national origin, is an "inherently suspect" classification, and that therefore statutes involving sex discrimination cannot be validated by the "reasonable classification" standard, but must be subjected to the scrutiny of the stricter standard. This doctrine was first asserted by the California Supreme Court in 1971.[49] Its reasoning was to a large extent echoed, two years later, in the deciding opinion of a plurality of the U.S. Supreme Court, who agreed that sex was indeed a suspect classification. In *Frontiero v. Richardson*,[50] a female Air Force lieutenant challenged the constitutionality of the requirement that she, in order to claim her husband as a "dependent" for the purpose of obtaining certain benefits, had to prove that he was dependent on her for over half of his support, whereas a man in the services could automatically claim his wife as a "dependent," regardless of her actual dependence on him. While eight of the justices agreed that the discriminatory requirement was unconstitutional, as a violation of the Due Process Clause of the Fifth Amendment, only four joined in the opinion of the Court which declared sex an "inherently suspect" classification. They argued:

> Since sex, like race and national origin, is an immutable characteristic determined solely by the accident of birth, the imposition of special disabilities upon the members of a particular sex because of their sex would seem to violate 'the basic concept of our system that legal burdens should bear some relationship to individual responsibility.' . . . And what differentiates sex from such non-suspect statuses as intelligence or physical disability, and aligns it with the recognized suspect criteria, is that the sex characteristic frequently bears no relationship to ability to perform or contribute to society. As a result, statutory distinctions between the sexes often have the effect of invidiously relegating the entire class of females to inferior legal status without regard to the actual capabilities of its individual members.[51]

The Aristotelian and Rousseauian functionalist modes of thinking about women, as seen in previous judicial opinions, seem here to be giving way to an approach that is akin to that of Plato in Book v of the *Republic*. The recognition that a person's sex is an accidentally determined characteristic, for which he or she is not responsible, and that it is frequently totally unrelated to that person's capabilities, leads this plurality of the Court to decide, as Plato did, that one who would discriminate between the sexes in any respect must bear the burden of proof that such discrimination is justified.

It would certainly be premature, however, to declare functionalist reasoning about women by the judiciary extinct. While this is not the place to provide an up-to-date chronicle of the precise constitutional status of sex-discriminatory legislation,[52] it is important to recognize that the old tendency to decide women's legal rights by asking what is woman's function, though apparently no longer argued explicitly, is still present in a disguised form in some high-court rulings. Two decisions, handed down in 1974 and 1976, indicate that the area of pregnancy is still one where the majority of members of the highest court are unprepared to treat women as equal human beings, in spite of the recent tendency of a minority of its members to relinquish the age-old functionalist reasoning with regard to women and their "natural" role within the family. The issue in both cases is the legal status of employee disability insurance programs which, though generally all-inclusive, exclude pregnancy-related disabilities from their range of coverage.

In *Geduldig v. Aiello*, with three of the subscribers to the "suspect classification" view of gender again dissenting, the Court ruled that because pregnancy is "an objectively identifiable physical condition with unique characteristics," discrimination on the basis of pregnancy is not sex-based discrimination. Therefore, the Court decided, a state disability insurance program which excluded pregnancy-related disabilities did not violate the Equal Protection Clause of the Fourteenth Amendment.[53] As Katherine Bartlett, reviewing the ruling, has noted, the Court's argument for the uniqueness of pregnancy is very weak, since the program covered "virtually every other disabling condition . . . regardless of its voluntariness, predictability, uniqueness, or 'normalcy.' " Clear examples of such cases are voluntary sterilization, sickle-cell anemia, prostatectomies, sex-change operations, and injuries resulting from accidents while drunk.[54] In fact, the Court's opinion is based mainly on the argument that the financial feasibility of the program would be imperiled by the inclusion of the disability involved in a normal pregnancy, which seems hardly legitimate reasoning in a case concerning the fundamental right of citizens to be treated equally under the law and their "basic civil right" to bear children. If something must be excluded because of the demands of economy, why pregnancy? The Court's answer is unconvincing:

> While it is true that only women can become pregnant, it does not follow that every legislative classification concerning pregnancy is a sex-based classification like those considered in *Reed, supra,* and *Frontiero, supra.* Normal pregnancy is an objectively identifiable physical condition with unique characteristics.[55]

What this last cryptic sentence is supposed to mean is far from clear. It seems unreasonable, to say the least, for the Court to distinguish between pregnancy and all the disabilities that are covered by the program, on the basis of either its objective identifiability or its uniqueness. For how is it that broken legs, measles, and the like, do not fall under the same categories?

In the second case, *General Electric Co. v. Gilbert,* which was decided in December 1976, a very similar disability insurance plan which likewise excluded pregnancy was tested against the sex-discrimination clause of the Civil Rights Act of 1964. Basing its decision on *Geduldig,* and specifically discounting the 1972 Equal Employment Opportunities Commission guidelines which specify that pregnancy-related disabilities are to be treated in employment policies and practices like other temporary disabilities, the Court decided that "an exclusion of pregnancy from a disability benefits plan . . . providing general coverage *is not a gender-based discrimination at all.*"[56]

The very notion that a classification revolving around pregnancy is not closely gender-or sex-related is offensive to common sense. As Justice Stevens points out in his dissenting opinion, a program which excludes the disabilities resulting from pregnancy "by definition" discriminates on account of sex, since "it is the capacity to become pregnant which primarily differentiates the female from the male."[57] The problem is, however, that the way women have been perceived, through the centuries, leads to the inability of many people, including the majority of Supreme Court justices, to perceive that discrimination against pregnancy is discrimination against women. Instead of reasoning from the fact that pregnancy is a primary differentiating characteristic of the female sex to the conclusion that to treat disabilities arising from that condition differently from other disabilities is to discriminate against women, they arrive at the conclusion that pregnancy is such a normal and natural function of womanhood that it is somehow unique, and not like other disabilities at all. As Bartlett points out with respect to the *Geduldig* case:

> The Court's decision . . . reflects an ill-defined perception that pregnancy is profoundly different from all other disabling conditions that plague or bless humankind. The notion that pregnancy is different from other disabilities with respect to a state disability insurance program suggests the familiar set of stereotypes—that women belong in the home raising children; that once women leave work to have babies, they do not return to the labor force; that pregnancy, though it keeps women from working, is not a 'disability' but a blessing which fulfills every woman's deepest wish; that women are and should be supported by their husbands, not themselves or the state. These stereotypes appear to be so deeply ingrained, so tied to fundamental beliefs about woman's place in the world as childbearer, that the Court apparently did not notice that they have nothing to do with the express purposes of the disability insurance program.[58]

While it would be absurd to reduce the entire experience of pregnancy to the status of a disability, there is no doubt that it is a condition which *involves* different degrees and durations of disability for different women and which prevents them temporarily from pursuing their normal work-lives. To refuse to recognize these disabling aspects of women's difference from men as entirely comparable with the other disabilities which people experience throughout their lives amounts to asserting that women's entire lives should be limited and conditioned by the factors of pregnancy and childbirth. Such decisions as the Supreme Court has given us recently with regard to the "uniqueness" of pregnancy amount in their effects to a strong reaffirmation of women's second-class status in all spheres of life outside of the household.

Thus, despite the opposite tendency of a minority of the justices, a majority of the Supreme Court continues to rely on implicit assumptions about the proper and natural role of women, and their functions and status within the family, in order to uphold discrimination against them. Only four of the Supreme Court justices, one of whom has since retired, have recognized that sex, as an accident of birth and in that sense similar to such characteristics as race or national origin, is inherently suspect as a legislative classification. The majority of the Court, then, continues to adjudge cases involving sex-discrimination by the more lenient standard of "reasonableness," and a number of their recent decisions serve to make us aware that the old underlying prejudices about what is reasonable in regard to the differences between the sexes have by no means entirely disappeared.[59]

Our review of judicial attitudes toward sex discrimination in U.S. law has demonstrated that, despite a readily discernible change that has begun to occur in very recent years, the study of political philosophers' modes of reasoning about women are by no means arcane or esoteric. Discrimination between the sexes with respect to their basic political rights and obligations, their educational and occupational opportunities, their economic and social standing, and their rights and duties with respect to each other in personal relationships, has been upheld by the courts on similar grounds to those appealed to by the philosophers. Like them, the judiciary, assuming the inevitability of the traditional structure of the family, has been far readier to refer to women's role or women's function than to acknowledge the importance of women's potential and their rights. They, too, have been inclined to view the "feminine" characteristics, the delicacy and dependency, of the women around them, as immutable factors—as the "natural" condition of women—rather than to recognize them as largely the effects of the patriarchal conditions of past and present society. They, like Aristotle and Rousseau, have all too often considered the pertinent question to be, "What are women *for*?"

12

Conclusions

This study has aimed to answer two questions, posed at the outset. The first of these asked whether the existing tradition of political philosophy could sustain the inclusion of women in its subject matter, on the same terms as men. The second asked what could be learned from an analysis of the treatment of women in political philosophy about the fact that the formal, political enfranchisement of women has not led to substantive economic, social or political equality between the sexes. In this final chapter, the findings of the study will be used to formulate answers to these two questions in turn.

The only place in political philosophy where women are already included on the same terms as men is Plato's guardian class in the *Republic*. There, the abolition of the private sphere of life, the control of reproduction, and the socialization of child-rearing and all domestic functions, result in the male and female guardians being both similarly educated and similarly employed. The natural differences between the sexes are narrowly conceived, and women's traditional functions are reduced to the physiological ones of pregnancy and lactation. Thus, while it makes no sense to talk of individual "rights" in the context of the *Republic*, the women of the guardian class are in a position of equality with the men.

In the works of all the other philosophers discussed, as well as in Plato's *Laws*, the existence of a distinct sphere of private, family life, separated off from the realm of public life, leads to the exaggeration of women's biological differences from men, to the perception of women as primarily suited to fulfill special "female" functions within the home, and consequently to the justification of the monopoly by men of the whole outside world. Let us now see what happens when we hypothesize the inclusion of women as complete equals, in all the theories we have examined. Will such an hypothesis alter the theories significantly? Will it thrust them out of shape, or reveal inconsistencies that are not apparent so long as women are assumed to be excluded from the major theoretical premises and conclusions? After this hypothesis has been applied to each of the political philosophers in turn, some general indications will be made concerning the adaptations necessary in any political theory if it is to treat women as the equals of men.

In the societies described in Plato's *Laws* and Aristotle's *Politics*, the *practical* problems caused by the transformation of women into citizens participating as fully as men in public life would be to some extent alleviated by the institution of slavery. This "solution," however, could be only a partial one; neither Plato nor Aristotle is happy with the prospect of prolonged contact between free children and slaves, and it is very doubtful that the management of the household could be expected to be carried out as closely in accordance with the best interests of the family if it were left entirely in the hands of slaves unsupervised by the mistress of the family. It is undeniable that the maintenance of each citizen's private household in these societies in which civic life is so important and time-consuming depends to a very large extent on the fact that women in Aristotle's case are totally excluded from the public sphere of life, and in Plato's *Laws* play a very secondary role.

There are deeper problems, however, involved in hypothesizing the complete equality of women within Plato's second-best and Aristotle's preferred polities. For both perceive the family as an aspect of private property, of which the wife herself is a major component. Male citizens in these two societies *own* their wives, and this is obviously untenable if men and women are to be equal. As is made clear in Chapter 3, Plato could not envisage the degree of participation in civic life that the female guardians enjoyed in the *Republic* as at all proper for the private wives of the *Laws*, in spite of the fact that his convictions about women's potential had become stronger by the time he wrote the *Laws*. In the second-best society, woman's "nature" must be prescribed for her, so as to befit her role as a wife. In the *Politics*, the life of the family is explicitly defined out of the realm of the political, which includes only its patriarch. Clearly, immense changes in both these conceptions of the family would have to be made in order to allow women to become equal family members, and equal citizens. Rather than an object of property, or a necessary condition for the provision of heirs and of daily requirements, the family would have to appear as an institution initiated and supported by its adult members as complete equals. This is a radical break from contemporary Greek notions, with which neither Aristotle's convention-based *Politics* nor Plato's traditional *Laws* is well equipped to cope.

In the case of the *Politics*, moreover, a still more serious problem arises when we hypothesize the equal treatment of male and female citizens. The teleological conception of the world on which Aristotle's entire political philosophy is founded depends on the premise that all the other members of the population—slaves and artisans as well as women—exist in order to perform their respective functions for the few free males who participate fully in citizenship. The "natures" of all these groups of people are defined in terms of their satisfactory performance of their conventional functions. If women were to be given status equal to men within the citizen class, the entire basis of Aristotle's functionalism would be undermined. If he were to deny the natural inferiority of women, the argument for which is based on the functions they performed in contemporary Athenian life, his parallel argument for the natural inferiority of slaves would also be placed in jeopardy. Once it is no longer agreed that women are by nature inferior and deficient in rationality, and exist only for the purpose of maintaining the household and bearing and rearing heirs, how can it be consistently maintained that the class of slaves exists only to perform its function of service, or that the class of artisans, because of the work it happens to do, is thereby unfitted for political life? Aristotle's identification of the hierarchical status quo with the natural, the necessary, and the good, cannot withstand the emancipation of women into political life. His system of politics is so extensively based on inequalities that to deny any aspect of the inequality jeopardizes the entire structure. How fragile the basis of that structure is becomes clear when the functional treatment of women is recognized as having no validity.

The introduction of women as equal citizens in Rousseau's ideal democratic republic would have, by contrast, the effect of resolving the obvious inconsistencies of his theory as it stands. It would resolve the considerable discrepancy between the egalitarianism and consensual basis of his ideas about government, and the extreme inegalitarianism of the patriarchal family that he upholds as natural and indispensable. His striking pronouncements about equality and freedom would no longer be contradicted by everything he says about relations between the sexes. Another problem the inclusion of women in public life would resolve is that dangerous conflict of loyalties discussed in Chapter 8 above. If women were no longer exclusively privately and personally oriented, they would be no more likely than men to be a danger to those wider loyalties that Rousseau valued so highly.

However, the problems arising from the transformation of women into equals are as great in the case of Rousseau as in the *Laws* and the *Politics*, and in a practical sense they are even more severe. For Rousseau's ideal republic requires at least as much civic participation as Aristotle's, and yet the private sphere of family life is crucial for him —not only as an economic base, as it was for the Greeks— but as a highly important aspect of affective life. Rousseau himself acknowledged political freedom to be so demanding that it might well be impossible to achieve without the institution of slavery to provide for the needs of daily life. Since he could not conceive of such a practice as legitimate, the issue is left unresolved. However, what *is* regarded as legitimate—since it follows from his premise that the patriarchal family is natural—is the exclusion from civic life, confinement to the private sphere, and functional definition of women.

Let us try to envisage equality of the sexes in a Rousseauian republic. First, the entire structure of the family would have to be radically altered, so as to be consistent with the equal rights and responsibilities of its adult members. Rousseau's entire conception of the relations between men and women, stemming from his great fear of dependency, except on a person one can control, would be overturned. Above all, husbands and wives would have to be able to trust one another—something Rousseau appears unable to envisage. Again, the woman's "nature" and entire mode of life could no more be defined in terms of the man's needs than he is defined in terms of hers. These requirements take us a long way from Emile and Sophie and from the chaste wives of Geneva whom Rousseau idealized.

Second, if women were to be politically equal, they, too, would have to spend a considerable amount of time in political meetings and other public activities. But Rousseau's republic is based on the institutions of the family, private property, and inheritance, and both private families and private holdings require a considerable amount of individual nurturance. While Rousseau says that the formal education of citizens is to be public, it is clear that he conceives of early child-rearing as a private activity, and sees the household as a place of refuge, for the man, from the tiring demands of the world outside. If all the adults of both sexes were to be as much preoccupied with civic activity as citizenship in a direct democracy requires, who would maintain this private sphere of life which Rousseau perceives as crucially important? It is clear that consider-able inroads would need to be made into the privacy and exclusiveness of the family, in order to allow women to participate fully as citizens.

Thus it would appear that, at least in an egalitarian society, one cannot achieve both the great intensity of civic life and the wholly private realm of family life without dichotomizing the spheres of operation of the sexes. Something has to give way, in Rousseau's world, if women are to be equal—either the extent of civic participation required of a citizen, or the eschewal of a class that exists to serve others, or the exclusiveness and total privacy of family life and property. The otherwise admirable egalitarian and participatory aspects of Rousseau's republic are, unfortunately, firmly founded on the exclusion of women.

As for John Stuart Mill, the inclusion of women is no longer merely hypothetical, for he made a determined effort to emancipate them into citizenship. However, in spite of his argument—so radical in its time—that political, educational and career opportunties should be open to women, he assumed that the exigencies of family life would restrict the full use of these opportunities to single women, whom he acknowledged would remain a small minority. To overcome these limitations and hypothesize substantive equality for married as well as single women would necessitate the radical alteration of Mill's conception of the family and its relations with the outside world. His assumptions that housework and child-care are functions which must necessarily be performed within the individual family, and that they are inevitably women's work, and unpaid work, would all have to be abandoned if the majority of women were to achieve anything approaching real equality with their husbands.

In Mill's liberal state, since he accepted representative as a practicable substitute for direct democracy, it is not so much the time-consuming nature of political participation which creates problems when we postulate the equality of women, though it certainly creates some. Jury service, for example, was regarded by Mill as an important and edu-cative aspect of citizenship, and yet it is inconceivable that he would have dissented from the U.S. Supreme Court's 1961 decision that women, as "the center of the home and family life," should not be subject to compulsory jury serv-ice. Likewise, the political education that Mill supposed would result from the democratization of the workplace and from direct participation in local government would be by and large inaccessible to married women.[1] For only after she has discharged what he perceives as "her" domes-tic responsibilities, Mill states clearly, should a wife assume outside activities or obligations. The more critical problem, however, is that by the time Mill wrote, family and eco-nomic life had become completely separated from each other by the development of the capitalist market economy, and the only way that women (other than heiresses) could achieve economic equality with men was by having the freedom and flexibility, as well as the training, to enable them to compete equally in selling their labor. There is, of course, no way that any married woman, however well qualified, who assumed the obligations Mill places on her, could compete in the occupational sphere with men.

There is no doubt that Mill—especially given the time at which he wrote—was a brave and far-thinking feminist. He refused to subscribe to many of the assumptions of pre-vious political theory about the exclusion of women from the political realm and the representative nature of the family's male head for all legal and political purposes. However, with Mill too, the strict separation of the private from the public realm, of the family from economic life, and the assumption that the day-to-day care of the family is woman's unpaid work, would all be undermined by the inclusion of women in his theory as the complete equals of men.

Though to varying degrees, all four political theories we have tested against the hypothetical inclusion of women on the same terms as men are considerably affected by this added requirement. In Plato's second-best *polis* and Aristotle's preferred one, in Rousseau's close-knit democratic republic and even to a large extent in Mill's liberal state, the sphere of public life is in many important respects premised on the existence of the private sphere of a family whose demands define woman's function and life style, and exclude her from equal participation and status in the world of economic and public life. It is clear that the structure of the family and the distribution of roles and responsibilities within it must be significantly altered in any theory in which women are to be equal human beings and equal participants in the public realm.

There are several significant respects in which political theories in general must change if they are to accommodate women as equal members of the political community. Political theorists as a class (though here Mill is an interesting partial exception) have made a number of assumptions concerning the family and its relation to society that are not consistent with the recognition of women as individuals equal to men. First, they have, sometimes contrary to appearances, made the family, rather than the adult human individual, the basic unit of their theories. The interesting and revealing corollary to this is that intrafamilial relationships—no matter how much power or authority they involve—are perceived as being outside the sphere of the political. Second, they have perceived human relationships within families as totally and qualitatively different from relationships between actors in the "political" realm—that is to say, the heads of families. It is important to discern how these prevalent assumptions about what should be the basic subject matter of political theory, and about the difference between intrafamilial and extrafamilial relations, would have to change in order to deal with equality between the sexes.

It is clear that Plato in the *Laws*, Aristotle, and Rousseau, regarded the male head of each family as its sole political representative. This is also true, and more paradoxically so, in the liberal theories of Hobbes, Locke, Kant, Hegel, and James Mill—paradoxically, because of the fact that liberalism is supposedly based on individualism. As Brian Barry has recently captured it, the "essence of liberalism" is "the vision of society as made up of independent, autonomous units who co-operate only when the terms of co-operation are such as to make it further the ends of each of the parties."[2] In fact, however, behind the individualist rhetoric, it is clear that the family, and not the adult human individual, is the basic political unit of liberal as of non-liberal philosophers. In spite of the supposedly individualist premises of the liberal tradition, John Stuart Mill was the first of its members to assert that the interests of women were by no means automatically upheld by the male heads of the families to which they belonged, and that therefore women, as individuals, should have independent political and legal rights. That these proposals should have appeared so dangerously radical in the climate of late nineteenth- and early twentieth-century opinion is ample testimony to the limitations of previous liberal individualism.

However, if the adult members of each family are to be regarded as equals, with lives of their own as well as the life they share as members of a family, the assumption that all their interests are common interests, which can be adequately represented by one of them alone and that one determined on grounds of sex, is clearly no longer tenable. No one would deny that, both because of the impotrant fact that they live together, and because of the strength of emotion that binds them, most families have far more interests in common than random groups of individuals would have. What must be recognized, however, but cannot be recognized by theorists who take as their basic unit for discussion not the individual but the family, is that there are many respects in which the interests of members of a family can either diverge from or clash with each other. This has become more clear as the old dichotomy of sex roles has been breaking down in recent years. When both husband and wife have independent lives, and particularly working lives, obviously they are far more likely to have opposing interests about such basic matters as where the family is to live. Whereas until recently, in the law as well as in political theory, the presumption has been that such matters must be decided by the family's male head, this type of assumption will clearly have to give way if women are to be equal.

This does not mean, however, that people must be treated, by political theories or by laws, always as isolated individuals and never as members of families or other long-term groups in which they choose to live with each other and to share responsibilities. Society is becoming atomized enough, even without the complete denial of the groups in which people live their intimate lives and in which they depend on each other for economic, emotional, and other forms of support. But to treat someone as, in certain respects, an equal member of a specifically related group, such as a family, is not the same as to assume the various positions and functions of persons within that group, and to define their rights and dictate their very opportunities in life, in terms of these assumptions.

Even in the case of legislation that—assuming the family unit—discriminates against *men*, the effect is generally to reinforce women's dependent position within that unit, and to restrict the choices of family members about how to order their lives.[3] It is not political theorists' and judges' acknowledgment of the existence of the family, in itself, but rather their assumptions about its patriarchal structure that has reinforced it as an institution which constrains rather than enhances people's opportunities to live free, creative and fulfilling lives.

At this point it is important to note that the fact that the family is the *only* socially recognized permanent relationship between people is discriminatory not only against women. The "normal" family, with dependent wife, is favored in many ways, both social and economic, at the expense of persons who are not part of such families.⁴ In order to correct this discrimination, a number of alternative living arrangements must be similarly recognized as constituting mutually supportive groups. These would consist of various numbers of people of either or both sexes, with or without children. Political theories and laws must be constructed in such a way as to recognize the dependence relationships and living arrangements that people choose for themselves, which will of course include families. However, they must also be constructed in such a way that they do not make assumptions about the various individuals' positions, obligations, sex roles, or functions within such groups. Only if these changes are made, will the forms of discrimination presently perpetrated both against all women, and against men who choose to live in groups less orthodox than the family, have a chance of being reduced.

The second mode of thought about the family that must be reassessed in terms of female equality is most prevalent with liberal thinkers, though it is also found in Rousseau. As was noted earlier, the liberal tradition assumes that the behavior of its political actors will be based on self-interest. Men with certain natural rights, or at least with certain passions requiring satisfaction, come together in political societies in order to defend themselves from invasion or harassment, and to compete with one another in a market environment where they are secure under the protective arm of the law. Relations within families, on the other hand, are perceived very differently. Theorists who have assumed a high degree of egoism to determine relations between individuals in the sphere of the market, have assumed almost total altruism to govern intrafamilial relationships.

The clearest example of this contrast is seen in the philosophy of Hegel, for whom the family and civil society are the utterly contrasting entities from which the state dialectically emerges—as a combination of the altruism of the former and the universality of the latter. When we read the passages about the family in the *Philosophy of Right* carefully, however, we can see that the unity of the family is founded on the refusal to cede to women any independent existence at all. One of the Additions to the section on the family asserts that, whereas men are like animals, women are like plants. Since women are not perceived as having any distinct life or interests at all, it is not difficult for Hegel to perceive the family as a place from which all discord and conflict of interest is absent, and where love and altruism reign supreme. The loving unity of Hegel's family is founded on the denial of a personality to its wife and mother.[5]

Similarly, Rousseau, in spite of his sequel about Emile and Sophie, in which the father's interests and will so clearly conflict with the welfare of his family and cause its ruin, maintained that the family operated on entirely different principles from those on which the outside world was based. He too, relying on the altruism of intrafamilial relations, persisted in regarding the patriarch as properly the sole representative of its interests, whereas he regarded any other instance of representation as an abdication of freedom.

Once one recognizes the existence of women as individuals in their own right, this assumption of the total unity of the family's interests becomes exposed for the myth that it always was. The clear contrast that has been pointed to by many philosophers between the altruistic, loving sphere of the family and the harsh, competitive world outside, is no longer as distinct. Perhaps this realization will result in a questioning of both sides of the exaggerated dichotomy—of the atomistic assumptions about the outside realm as well as the unrealistic degree of altruism that has been supposed to characterize family relationships. If, as seems likely, the assumed love and altruism of the family, founded as it is upon the radical inequality of women, has served to soften the full impact of a world of self-interested individuals, maybe one of the results of treating women as beings with their own personalities and interests will be to expose the full implications of a theory in which self-interest is assumed to be the norm for economic and political life. Without the total selflessness that was supposed to exist within families, the total self-interestedness that liberalism assumes exists outside of them may seem more in need of reconsideration.

It should by now be clear that it is by no means a simple matter to integrate the female half of the human race into a tradition of political theory which has been based, almost without exception, upon the belief that women must be defined exclusively by their role within the family, and which has thus defined them, and intrafamilial relationships, as outside the scope of the political. There is no way in which we can include women, formerly minor characters, as major ones within the political drama without challenging basic and age-old assumptions about the family, its traditional sex roles, and its relation to the wider world of political society.

Before we leave the subject of the adaptations to political theory that would be made necessary by the absolutely equal treatment of women, we should note one respect in which democratic theories would thereby be rendered more internally consistent. For any theorist who aims at genuine political equality, the transformation of the family into a more egalitarian group should be welcome for reasons affecting the health of the political community as a whole. If the family is to lose the last vestiges of its patriarchal character, and to become a democratically run institution in which the only differential in terms of authority is the temporary one of age, this will surely affect the potential of the family as a socializing agency for the wider political community. The patriarchalism of the seventeenth century is the clearest parallel that has been drawn by political theorists between familial and governmental structures of authority and obedience.[6] Clearly, in the view of such theorists, the hierarchical nature of the family made it an exemplary socializing agent for the hierarchical world of king and subjects. For democratic or egalitarian political theorists, however, it would seem that a family structure that is as democratic and egalitarian as possible would best serve the function of preparing future citizens for a life of political patricipation and equality.

It is now a generally accepted proposition that, as sociologist T. B. Bottomore recently wrote, "the institutions which exist in the differing spheres of society are not merely co-existent but are connected with each other by relations of concordance or contradiction and mutually affect each other."[7] This means, of course, that we cannot ignore the significant relationship that exists between the structure of the family and the structure of the wider political society of which it is a part. This idea has been developed more explicitly by Harry Eckstein, who argues that the stability of any political order is dependent upon the "congruence" between governmental authority structures and other such structures in the society, including those of work places, pressure groups, schools, and, most significantly, in the present context, the family.[8] Eckstein concludes that, since democratization of some of these, including the family, is unfeasible, without "seriously dysfunctional consequences," the need for congruence requires that stable governments must not be "extremely, i.e. purely, democratic," but rather should include "a healthy element of authoritarianism."[9] The odd thing about this conclusion, especially considering Eckstein's perception of "manifest egalitarianism" between the sexes in his study of Norway[10] (to which the "congruence" theory forms part of the Appendix), is that he does not distinguish clearly between the respects in which families can be democratic—i.e. in relations between their adult members, including the children as they become mature—and the respects in which democratic decisions would be absurd—such as whether a three-year-old should go to nursery school. No one, surely, would disagree with Eckstein's statement that "an infant cannot be cared for democratically."[11] However, this does not mean that, in many respects, families cannot differ greatly in their authority structures. Surely the degree of equality that exists between the parents, and the degree to which the children themselves are respected as human beings and consulted about family decisions as they grow older, will make a very strong impression on them, which they will take with them as part of their personality structure into other areas of life, including their relationships to their fellow citizens and their government.

The direct opposite of congruence—the paradox of a patriarchal family in a highly democratic society—is seen most clearly in Rousseau. At the beginning of *Emile*, he asserts that the family is the principal socializing unit for the preservation of society, that good mothering is the key to the revival of republican consciousness, and that the natural feeling of love for the "little fatherland" is the essential basis for the love that its citizens owe the state. Significantly, he also subscribes to a general proposition very similar to the theory of congruence as described above. In the *Letter to d'Alembert*, justifying the existence of civic clubs, he asserts, "There is no well-constituted state in which practices are not to be found which are linked to the form of government and which help to preserve it."[12] Clearly, however, Rousseau's family, governed as it is by its patriarchal head, on whom it is entirely dependent for its welfare, is no fit environment for the development of democratic sentiments or an egalitarian consciousness in those who are the state's future citizens. The family is the one place in Rousseau's ideal republic where the idea of the general will is given no application at all, and it is impossible to see how the young citizens could grow up with any notion of the equal dignity of their fellow human beings in an institution in which the notion of equality even between adults is totally absent and one adult member exerts absolute rule over the other. As a socializing agent for his democratic republic, Rousseau's patriarchal family is a disaster.

We have already concluded that the equality of women cannot be achieved in any political theory without the radical restructuring of the family. Now, in turn, we can see that such a transformation of the family cannot occur, either within a theory or in the actual world, without having considerable effect on the related political order. If our aim is a truly democratic society, or a thoroughly democratic theory, we must acknowledge that anything but a democratic family, with complete equality and mutual interdependence between the sexes, will be a severe impediment to this aim.

We will turn now to the second question raised in the Introduction. Why is it that the formal, political enfranchisement of women has not led to substantial equality between the sexes, and what light can our study of the treatment of women in political theory shed on this inquiry? Here, of course, we shall be far more concerned than hitherto with the position of women in the real world of contemporary society.

The women who struggled for the vote, in the early twentieth century, were not unaware that its achievement would be only the beginning of a much broader struggle for equality. In 1923, the National Women's Party explained why it was proposing an equal rights amendment, to overcome the limitations of the female suffrage amendment:

> As we were working for the national suffrage amendment . . . it was borne very emphatically in upon us that we were not thereby going to gain full equality for the women of this country, but that we were merely taking a step, but a very important step, it seemed to us, toward gaining this equality.[13]

The persistence of sex discrimination in the legal field alone has shown these women to have been absolutely right in their assumption that the vote was only a first step. Their attempts toward an equal rights amendment were, needless to say, unsuccessful.

As most present-day feminists agree, the political emancipation of women brought with it very little of substance with respect to their economic and social position, and their actual life experience. In spite of the prevalent assumption that women have it within their power to be the equals of men, simply by taking up the equal opportunities offered them, the status of women in this country, measured in terms of occupation, education and income, has been gradually but persistently declining over the last few decades.[14]

This finding must be considered in the light of the fact that an increasing number of women, married as well as single, have been entering the labor force. Whereas in 1940, only 26 percent of women were in the paid labor force, in 1977, 48 percent were, and they comprised over 40 percent of the total full-time active work force.[15] Moreover, most women work primarily for reasons of economic necessity: in 1975, 42 percent of women in the labor force were unmarried, widowed, divorced or separated and an additional 14 percent had husbands who earned less than $7,000 per year.[16] These facts about women's participation in the labor force certainly belie the notion that women work either to while away the time or for "pin-money."

In spite of the efforts of government—through the Equal Pay Act of 1963 and Title VII of the Civil Rights Act of 1964—to improve the position of women workers, it has instead been declining. As the U.S. Supreme Court acknowledged in a 1974 opinion, "Whether from overt discrimination or from the socialization process of a male-dominated culture, the job market is inhospitable to the woman seeking any but the lowest paid jobs."[17] Calling attention to the lack of encouraging results of the Equal Pay Act and Title VII, the Justices stated that "firmly entrenched practices are resistant to such pressures," and cited data to show that women working full time in 1972 had a median income of only 57.9 percent of the male median—six points *below* what women had achieved in 1955. In 1970, while 70 percent of men earned over $7,000, only 26.1 percent of women working full time earned this amount or more.[18] Moreover, while part of this pay differential is doubtless due to differences in training or education, certainly much of it is not. In 1972, the median annual income of women with four years of college education was exactly $100 more than that of men who had not completed a year of high school. In spite of the Equal Pay Act, women are frequently paid far less than men for doing identical or almost identical work. Women in sales work, for example, in 1970, averaged less than half of what the average salesman was paid, and professionally and technically trained women have an income of 67.5 percent of that of their male counterparts.[19]

The disparity in remuneration that *is* due to training or educational differentials is, of course, itself indirectly attributable to sexism, as is evident both in admission policies for such training and educational institutions, and in the self-images and expectations that girls and boys absorb during the socialization process. Though the expectations and aspirations of women are changing, particularly in the middle class, they are still very different from those that men are encouraged to develop.

The continuing inequality of women, and not only of those within the work force, clearly performs important functions for the capitalist economy in which we live. Outside of the recognized work force, women perform the functions held to be natural to their sex—child-rearing and housework—which are given no economic recognition at all. As a number of feminists have pointed out, conventional notions of the family and its sex roles have facilitated the distinct separation of the public and private spheres, and of productive labor into two types.[20] On the one hand, there is that recognized as productive labor, which is performed in work places outside of the home by both men

FUNCTIONALISM, FEMINISM AND THE FAMILY

and women, and is paid, though at rates which continue to correlate to a high degree with the sex of the worker. On the other hand, there is that, though in fact productive labor but not recognized as such, which is still performed largely by women within the home, and is unpaid—the labor involved in the reproduction, nurturance, health and welfare of the work force. There is no denying that what housewives and mothers do is work, nor that it is necessary. However, it is frequently not regarded as work: "working mothers" are mothers who work *outside* their homes, only. The bearing and rearing of children, particularly in this age of population consciousness, are all too frequently perceived as a luxury and indulgence of private life, rather than as a process of overwhelming social importance.

As for women's growing participation in work outside the home, it has been an essential factor in the shaping of the contemporary labor force.[21] With the convenient but largely mythical justification that as part of the family structure they are adequately supported by men, women are providing an increasingly vast amount of labor at very cheap rates compared with those at which men are paid. In addition to the vast influx of women into the expanding sales and service sectors, the proportion of women in what were previously regarded as "male" jobs is increasing rather than decreasing. In many important industries, women, with little specialized training, and with a socialization which makes them view their participation in the labor force as a less important aspect of their lives, are performing, for a fraction of the pay, jobs which before they were fragmented and highly mechanized were performed by highly skilled and well-paid workers, who were almost always men. The obvious advantages of this to the capitalist are that the cost of labor is far lower (the average full-time female worker's wage would have to increase by 75 percent in order to equal the average male's), and that his ability to control the labor force is greater. Since the women who now perform the work are far less highly trained and unionized than the men who used to do it, they are more easily disciplined, fired and replaced. In addition, the large-scale participation of women in the labor force is a crucial factor in maintaining a high unemployment rate, which also increases the control of employers over employees.

The connection of all the above data on the contemporary inequality of women with the treatment of women by political theory is that, as in the past, the continuing oppression of women is ideologically supported by the survival of functionalist modes of thought. Just as women have been defined functionally in relation to men, and therefore deprived of the education, rights and opportunity to participate in the political realm, so today, women, though enfranchised citizens, are handicapped by the fact that neither their socialization nor their training, neither the expectations placed on them nor the opportunities or rewards afforded to them in their adult lives are such as to enable them to achieve economic, social, or political equality with men. The traditional, supposedly indispensable, nuclear family is used as the connecting link by which the basic biological differences between the sexes are expanded into the entire set of ascribed characteristics and prescribed functions which make up the conventional female sex role. It is the definition of women in terms of their wife-mother role that continues to be used, as we have seen, by the courts, and by society at large, to justify many kinds of discrimination against them, particularly in the spheres of education and employment.

Though it is clear that the injustices suffered by women in the work force cannot end until those in the sphere of education are eradicated, women's educational experience continues to be restricted by the expectation that they are essentially destined for "home-making." This expectation, moreover, follows them into the work place. As one sociologist wrote recently, "Discrimination on the basis of sex undoubtedly does exist in the occupational market, often motivated by the presumed rational economic concern over the marriage-pregnancy-maternity cycle and its accompanying absenteeism, though evidence does not support this concern."[22] The exploitation of women in the labor force is accentuated by the fact that they are frequently relegated to low-paid "women's work." "By extension [from the family], in the larger society women are seen as predominantly fulfilling nurturing, expressive functions . . . [and] intellectually aggressive women are seen as deviants."[23] This mode of thought about women's work is clearly identifiable in the work of Talcott Parsons and Erik Erikson, analyzed above. By means of consigning many women to functions allegedly related to their reproductive capacity, they are maintained in a permanently unequal position in the labor force. This in turn both discourages women from seeking promotion or, if they have the option, from seeking work at all, and reinforces the idea that they are not capable of performing the more demanding and prestigious jobs. That "woman's place is in the home" is to a large extent a self-fulfilling prophecy.

In the light of all this, it is not surprising that a strong section of the contemporary feminist movement calls for the abolition of the family, as an institution which has in the past proved so oppressive to women. Ann Oakley, for example, attacks the family itself as well as Parsons' analysis of it.[24] She argues that the abolition of the housewife role and of the automatic assumption that women will rear children are necessary steps toward the equality of women, but that they are, in themselves, not sufficient. Marriage will have to be abolished also, as a "basic impediment to occupational sex-equality." I would agree that, under present conditions, both of work and of marriage, it is undoubtedly true that marriage is such a "basic impediment." This is testified to, for example, by the fact that in England female professional workers are between three and four times more likely to be unmarried than male professionals. However, this is not to say that, given radical changes in the structure and conditions of work, an altered family structure could not coexist with sexual equality in the occupational sphere.

Shulamith Firestone goes one large step further, and looks forward not only to the abolition of the family, but to the time when women will be completely freed from pregnancy and childbirth.[25] As we have previously indicated, Firestone is, of course, correct in asserting that the family has "reinforce[d] biologically based sex class," and that "the family structure is the *source* of psychological, economic, and political oppression."[26] But, again, this is not to acknowledge that *any* family structure would be incompatible with the equality of the sexes. Moreover, Firestone in fact commits the same error as many antifeminists in perceiving the entire nurturing and domestic female sex role as necessarily implied by women's reproductive biology. "Nature produced the fundamental inequality," she asserts, ". . . half the human race must *bear and rear* the children of all of them."[27] Unlike the antifeminists, who thereupon conclude that the whole female sex role is inevitable, Firestone concludes that the only way to liberate women is to replace natural with artificial reproduction.

It is essential to recognize, however, first, that without the connecting link of the division of sex roles in the family there is no reason why female child-*bearing* should entail child-*rearing* by women alone. Second, Firestone's conviction that an artificial means of reproduction is an essential prerequisite to female equality is largely based on the fact that she perceives women's reproductive function as "barbaric," "clumsy [and] inefficient," "tyrannical" and "fundamentally oppressive."[28] Surely, however, though the reproductive process may have oppressive and barbaric attributes for women in a sexist society where it is to a very large extent controlled by men, there is no justification for such harsh judgments regarding the experiences of pregnancy and childbirth in themselves. It is not the fact that women are the primary reproductive agents of society, in itself, that has led to their oppression, but rather that reproduction has taken place within a patriarchal power structure, has been considered a private rather than a social concern, and has been perceived as dictating women's entire lives, and as defining their very nature.

Many other feminists have warned of the facile and misguided nature of demands for the abolition of the family. Though they regard the existing family structure as an institution which oppresses women in the process of serving important functions for capitalism, and the ideology of the family as an age-old reinforcement of women's inequality, they do not consider that purely negative attacks against it are the answer to anything.[29]

The feminist struggle against the "dictates of Nature" is clearly exemplified by Juliet Mitchell's work, as is the perception that the "lynchpin" of this line of argument is the idea of the family. "Like woman herself," Mitchell explains,

> the family appears as a natural object, but is actually a cultural creation. There is nothing inevitable about the form or role of the family, any more than there is about the character or role of women. It is the function of ideology to present these given social types as aspects of Nature itself. . . . The apparently natural condition can be made to appear more attractive than the arduous advance of human beings towards culture.[30]

Her aim is the equality of women as a result of the triumph of culture over nature. First in a brilliant pamphlet, later enlarged into a book, she argues that the root of the problem of women's role is that their functions within the family have been regarded as intrinsically bound together.[31] Only when it is recognized that reproduction, sexuality and the socialization of children, though fused in the traditional female sex role, are in fact separable from each other, can women be freed from the stereotypes and functionalist definitions of the past.

As we have seen in the course of this study, what has been alleged to be women's nature has been used throughout history and into the present to justify keeping the female sex in a position of political, social and economic inequality. It is evident, from arguments ranging from Aristotle to leading scholars and Supreme Court Justices of the twentieth century, that women's nature has been prescriptively defined—defined, that is, in terms of the functions they have served in a male-dominated world, and, particularly, within the patriarchal family, which, with its distinct sex roles, has also been designated as in accord with the dictates of nature. Women's significant but few and specific biological differences from men—the capacity to bear and suckle children, and lesser muscular strength—have been held to entail a whole range of "natural" differences—moral, intellectual, emotional—between the sexes. Because of the enforcement of such notions by political systems, laws, institutions, and socialization processes, women have been stunted and crippled as human beings, and persons of both sexes have been unable to develop freely their own personalities and potential.

Those who perceive the qualities approved in women today, or who perceived the characteristics of women in the fourth century B.C. or at any time since, as "women's nature," refuse to acknowledge that women have been produced, or at the least, very much shaped, by the societies in which they have lived—societies which have always been male-dominated. As both Plato and John Stuart Mill were well aware, no one knows what women's nature is like, as distinct from men's, and no one will know, until members of the two sexes are enabled to develop in the absence of differential treatment during the socialization process and throughout their lives. Even if we *did* know what women's nature is like, moreover, it is worth pausing to ask what repercussions should follow from this, either in theory or

FUNCTIONALISM, FEMINISM AND THE FAMILY

in practice. In other words, what value does "nature" have as a standard by which to test human norms, institutions or practices?

As a number of feminists have pointed out, and as Marx clearly recognized when discussing relations between the sexes, modern civilization is a very long way from nature, and the process of human history has been to a large extent the conquest of nature and the superimposition onto it of culture. Thus *human nature*, when this is understood to mean the fundamental characteristics of human beings, is not something which has been fixed and will continue to be fixed for all time, but is rather an achievement, a result of thousands of years of history. Men and women, individually and in their relationships with each other, have the potential for becoming more and more specifically human and differentiated from the other animals, and, to a large extent, it is by being freed from the constraints of necessity imposed on them by nature that humans can achieve the fullness of their human potentiality.[32]

The demands of nature, moreover, have applied not only to the sphere of production, but also to the sphere of reproduction. Much of Marx's writing, of course, is concerned with the historical process of humanity's freeing itself from the constraints of arduously producing its means of subsistence, and the eventual achievement of that "realm of freedom" in which all human beings will be able to create, and to live lives that are no longer animal, but truly human, because for the first time truly social. Clearly, the nature of people must be affected considerably by whether they need to spend two or twelve hours a day toiling in order to feed and clothe themselves, and by the conditions under which this production takes place. But there is another side to the picture, and one of particular importance for women. This is the freeing of human beings—and primarily women, because of their biology—from the life-long constraints of the need to reproduce. The scientific breakthroughs that have prolonged life, eradicated epidemics, and drastically reduced infant mortality, mean that there is now no need for women to spend more than a tiny fraction of their lives in bearing enough children to maintain the population level. Moreover, the provision by technology of increasingly reliable methods of birth control and increasingly safe methods of abortion means that each woman can choose both if and when she will bear children. Just as the characteristics of the means of production affect people's development and their nature, so do the characteristics of the means of reproduction. It could surely not be claimed that the nature of a woman who knows that at any moment over a thirty-year period she may become pregnant, and that in order to raise two children she must bear twelve, is the same as the nature of a woman who can control her body to the extent of spending two planned years of her life engaged in the physical process of reproduction, with the same end result. By reasoning parallel to Marx's concerning the realm of production, women can achieve freedom and a fully developed human nature only when the reproduction and rearing of children becomes a freely chosen activity, and when it no longer dictates the entire mode of life of the female sex.

For these conditions to come about, however, more than a revolution in technology is required; a revolution in conditions and ideas must occur with it, and although this has clearly begun, it is by no means completed. This latter revolution must accomplish two ends. First, it must make motherhood a freely chosen option for women. Contraception in itself, of course, does not make childbearing optional, if female socialization is overwhelmingly weighted toward motherhood, or if women are not reinforced or highly rewarded in other spheres of their lives. Second, the revolution must succeed in clearly separating out those aspects of reproduction which are biologically women's— necessarily, pregnancy, and if it is opted for, lactation— from all those long-term aspects of child-rearing which are not necessarily women's work, but have been made to seem so on account of the accepted structure of the family. As we have seen in the case of Firestone, some feminists as well as antifeminists have fallen into the trap of perceiving child-rearing as inseparable from childbearing, which means of course that as long as the latter is a female function, so must the former be.

Now that technology has given women the means of controlling reproduction (in principle, though by no means universally in practice), there is a far greater possibility of achieving a separation of functions. The fact that many women have now, and it is to be hoped all women will have in the future, complete freedom of choice as to whether to bear children at all, and when to bear those they choose to have, means that women's lives need not be perceived, by either themselves or society, as dictated by the physical demands of maternity.

As for the socialization of young children, while it is clearly of immense significance, there is no reason why it should be done by one woman, the biological mother. There is, indeed, no reason why it should be done by one person alone, or by women only. In this area, the structure of the family that has predominated throughout history must change radically if women are to achieve equality with men. And yet there are clearly many people who still believe that the conventional division of roles between the sexes, and most particularly where child-rearing is concerned, is both of critical importance to the maintenance of civilization, and indispensable for the preservation of the family unit. Parsons and Erikson, as we have seen, clearly exemplify this mode of thinking. George Gilder's recent and popular books, *Sexual Suicide* and *Naked Nomads*[33] are based on the same assumptions, with the added belief of the author that men, being fundamentally less civilized, require to be continually "socialized" by women even throughout their adult lives. And when Richard Nixon vetoed the child-care bill of 1971-72, he did it on the grounds that it would lead to the "destruction of the American family."[34] He was clearly including in his definition of "the American family" the arrangement whereby children are cared for completely within the individual family unit, with the mother devoting herself to this purpose while the father provides the family's entire support. In fact, more than half of existing American families do not fit this prescriptive definition, and it is perfectly feasible to envisage and work toward a family structure in which none of these assumptions are made. It is clearly the historical inequality within the family that provokes the iconoclastic urge to destroy it. The inequalities of the past, however, need not preclude the achievement in the future of a family structure that is consistent with sexual equality.

We must aim toward a time when child-rearing will be equally shared between the sexes. This is essential, if women are to enjoy equality, for three reasons. First, the great majority of women, who are mothers, can never be men's equals in the work force or in any realm of activity outside the home while only their working lives are subject over a period of years to the effects of the total responsibility for child-rearing. Women presently are handicapped in the realm of work and public activity not only by the fact that most, by far, still actually do take a disproportionate amount of responsibility for housework and child-care, but also because, even if they do not, this is the expectation of the world in general—of employers, courts, voters, and other persons and institutions who have power over what women will be able to do in the outside world, and who discriminate against them to the extent documented above.

Second, only when men share equally in such tasks as housework and child-rearing will they come to be valued equally with those "masculine" tasks which society presently acknowledges to be productive and rewards with money, and sometimes with prestige. There will be no such thing as an inferior class of "women's work," and no relegation of women alone, in the work force as in the home, to nurturing, "expressive," supportive and under- or unpaid work.

Third, it is clearly by identification with the parents, as Parsons recognizes, that children learn traditional sex roles. Girls and boys will not grow up with open-minded ideas about themselves and the kinds of lives they want to lead until they perceive adults, and especially those closest to them—their parents—filling, and expressing themselves in, all types of roles. None of these three aims can be achieved until housework is shared and "parenting" takes the place of "mothering."

For this to take place, there will have to be many changes involving the merging, to a considerable extent, of what have up till now been regarded as the private and unproductive functions of family life, and the public, productive work of the market economy. On the one hand, much of the work of the private household, and especially the most time-consuming part of it, child-care, can be done outside of the home. Good, accessible and subsidized day care facilities, staffed by both sexes, will be a partial solution. In addition, however, the structure and conditions of work outside the home will have to relinquish the inflexibility they have been able to develop on the assumption that women take responsibility for home and family. Employers and institutions will have to change their attitudes toward men and women. They must cease to consider women as dependents and adjuncts of their husbands, ready to move like part of the furniture whenever his job requires it, expected to give their time gratuitously for the furtherance of their men's careers, to accept low pay and insecurity of tenure for the work they undertake outside the home because it is assumed that they are really supported by a man, and willing to assume total responsibility for the raising of children. Employers and institutions, as well as the law, must acknowledge that fathers have as much responsibility as mothers for the care of their children. Only when a new flexibility develops, and it is conceded that the eight-hour day is no more sacred than the ten-hour or twelve-hour day was once held to be, will we be able to achieve a society in which both men and women share in the pleasures and burdens of the tasks that are now so arbitrarily divided between them. Whether such changes can be accomplished within the structure of capitalism is a question which must be considered outside the scope of this work. Suffice it to say that, given the obvious advantages that capitalism derives from the present sex-role differentiation—particularly the cheap or gratuitous labor provided by women— changes such as are outlined above can be expected to be resisted strongly by those with economic power and an interest in maintaining the status quo.

We have reached a point in technological and economic development at which it should be possible to do away with sex roles entirely, except for the isolated case of woman's freely chosen exercise of her procreative capacity. Women today (in principle though not yet in practice) are in a position which is in an important respect analogous to that of the female guardians of Plato's *Republic*. While the reproductive processes of the guardians were to be controlled by the philosophic rulers of the ideal state, however, modern technology has given women for the first time control over their own bodies and freedom from the demand that they spend their adult lives in reproduction. While for Plato it was necessary to abolish the family in order to achieve such control, this is no longer a prerequisite for being able to plan the number and timing of pregnancies. In the modern age, then, as in Plato's *Republic*, there is no rational basis for defining women's nature and prescribing their entire lives in terms of their sexual and reproductive functions.

As we have seen, attempts are still being made to retain the ancient practice of defining women in terms of the functions they serve. Such attempts, however, can be refuted by means of rational analysis of the separate functions which women and the family presently serve, and by acknowledgment that practically all of these functions can be fulfilled by men and women, rather than divided along sex lines. The tendency to regard men as complete persons with potentials and rights, but to define women by the functions they serve in relation to men, is clearly unjustifiable. While fully consistent with a hierarchical conception of a good society such as Aristotle's, in which only the few males at the top were regarded as fully human, it is jarringly out of place in a society which claims to be founded on the principle of human equality. In such a society, women must be treated in every respect—politically, socially, economically—as the equals of men. They must be set free from assumptions about the kinds of work they are suited for, and enabled to attain equal status with men in the work force and in all other parts of the economic and political realm. Women cannot become equal citizens, workers, or human beings—let alone philosopher queens— until the functionalist perception of their sex is dead.

Appendix to Chapter 2

The scholarly commentaries on the first of Plato's "waves of paradox" have been overwhelmingly hostile to the idea that women should have a place equal to men's, even in the most utopian of societies. Recently, Christine Pierce has written a most interesting article about this aspect of Plato scholarship. She concludes that the lengths to which " 'pure' scholars, rational men" have been driven in giving "questionable interpretations of passages in *Republic* v which are clear and straightforward" is a striking instance of the "tendency to superimpose the mores and beliefs of one's own society on figures of philosophy's past."[1] Her paper deals most adequately with the rejections of Plato's radical proposals about women by the older generation of scholars—A. E. Taylor and Ernest Barker—and she exposes the lack of foundation of Leo Strauss's charge that the attempt to treat women as equal is simply one of those instances where, by "abstracting from" the body and from *eros*, Plato is subtly indicating that the just city is against nature and therefore impossible. The only aspect of the article which leaves important ground uncovered is its treatment of Allan Bloom's approach to Plato on women.

Bloom's translation of the *Republic* has rapidly become recognized as the most accurate available, and for this reason it is essential to point out the mistakes and absurdities contained in his commentary on sections 449a-473c. Whereas up to this point, Bloom says, what Socrates has suggested has been "severe, but not outlandish," the first two waves of Book v are "absurd conceits" which "have never existed in reality or in the thoughts of serious men."[2] Book v, Bloom concludes, "in its contempt for convention and nature, in its wounding of all the dearest sensibilities of masculine pride and shame, the family, and statesmanship and the city" is "preposterous, and Socrates expects it to be ridiculed."[3] Its purpose is, Bloom alleges, to prove to Aristophanes that Socrates can write a funnier comedy than he.[4]

Moreover, while Socrates himself asserts that his third wave of paradox is "the biggest and most difficult," Bloom says that "the notion of philosopher-kings is not in itself paradoxical for us," and that "modern men" are likely to find this third wave "far less reprehensible" than either the abolition of the family or the granting of an equal role to women.[5] In an extension of Strauss's argument, he sets out to show that Socrates' "forgetting" of the body, in his discussion of the treatment of the female guardians, is indeed an indication to the reader of the essential impossibility of the ideal city.

First, Bloom takes up Socrates' proposal that the two sexes exercise together naked. He first argues that this is impossible because it would lead to licentiousness. Public nakedness, he asserts, is permissible where it is not likely to lead to sexual desire, and he uses the example, which seems sublimely naive in the Greek context, that "men can be naked together because it is relatively easy to desexualize their relations with one another"![6] Later, however, Bloom reverses his position and argues that public nakedness of men and women is nonsense because "shame is an essential component of the erotic relations between men and women,"[7] which in turn are essential for the preservation of the city. Apparently, the fear here is that nakedness will lead to sexual indifference. Apart from the fact that it is explicitly denied that this will happen, by both Socrates and Glaucon, the continued existence of countless primitive tribes who habitually go naked would seem sufficient to dispel Bloom's fear, and the overwhelming evidence of strong eroticism amongst Greek men adds weight to this. As for the first, contradictory concern, that nakedness would cause uncontrolled sexuality, Socrates acknowledges that "irregular intercourse" will be a temptation, but states

that the rulers of the city will be able to effect the necessary
regulation of sexual relations.[8] Altogether, Bloom's attempt
to show that an equal role for women is impossible seems
not only unfounded but also rather presumptuous in view
of the fact that in Plato's text Socrates and his audience
agree that it is possible. Even in the case of the third wave,
the most paradoxical of all, Socrates insists that he is not
"speaking of impossibilities."[9]

As Christine Pierce has demonstrated, Bloom next takes
Plato's assertion that men as a class are more capable than
women as a class, and interprets it to mean that "the best
women are always inferior in capacity to the best men,"
which it clearly does not.[10] Concluding from this that "it
is then highly improbable that any women would even be
considered for membership in the higher classes" on
grounds of merit, he has to find an explanation for the
fact that Socrates does indeed include women in these
classes. The major reason, Bloom concludes, which Socrates
finds it necessary to lie about (Plato *usually* tells us when
he is lying. Why not this time?), is that women are needed
in the upper ranks in order to reproduce them. It is, then,
their essential difference from, not their similarity to men
—whatever the text says to the contrary—that legitimates
the inclusion of women in the guardian class. Now, as
Pierce reminds us, this would have been a very dangerous
thing for Plato to do. For clearly the female guardians are
not to have their function restricted to procreation, but
are to share in all aspects of ruling and defending the city.
As we are explicitly told, they are to be philosophers, too.
However, Plato has stressed the very great dangers involved
in letting anyone unqualified by nature enter the ranks of
the guardians; such meddling, he says, could lead to "the
destruction of the city."[11] It seems hardly likely, then, that
he would have tolerated the admission of women into the
highest rank of all, if he considered that they lacked the
necessary abilities.

Clearly, Allan Bloom is a latter-day example of a series

of scholars who have found Plato's arguments about women in *Republic* v both incredible and intolerable. He and Strauss, however, unlike the earlier critics, have attempted to exonerate Plato of apparent absurdity by persuading us that he didn't really mean what he seems to mean. Bloom, to give him credit, is the only one honest (or brazen) enough to admit that Socrates' wounding of "the dearest sensibilities of masculine pride" has helped to provoke his reaction. The irony of it all is that Socrates foresees all such reactions to his proposals, and allows for the fact that they will seem ridiculous in many ways to people such as Bloom who are used to a totally different order of things. Despite this, he hopes that the reason of his argument will triumph, and that rational men will realize that nothing is ridiculous but evil, and that it is not equality between the sexes that is unnatural, it is "the way things are nowadays (that) proves to be, as it seems, against nature."[12] Book v, then, is not a comedy, but Bloom's commentary on it seems to be, and Socrates has the last laugh.

Notes

INTRODUCTION

1. *The First and Second Discourses*, p. 101.

2. One of the earliest feminists to point out this anomaly was Mary Wollstonecraft, whose *A Vindication of the Rights of Woman* is a pioneer work in the correction of the language and orientation of liberalism, exemplified in her time by Thomas Paine and the French Declaration of the Rights of Man. For two recent discussions of the sexism inherent in our language, see Elizabeth Lane Beardsley, "Referential Genderization," and Sheila Rowbotham, *Woman's Consciousness, Man's World*, pp. 34-38.

3. *Kant's Political Writings*, trans. H. B. Nisbet, ed. Hans Reiss. Cambridge, 1970, pp. 43-47, 78, 158-159.

4. Excerpts from the *Adams Family Correspondence*, in Alice Rossi, *The Feminist Papers*, New York, 1973, pp. 9-11.

5. See for example the beginning of Chapter 11 below, for Jefferson's views on this issue.

6. *The Utopian Vision of Charles Fourier*, pp. 195-196.

7. *Karl Marx, Early Writings*, p. 154.

CHAPTER 1

1. Hesiod, *Works; Theogony*, p. 585 and cf. pp. 570ff.; *Works and Days*, pp. 73ff.

2. *Works and Days*, pp. 400f. and pp. 370f.

3. M. I. Finley, *The World of Odysseus*, p. 138.

4. For examples of this, see Plato, *Symposium*, 181a-d; also Finley, *The World of Odysseus*, p. 151.

5. Homer, *Odyssey*, VII, 50-60, and see Finley, *The World of Odysseus*, pp. 103-104 and 150.

6. Finley, *The World of Odysseus*, p. 83.

7. A. W. Adkins, *Merit and Responsibility; A Study in Greek Values*, pp. 30-36; Alasdair MacIntyre, *A Short History of Ethics*, Chap. 2.

8. Adkins, *Merit and Responsibility*, pp. 32-33.

9. *Merit and Responsibility*, pp. 36-37.

10. Finley, *The World of Odysseus*, p. 148; Adkins, *Merit and Responsibility*, pp. 40 and 43.

11. *Odyssey*, XI, 330.

12. John Addington Symonds, *A Problem in Greek Ethics*, p. 64; Jean Ithurriague, *Les Idées de Platon sur la condition de la femme*, pp. 38, 47; Sarah B. Pomeroy, *Goddesses, Whores, Wives, and Slaves*, Chap. 4 and 5.

13. Xenophon, *Oeconomicus*, in *Xenophon's Socratic Discourse*, trans. Carnes Lord and ed. Leo Strauss, Ithaca, 1970, p. 29 and cf. pp. 30-33.

14. Ehrenberg, *The People of Aristophanes*, pp. 202 and 295; *Society and Civilization in Greece and Rome*, p. 59; cf. Ronald B. Levinson, *In Defense of Plato*, p. 83.

15. Symonds, *A Problem in Greek Ethics*, p. 51; and as sources for this paragraph as a whole, see p. 33 and p. 64; Glenn Morrow, *Plato's Cretan City*, p. 285, n. 111; Levinson, pp. 82-85; Ithurriague, pp. 47-48; Grube, *Plato's Thought*, pp. 87-88; H. D. Rankin, *Plato and the Individual*, pp. 83-84; Alvin Gouldner, *Enter Plato*, p. 62.

16. Sophocles, *Ajax*, pp. 291-293; Aristotle, *The Politics*, I, xiii, 11; cf. *Lysistrata*, pp. 41-42, and Ehrenberg, *The People of Aristophanes*, p. 202.

17. Thucydides, *The Peloponnesian War*, I, vi, p. 109.

18. Demosthenes, *Private Orations*, III, p. 122; cf. Ehrenberg, *Society and Civilization*, p. 26, for confirmation that this was a prevalent attitude.

19. Sophocles, *Antigone*, 570.

20. Xenophon, *Symposium*, II, 9, in *The Works of Xenophon*, trans. H. G. Dakyns, London, 1897.

21. *Meno*, 72d-73b.

22. *Protagoras*, 342.

23. *Symposium*, 175e; *Ion*, 540; and Levinson, *In Defense of Plato*, p. 129.

24. *Laws*, 817c; *Letters*, VIII, 355c; *Thaetetus*, 171e.

25. *Republic*, 387e-388a, 395, 431b-c, 605d-e; *Laws*, 639b.

26. *Laws*, 836e.

27. Gregory Vlastos, "The Individual as an Object of Love in Plato," in *Platonic Studies*, pp. 24-25.

NOTES TO 2. PHILOSOPHER QUEENS AND PRIVATE WIVES

28. *Symposium*, 181a-d.
29. *Symposium*, 189d-193c, but especially 192.
30. *Symposium*, 208e and 211e; cf. Thaetetus, 150.
31. "The Individual as an Object of Love," p. 42.
32. *Symposium*, 209c.
33. Cf. Levinson, *In Defense of Plato*, p. 121.
34. *Timaeus*, 42a-d.
35. In the *Statesman*, too, an "original age" is depicted, in which men were not reproduced by women, but sprang full-grown from the earth, and subsequently developed backward to childhood and then vanished. It was only after God forsook the human race that it had to propagate itself and to develop from infancy to old age. Not only Hesiod and Plato, but Aristotle, the Christian tradition, and Rousseau, all have their own versions of this revealing myth of a time before women lived with men.
36. *Timaeus*, 42a-d; also 90e and 91d.
37. *Laws*, 781a-b.
38. *Laws*, 944d-e.
39. Cornford, "Psychology and Social Structure in the *Republic* of Plato," p. 252; *In Defense of Plato*, p. 129.

CHAPTER 2

1. *Republic*, 420b.
2. *Statesman*, 297b; cf. *Laws*, 630c, 644-645, 705d-706a, 707d; *Euthydemus*, 292b-c; see also Sheldon Wolin, *Politics and Vision*, pp. 34-36.
3. *Laws*, 731e.
4. *Laws*, 743d-e.
5. Morrow, *Plato's Cretan City*, p. 101; see also *Laws*, 736e.
6. *Republic*, 372e-373e, and VIII passim.
7. *Republic*, 462a-e.
8. *Republic*, 462a-e.
9. *Laws*, 739c-740a.
10. *Republic*, 416c-417b.
11. *Republic*, 416c-d.
12. *Republic*, 417a-b.
13. *Republic*, 423e; *Laws*, 739c.
14. *Republic*, 423e.

15. *Republic*, 423e, 462, 464; *Laws*, 739c, 807b.
16. Cf. Grube, *Plato's Thought*, p. 89.
17. *Republic*, 464c-d.
18. *Laws*, 805e.
19. *Republic*, 547b, 548a.
20. *Republic*, 549c-e.
21. Morrow, *Plato's Cretan City*, p. 102, n. 13, where he notes that in Athens custom forbade the alienation of the family land. The connection in classical Greek thought and practice between the wife and the custody of the household property is amply confirmed in the descriptions of household management given by Xenophon and Aristotle.
22. M. I. Finley, *The Ancient Greeks*, pp. 123-124; Ehrenberg, *Society and Civilization*, p. 59.
23. Finley, *The Ancient Greeks*, p. 124.
24. *Laws*, e.g. 866 and 873e.
25. *Euthyphro*, 4a-b.
26. *Plato's Thought*, p. 270; see also A. E. Taylor, *Plato, the Man and his Work*, p. 278.
27. "On Plato's Republic," in *The City and Man*, p. 117.
28. Taylor, p. 278; see also Grube, p. 270, and Strauss, p. 117.
29. Ithurriague, *Les Idées de Platon*, p. 53.
30. Grube, p. 270.
31. See Chapter 8, circa notes 62-65.
32. "Plato and the Definition of the Primitive," p. 126.
33. *Timaeus*, 18c-e.
34. *Republic*, 463c-e.
35. *Republic* 464d-e, 465a-b, 471c-d.
36. "The Individual as an Object of Love," p. 11.
37. Rousseau, *Emile, Oeuvres Complètes*, Pléiade Edition, Vol. 4, pp. 699-700 (my translation).
38. For examples of each of these three positions respectively, see, e.g., Christine Pierce, "Equality: *Republic* v," 6; Strauss, "On Plato's Republic," p. 116; A. E. Taylor, *Plato, the Man and his Work*, p. 278. The objections of William Jacobs ("Plato on Female Emancipation and the Traditional Family," forthcoming in *Apeiron*) have caused me to revise my original wording of this passage.
39. *Republic*, 370; this is graphically illustrated by the assertion at 406d-407a, that if one can no longer perform one's task, it is worthless to go on living.

40. *Republic*, 454b, and see 454-456 in general for source of this paragraph.
41. *Republic*, 460b.
42. *Republic*, 540c.
43. Strauss, "On Plato's Republic," Part 2 of *The City and Man*, pp. 116-117; Allan Bloom, Interpretive Essay to *The Republic of Plato*, pp. 382-383.
44. *Republic*, 451c and 453d.
45. *Laws*, 806a-c.
46. *Republic*, 417a-b.
47. *Republic*, 592b; *Laws*, 739
48. *Laws*, 805a-b.
49. *Laws*, 805c-d.
50. *Laws*, 740a-c.
51. *Plato's Cretan City*, pp. 118-119.
52. *Laws*, 866a, 868b-c, 871b, 879c. See Morrow, pp. 120-121.
53. *Laws*, 772d-773e, 774e.
54. *Laws*, 773c.
55. *Laws*, 923e. I am grateful to William Jacobs for helping me to clarify this point. Private correspondence, 1977.
56. *Laws*, 928e-929a.
57. Morrow, p. 113, note 55.
58. *Laws*, 784b, 929e, 930b, 882c. See Morrow, p. 121.
59. *Laws*, 784d-e.
60. *Laws*, 937a-b.
61. *Republic*, 540c. The fact that Plato's rulers have always been referred to as philosopher kings tends to suggest that the reminder indeed was, and still is, necessary.
62. *Laws*, 741c, 759b, 764c-d, 800b, 813c, 828b, 784a-c, 790a, 794a-b, 795d, 930.
63. *Laws*, 961.
64. *Laws*, 765d-766b.
65. Levinson agrees with this conclusion (*In Defense of Plato*, p. 133), and Morrow notes that Plato nowhere suggests that women should perform the basic civic function of attending the assembly of the people (*Plato's Cretan City*, pp. 157-158).
66. *Laws*, 785b.
67. *Laws*, 947b-d, 764e.
68. *Laws*, 804e-805a, 806b.
69. *Laws*, 794c-d.
70. *Laws*, 833c-d, 834a, 834d.

71. *Laws*, 785b.
72. *Laws*, 808a, 808e.
73. *Laws*, 833d.
74. Compare *Laws*, 781c-d with *Republic*, 452a-b.

CHAPTER 3

1. *Phaedrus*, 207d-e.
2. Theognis writes, for example:
> To make the foolish wise, the wicked good,
> That science never yet was understood. . . .
> . . . human art
> In human nature has no share or part. . . .
> No scheme or artifice of human skill
> Can rectify the passions or the will.

The Works of Hesiod, Callimachus and Theognis, p. 442.
The commentary asserts that in the long-debated question of whether virtue and vice are innate, Pindar and Euripides, too, came down on the affirmative side.

3. Education, for Plato, could include anything from drinking parties to legislation on all kinds of matters (*Laws*, 641).
4. F. M. Cornford, *From Religion to Philosophy*, p. 73.
5. *Laws*, 794d-e.
6. *Laws*, 834d.
7. *Republic*, 424a.
8. *Republic*, 370a.
9. *Timaeus*, 86d-87b.
10. *Phaedrus*, 269d.
11. *Laws*, 740a.
12. *Republic*, 377b.
13. *Republic*, 378d-e.
14. *Republic*, 424e-425c; see also *Laws*, 797, 816.
15. *Republic*, 410c-411e.
16. *Republic*, 375.
17. *Republic*, 423d-e.
18. *Republic*, 514a.
19. *Laws*, 804b; *Plato's Cretan City*, p. 541.
20. *Laws*, 641c, 788-789, 792e, 765e, 741a.
21. *Laws*, 766a.

NOTES TO 3. FEMALE NATURE AND SOCIAL STRUCTURE

22. See, e.g., Gouldner, *Enter Plato*, p. 228; Grube, Plato's Thought, pp. 268-269; Alasdair MacIntyre, *A Short History of Ethics*, p. 44.

23. *Republic*, 382a-d, 389b.

24. *Republic*, 387-389.

25. *Republic*, 426d-e.

26. *Republic*, 451e.

27. *Republic*, 455d; Pierce, "Equality: *Republic* v," 9.

28. *Republic*, 455d-e.

29. Even though Socrates says that it is the least paradoxical of his three great waves, he seems more sensitive to the apparent ridiculousness of his proposal here than anywhere else in the *Republic*.

30. "Equality: *Republic* v," 3.

31. *Laws*, 804e-805a.

32. *Laws*, 794c-d.

33. *Plato's Cretan City*, p. 329.

34. *Laws*, 795a-c.

35. Cf. *Laws*, 795c with 805a-b.

36. Thus, in playing music, it does not matter if the hands are used and developed differently, and likewise, right at the end of the passage about ambidexterity, Plato divides the supervision of the children between the officers according to the sex of the latter. The women, he proposes, will see to the games and meals, while the men take charge of the lessons (795). How this division of labor would affect the young girls' perception of themselves and their sex, Plato does not consider. He simply seems to think that in some spheres it is necessary for the good of the city for women to be utilized in the same way as men, and that in others, since the distribution of roles is immaterial for the general welfare, women might just as well stick to their traditional nurturing roles, and men to their traditional intellectual ones.

37. Cf. Aristotle's *Metaphysics*, Book Alpha, 986a. I am indebted to Victor Menza for pointing out this connection. See also Caroline Whitbeck, "Theories of Sex Difference," *The Philosophical Forum*, Vol. 5, Nos. 1-2, 1973-1974, 57-60.

38. *Laws*, 795b.

39. *Laws*, 795d.

40. *Republic*, 592b; *Laws*, 739c-d.

41. *Laws*, 810d-e.

42. *Laws*, 746b-c.

43. *Laws*, 797ff.

44. *Laws*, 781. Bury does not translate the *physis* which is present in the Greek.

45. *Timaeus*, 87b.

46. *Laws*, 802d-e.

47. *Republic*, 410c-411e; *Laws*, 802c.

48. Glenn Morrow seems to have missed the prescriptive character of the passage; according to him, it indicates Plato's awareness of "the specific differences between the psychical nature of women and that of men" (*Plato's Cretan City*, p. 331).

49. Introduction to the *Iliad*, by E. V. Rieu, p. xx. See also J. H. Finley, *Four Stages of Greek Thought*, p. 92, on the *nomos/physis* dichotomy in general.

50. *Plato and the Individual*, p. 92.

51. *Laws*, 636b-c, 836c-d.

52. *Laws*, 839a, 840d-e.

53. See Levinson, *In Defense of Plato*, p. 135.

54. *Laws*, 836c-d.

55. *Laws*, 839c-d.

56. *Republic*, 452a.

57. *Laws*, 838a-d.

58. *Republic*, 458e.

59. *Laws*, 806b.

CHAPTER 4

1. *The Philosophy of Right*. Trans. T. M. Knox, Oxford, 1952, p. 11.

2. Aristotle, *Nichomachean Ethics*, VI, 1139b.

3. *Nichomachean Ethics*, VII, 1145b.

4. See D. J. Allan, *The Philosophy of Aristotle*, p. 124, and G. E. R. Lloyd, *Aristotle: The Growth and Structure of his Thought*, p. 206.

5. *Politics*, I, 1253a.

6. *De Anima*, II, 412b.

7. *De Anima*, II, 412b.

8. *De Anima*, I, 407b; cf. II, 415b.

9. *Generation of Animals*, V, 789b.

10. *Politics*, VI, 1333a.

11. *Politics*, I, 1256b; cf. also I, 1253a, for an example of nature's "economy."

12. *Nichomachean Ethics*, I, 1097b.

13. *Nichomachean Ethics*, I, 1098a.

14. *Politics*, I, 1252b.

15. *Nichomachean Ethics*, X, 1177b.

16. *Politics*, VII, 1328a.

17. *Politics*, I, 1255a, 1252a, 1255b.

18. *Nichomachean Ethics*, VIII, 1161a.

19. *Nichomachean Ethics*, VIII, 1162a; *Eudemian Ethics*, VII, 1238b.

20. *Politics*, III, 1278b.

21. *Eudemian Ethics*, VII, 1242b.

22. Politics, III, 1277b. See Jean Bethke Elshtain, "Moral Woman and Immoral Man," *Politics and Society*, Vol. 4, 1974, 453-456, for a discussion of these aspects of Aristotle's functionalism.

23. See Chapter 3 above.

24. E.g., *Nichomachean Ethics*, II, 1103a, passim.

25. E.g., *Art of Rhetoric*, I, 1370a.

26. *Politics*, I, 1252b.

27. *Politics*, I, 1253b.

28. *Politics*, I, 1254a.

29. *Politics*, I, 1253a.

30. *Politics*, I, 1254b.

31. *Politics*, I, 1252b.

32. *De Anima*, II, 415a. The reason reproduction is the "most natural" function of living beings is that it is their only means of achieving immortality. As is clear from what follows, however, it is only the male who achieves immortality, since it is he, according to Aristotle, who furnishes the child with its soul.

33. *Generation of Animals*, II, 732a; cf. I, 727b and II, 738b.

34. *Generation of Animals*, IV, 767b, 775a.

35. *Generation of Animals*, I, 728a, IV, 766a.

36. *Generation of Animals*, I, 729a, 731a.

37. *Politics*, VII, 1334b-1335b.

38. See Barker's note 2, *Politics*, p. 327.

39. *Nichomacheañ Ethics*, VIII, 1162a; *Politics*, III, 1277b.

40. *Politics*, II, 1261a-b.

41. *Politics*, II, 1264b.
42. *Nichomachean Ethics*, v, 1134b.
43. *Nichomachean Ethics*, v, 1138b.
44. *Nichomachean Ethics*, VIII, 1161a.
45. *Nichomachean Ethics*, VIII, 1158b.
46. *Oeconomica*, III, 141.
47. *Eudemian Ethics*, VII, 1238b.
48. *Merit and Responsibility*, especially pp. 30-31 and 341-342.
49. *Merit and Responsibility*, p. 342.
50. *Politics*, v, 1312a, where Aristotle gives, without comment, an example of a monarch who was killed, "from the motive of contempt," by a man who saw him carding wool among women. Oddly enough, it is not so much the actual content of the work done by these subordinate classes of people that Aristotle cites as the reason it is so degrading, but rather the fact that it is done at the behest of other people. See *Politics*, VIII, 1337b.
51. *Eudemian Ethics*, II, 1218b-1219a.
52. *Poetics*, XV, 1454a.
53. *Politics*, III, 1276b.
54. *Politics*, III, 1277b.
55. *Politics*, I, 1260a.
56. *Politics*, I, 1260a.
57. *Art of Rhetoric*, I, 1361a.
58. *Poetics*, XV, 1454a.
59. *Politics*, III, 1277b.
60. *Politics*, I, 1260a.
61. *Eudemian Ethics*, VII, 1237a.
62. *Art of Rhetoric*, I, 1367a.
63. "Aristotle," in *History of Political Philosophy*, ed. Leo Strauss and Joseph Cropsey, pp. 74-76.
64. Ferguson, *Aristotle*, pp. 139-140.
65. Ross, *Aristotle*, p. 242.
66. *Aristotle*, pp. 243 and 249.
67. *Aristotle*, pp. 245-246.
68. *The Philosophy of Aristotle*, p. 161.
69. *Aristotle: The Growth and Structure of his Thought*, pp. 264-265, 296.

CHAPTER 5

With the exception of the *Letter to d'Alembert*, translated by Allan Bloom (Cornell, 1968), and *The First and Second Discourses*, translated by Roger D. and Judith R. Masters (New York, 1964), references to Rousseau's works are in general to the *Oeuvres complètes*, Vols. 1-4, Pléiade Edition, Paris, 1959-1969, henceforth cited as *O.C.* The translations from this edition are my own. In addition, as specified below, I have used the Hachette *Oeuvres complètes* and the *Correspondance générale* a few times, for works not yet included in the Pléiade edition.

1. See, e.g., Hegel, *The Philosophy of Right*, Par. 166 and Add. 107, for a prime example of this type of reasoning about the capacities of women.

2. Eva Figes, *Patriarchal Attitudes*, p. 42.

3. On this subject, see Ronald Grimsley, *Jean-Jacques Rousseau*, Chap. 3, especially pp. 104-115.

4. *Emile*, *O.C.* 4, p. 709, and see below, p. 204.

5. See, e.g., *Confessions*, *O.C.* 1, p. 317.

6. *Confessions*, p. 573; *Rousseau juge de Jean-Jacques*, *O.C.* 1, p. 687.

7. *Rousseau juge de Jean-Jacques*, p. 933.

8. Pierre Burgelin, "L'Education de Sophie," 113.

9. Letter to M. Lenieps, 1758, *Correspondance générale de Jean-Jacques Rousseau*, 4, p. 115.

10. See, e.g., *Lettres morales*, *O.C.* 4, pp. 1090-1092.

11. *Letter to M. d'Alembert*, p. 83.

12. *Emile*, pp. 380-381, and *Emile et Sophie*, *O.C.* 4, p. 900.

13. *Emile*, p. 324.

14. Montesquieu, *Persian Letters*, passim, e.g., Letters 26, 38, 63.

15. Montesquieu, *Spirit of the Laws*, 1949, pp. 252 and 258.

16. Helvétius, *A Treatise on Man*, Vol. 1, p. 156.

17. d'Holbach, *Système sociale*, p. 122, my translation.

18. *Encyclopédie ou dictionnaire raisonné des sciences, des arts et des métiers*, eds. Diderot and d'Alembert, Vol. 6, pp. 469-477.

19. Burgelin, in a discussion, reported in *Annales Jean-Jacques Rousseau*, 35, p. 136.

20. "Sur les Femmes" and "Essai sur les Evénements Importants dont les Femmes out été la Cause Secrette," *O.C.* 2, pp. 1254-

1255 and 1257-1259; see that volume's Introduction, p. ci, for dating.

CHAPTER 6

1. See, e.g., references cited in notes 15 and 18 of Chapter 5, above.

2. *Discourse on the Origin of Inequality, First and Second Discourses*, pp. 77, 104 and 229; Letter to M. Lenieps, *Correspondance générale*, 4, p. 114.

3. *Emile, O.C.* 4, pp. 692 and 736.

4. Preface to the *Discourse on the Origins of Inequality*, pp. 96-97.

5. E.g. by A. O. Lovejoy, "The Supposed Primitivism of Rousseau's Discourse on Inequality," *Essays in the History of Ideas*, Baltimore, 1948.

6. *Discourse on Inequality*, p. 104.

7. *Discourse on Inequality*, p. 134.

8. *Discourse on Inequality*, p. 135.

9. *Discourse on Inequality*, p. 213-220.

10. *Discourse on Inequality*, p. 215, quoting Locke.

11. *Discourse on Inequality*, p. 215.

12. *Discourse on Inequality*, p. 216.

13. *Emile*, p. 524.

14. I am not suggesting that Rousseau would have agreed to this conclusion. Nevertheless, it follows logically from his arguments about the state of nature.

15. *Discourse on Inequality*, p. 127.

16. *Discourse on Inequality*; see pp. 128-132 on man's goodness in the original state of nature, and note from pp. 146-149 that quarrels and fights, jealousies and discord are supposed to have begun as soon as regular contact between individuals, differentiation of families, and rudimentary property were established.

17. *Discourse on Inequality*, p. 151; *Emile*, p. 859; *La Nouvelle Héloïse, O.C.* 2, e.g. pp. 79-84; *Letter to d'Alembert*, pp. 60-65.

18. "The Supposed Primitivism," p. 31.

19. *Discourse on Inequality*, p. 147.

20. *Discourse on Inequality*, p. 147.

21. *Discourse on Inequality*, p. 154; "it is impossible to con-

ceive of the idea of property as arising from anything except manual labor."

22. *Discourse on Inequality*, p. 166.

23. *Discourse on Inequality*, p. 135.

24. *Discourse on Inequality*, p. 151.

25. *The Social Contract*, O.C. 3, p. 352.

26. *Emile*, p. 797.

27. *Emile*, p. 859.

28. *Emile*, p. 865.

29. *Discourse on Political Economy*, O.C. 3, p. 242-243 and *The Social Contract—First Draft*, O.C. 3, p. 299. These arguments are discussed further in Chapter 7 below.

30. *Emile*, p. 697.

31. *Letter to d'Alembert*, p. 85.

32. *Emile*, pp. 697-698.

33. *Emile*, pp. 692-693.

34. *Emile*, pp. 692-693.

35. *Letter to d'Alembert*, p. 84, and see *Lettres morales*, O.C. 4, p. 1110.

36. *Emile*, p. 693.

37. *Emile*, p. 694.

38. *Emile*, p. 697.

39. *Emile*, p. 698.

40. *Emile*, pp. 693, 766.

41. *La Nouvelle Héloise*, p. 128.

42. *Emile*, p. 702.

43. *The Social Contract*, p. 352.

44. *Discourse on Inequality*, p. 163.

45. Roger Masters, in *The Political Philosophy of Rousseau*, concludes after much discussion of the subject that, since "all references to savage man' in his original condition could be extended to the primitive nuclear family . . . without thereby changing any of the fundamental conclusions of Rousseau's analysis . . . even if the family is natural to the human species, Rousseau's conclusions from his account of the state of nature will be unchanged" (p. 131). Very clearly, however, with respect to the naturalness of the subordinate role of women, they will be greatly changed.

46. "Sur les Femmes," O.C. 2, p. 1254.

47. *Letter to d'Alembert*, p. 83.

48. *Letter to d'Alembert*, p. 87.

49. *The Social Contract*, p. 431, and see below, Chapter 7, for further discussion of this issue.

50. *Emile*, p. 495.

51. *Discourse on Inequality*, p. 138.

52. *Discourse on Inequality*, p. 111.

53. *Discourse on Inequality*, p. 218 (Rousseau's notes).

54. *Emile*, p. 495.

55. *The Social Contract*, p. 353.

56. *Emile*, p. 281, and see editor's note, p. 1325.

57. *Emile* (Preface), p. 242.

58. *Emile*, pp. 246-247.

59. *Emile*, p. 767.

60. *Emile*, p. 430.

61. *Discourse on Political Economy*, pp. 251 and 260.

62. *Considerations on the Government of Poland*, O.C. 3, pp. 965-966; and Chap. 4, passim.

63. *Letter to d'Alembert*, pp. 103 and 112.

64. At note 59.

65. *Emile*, pp. 703-707, 719 and 733-734.

66. *Emile*, pp. 350-351.

67. *Emile*, pp. 734-735, and 750.

68. *Emile*, p. 699.

69. *Emile*, pp. 703-704.

70. *Emile*, p. 711.

71. *Letter to d'Alembert*, p. 103.

72. "Sur les Femmes," p. 1255.

73. "Sur les Femmes," p. 1255.

74. John Locke, *Second Treatise on Civil Government*, Chap. 7, 82.

75. *Discourse on Political Economy*, p. 242.

76. A most striking recent example of this appears in the statement by Jan Morris, the English writer who recently underwent a change of sex. "I was afraid that the change would mean the loss of my gift of writing," she says, "but that seems intact. I do notice that the latest book . . . is more concerned with detail and with people than with the grand sweep of things. I guess I've lost some of that male arrogance" (*Newsweek*, 1974). Even a person who has been a member of both sexes is here under the impression that their mental powers are different! Anyone would think he/she had undergone brain surgery.

77. *Emile*, p. 720.
78. *Emile*, p. 736 (emphases added).
79. *Emile*, p. 791.
80. *La Nouvelle Héloise*, p. 128 (emphasis added).
81. *La Nouvelle Héloise*, p. 55.
82. *Emile*, p. 730.
83. *Emile*, p. 737.
84. *Emile*, p. 720.
85. *La Nouvelle Héloise*, p. 374.
86. *Men and Citizens*, p. 199.
87. *Emile*, p. 720.
88. *Emile*, pp. 693-698, especially p. 693.
89. *Emile*, p. 245.
90. See, e.g., Pierre Burgelin, Introduction to *Emile*, p. cxxii, and "L'Education de Sophie," p. 114; Masters, *The Political Philosophy of Rousseau*, p. 21.
91. *Emile*, p. 703.
92. *Emile*, p. 732.
93. *Emile*, pp. 704-705; *Letter to d'Alembert*, pp. 88-89.
94. *Letter to d'Alembert*, p. 82.
95. "Fragments pour *Emile*," *O.C.* 4, p. 872, quoted from the *Economics* Book III, i, now considered to have been written by one or more of Aristotle's disciples.
96. *Emile*, p. 705.
97. *Letter to d'Alembert*, p. 100.
98. *Letter to d'Alembert*, p. 100.
99. Letter to M. Lenieps, *Correspondance générale*, 4, p. 114.
100. *Letter to d'Alembert*, p. 107, note.
101. *La Nouvelle Héloise*, p. 450.
102. *La Nouvelle Héloise*, p. 450; also *Letter to d'Alembert*, p. 107. Rousseau, however, considered the principle of the social separation of the sexes to be suitable only for such peoples as have not yet been corrupted—a requirement fulfilled both by the Wolmars and by his idealized Genevans, but by very little of the real world. In corrupt societies, keeping the sexes apart should not even be attempted, since all they could hope for was to "ascend again, if it is possible, to the point of being only corrupt" (*Letter to d'Alembert*, p. 110).
103. *La Nouvelle Héloise*, p. 450.
104. *Discourse on Inequality*, p. 216.

CHAPTER 7

1. Shklar, *Men and Citizens*, p. 19 and see p. 30. See also Jean Starobinski, "La Pensée politique de Jean-Jacques Rousseau," in S. Baud-Bovy, et al., *Jean-Jacques Rousseau*, pp. 84-85.

2. *Confessions*, O.C. 1, pp. 31 and 514.

3. *Discourse on Inequality, First and Second Discourses*, p. 78.

4. *Emile*, O.C. 4, p. 524.

5. *Discourse on Inequality*, pp. 159-160.

6. *Emile*, p. 524.

7. *Emile*, p. 524.

8. *The Social Contract*, O.C. 3, p. 354.

9. *Emile*, p. 841.

10. *The Social Contract*, p. 367.

11. *Considerations on the Government of Poland*, O.C. 3, p. 973-974.

12. *Discourse on Inequality*, pp. 167-168; *The Social Contract*, pp. 355-358; *Emile*, p. 839.

13. E.g., by Masters, *The Political Philosophy of Rousseau*, p. 424; Shklar, *Men and Citizens*, p. 18.

14. *The Social Contract*, p. 431.

15. *Emile*, p. 701.

16. *Discourse on Inequality*, Dedication, p. 89.

17. "Fragments pour *Emile*," O.C. 4, p. 872.

18. *Emile*, p. 865.

19. The following three paragraphs draw on *Discourse on Political Economy*, O.C. 3, pp. 241-242, and First Draft of *The Social Contract*, pp. 297-300.

20. See, e.g., *Letter to d'Alembert*, p. 85; *Emile*, pp. 697-698; *Emile et Sophie* ou *Les Solitaires*, O.C. 4, p. 904.

21. *Letter to d'Alembert*, p. 83.

22. *Emile et Sophie*, p. 904; *La Nouvelle Héloise*, *passim*; *Confessions*, pp. 344-345 and 594-595.

23. *La Nouvelle Héloise*, Second Preface, O.C. 2, p. 24.

24. *Discourse on Political Economy*, p. 247.

25. *Emile*, p. 695. For an interesting account of Rousseau's antifeminism which attributes it largely to his fear of women, see Victor G. Wexler, " 'Made for Man's Delight': Rousseau as Antifeminist."

26. *Letter to d'Alembert*, p. 47.

27. *Emile*, p. 731.

28. Vers: "Sur la Femme," *Oeuvres complètes*, Hachette, Vol. 6, p. 28.

29. *Discourse on Inequality*, p. 137.

30. *Discourse on Inequality*, p. 135.

31. *Emile*, p. 740.

32. *La Nouvelle Héloise*, pp. 265-278; Rousseau's note, p. 278.

33. *Emile*, pp. 668 and 742.

34. *Emile*, p. 659.

35. Letter to M. Lenieps, p. 115.

36. *Emile*, p. 709.

37. *La Nouvelle Héloise*, p. 194.

38. *La Nouvelle Héloise*, Second Preface, p. 24.

39. *Discourse on the Arts and Sciences, First and Second Discourses*, pp. 52-53.

40. *Emile*, p. 742; *La Nouvelle Héloise*, pp. 220 and 229; *Confessions*, p. 171; *Réponse à M. Bordes, Oeuvres complètes*, Hachette, Vol. 1, p. 50.

41. *Discourse on Political Economy*, p. 257; *Discourse on Inequality*, p. 167; *The Social Contract*, p. 356.

42. *Confessions*, pp. 379-380; *Reveries, O.C.* 1, pp. 1051-1053, 1059.

43. *Reveries*, p. 1059.

44. *Discourse on Inequality*, p. 140.

45. *Discourse on Inequality*, p. 151.

46. See, e.g., Masters, Introduction to *The First and Second Discourses*, p. 24; Shklar, *Men and Citizens*, pp. 155-156.

47. *Emile*, p. 311.

48. *Emile*, p. 841.

49. *Discourse on Political Economy*, pp. 248-249 and *The Social Contract*, p. 356.

50. On this subject, see Chap. 3, "The Empire of Opinion," in Shklar, *Men and Citizens*, pp. 75ff.

51. *Reveries*, p. 1079.

52. *Discourse on Inequality*, p. 155.

53. *Emile*, p. 253.

54. *Letter to d'Alembert*, pp. 79-80.

55. *Discourse on Inequality*, pp. 37-38; *La Nouvelle Héloise*, pp. 231-236.

56. *Discourse on the Arts and Sciences*, p. 64. Masters, however,

translates "autrui" as "another"; I have substituted "others," an alternative which seems to fit Rousseau's context better.

57. *Emile*, p. 857.

58. *Emile*, pp. 420-422.

59. There is one passage, however, in which, curiously, the opinions of the passers-by *are* used as a pressure on the child to behave (*Emile*, pp. 367-368).

60. *Emile*, p. 320.

61. *Emile*, p. 782; see also p. 671.

62. *Letter to d'Alembert*, p. 81.

63. *Emile*, p. 713.

64. *Emile*, p. 701.

65. *Emile*, pp. 710, 741, 750, 766.

66. *Emile*, pp. 710-711. See also pp. 745, 755.

67. *Emile*, pp. 704, 731, 767, 768-769.

68. *Emile*, p. 768. While Julie's education, though no systematic account is given of it, is much more thorough and intellectual than Sophie's (see, e.g., *La Nouvelle Héloise*, p. 59), Julie is unique in that she was conceived as Rousseau's ideal woman for himself, in the persona of the philosopher Saint-Preux. It seems reasonable to regard the education of Sophie, the helpmeet for the more ordinary natural man, as Rousseau's more typical prescription for female education.

69. *Emile*, p. 791.

70. *Emile*, p. 749.

71. *Discourse on the Arts and Sciences*, pp. 52-53.

72. *Emile*, p. 735, note; *Letter to d'Alembert*, pp. 82-83.

73. See Burgelin, Introduction to *Emile*, p. cxxiii.

74. *Emile*, p. 751.

75. *Emile*, pp. 702-703.

76. *Emile*, p. 749.

77. *Emile*, pp. 709-710.

78. *Emile*, p. 716.

79. *La Nouvelle Héloise*, Second Preface, p. 24, and *Letter to d'Alembert*, p. 129.

80. *La Nouvelle Héloise*, p. 257. It is interesting to note that only when Claire's husband dies does she feel young and attractive again.

81. *Emile*, p. 721.

82. *Emile*, p. 721.

83. *Emile*, p. 730.

CHAPTER 8

1. *Emile, O.C.* 4, pp. 835, 855-857.
2. *Emile,* p. 823.
3. *Emile,* p. 493.
4. *Emile,* p. 858.
5. *Emile,* p. 858; see also p. 818.
6. *Emile,* pp. 858-859.
7. *Emile,* p. 860.
8. *Emile et Sophie, O.C.* 4, p. 914.
9. *Men and Citizens,* p. 150.
10. *Emile,* pp. 249-250.
11. *Emile et Sophie,* p. 918.
12. *Emile,* p. 763.
13. *Emile et Sophie,* p. 904.
14. *Emile,* pp. 911-912.
15. *Emile,* p. 884. Emile reports that "the last day of her life showed me (charms) that I had not known of."
16. *Emile,* p. 887.
17. *Emile,* p. 751.
18. "L'Education de Sophie," pp. 126-127. See *Emile,* p. 762.
19. *Confessions, O.C.* 1, p. 430.
20. It is significant that only the women in Rousseau's novels appear to have any parents, and therefore, to be faced with the potential conflict of family duty with their own feelings and consciences.
21. *La Nouvelle Héloise, O.C.* 2, p. 96.
22. *La Nouvelle Héloise,* p. 103.
23. *La Nouvelle Héloise,* p. 212.
24. *La Nouvelle Héloise,* p. 201.
25. *La Nouvelle Héloise,* pp. 226-227.
26. *La Nouvelle Héloise,* p. 340.
27. *La Nouvelle Héloise,* p. 401.
28. *La Nouvelle Héloise,* p. 528.
29. *La Nouvelle Héloise,* p. 694.
30. *La Nouvelle Héloise,* p. 664.
31. *Men and Citizens,* p. 120. René Schaerer, too, says that Julie plays the part of the redeemer, "Jean-Jacques Rousseau et la Grande Famille," in *Jean-Jacques Rousseau,* Baud-Bovy, et al. p. 199.
32. *Emile,* p. 709.

33. *Emile*, p. 249.
34. *La Nouvelle Héloise*, p. 612; *Emile*, p. 251.
35. *Emile*, p. 249.
36. *Emile*, p. 249; Réponse à M. Bordes, p. 60.
37. *Considerations on the Government of Poland*, O.C. 3, p. 966, and see Chap. 4; also *Letter to d'Alembert*, pp. 125-126.
38. *Letter to d'Alembert*, p. 111; *Emile*, pp. 250-251.
39. *Emile*, pp. 249-250.
40. *Emile*, p. 251 (emphasis added).
41. *Emile*, pp. 483-484, and see p. 654: "as a member of society he must fulfill its duties."
42. *Emile*, p. 823.
43. *The Social Contract*, O.C. 3, p. 351.
44. *Emile*, pp. 493-494; *Confessions*, p. 414. For two recent and interesting discussions of Rousseau's philosophy of love, see John Charvet, *The Social Problem in the Philosophy of Rousseau*, pp. 114-117, and Elizabeth Rapaport, "On the Future of Love: Rousseau and the Radical Feminists," pp. 185-205.
45. See Second Preface to *La Nouvelle Héloise*, pp. 15-16, and text pp. 372-373.
46. *Emile*, pp. 775-776.
47. *La Nouvelle Héloise*, p. 372.
48. See, e.g., *Confessions*, p. 424.
49. *La Nouvelle Héloise*, p. 223.
50. *La Nouvelle Héloise*, p. 147.
51. *La Nouvelle Héloise*, pp. 56 and 312.
52. *La Nouvelle Héloise*, p. 194.
53. *Emile*, p. 819.
54. *Correspondence générale*, Vol. 4, p. 827.
55. *Letter to d'Alembert*, p. 118.
56. *Letter to d'Alembert*, p. 117.
57. *Emile*, p. 866.
58. *Emile*, p. 866.
59. *La Nouvelle Héloise*, p. 372.
60. *La Nouvelle Héloise*, p. 373.
61. *Letter to d'Alembert*, p. 47.
62. *Greedy Institutions*, p. 139.
63. *Greedy Institutions*, p. 140, from Rosabeth Kanter, *Commitment and Community*, Cambridge, Mass., 1972, p. 87.
64. *La Nouvelle Héloise*, pp. 449-450.

65. See Coser, Chaps. 7, 8, 9 and 10; Plato, *Republic* v; Campanella, *The City of the Sun*, pp. 282-293; Fourier, *The Utopian Vision of Charles Fourier*, Parts 5, 6, and 7.

66. *Letter to d'Alembert*, p. 131.

67. Compare *Considerations on the Government of Poland*, pp. 970-971 with *Discourse on Political Economy*, *O.C.* 3, p. 241.

68. *Discourse on Political Economy*, p. 261.

69. *Emile*, pp. 248-249.

70. *Discourse on Political Economy*, p. 246.

71. *The Social Contract*, p. 361.

72. *The Social Contract*, p. 438.

73. *Discourse on Political Economy*, pp. 286, 263-264.

74. *O.C.* 3, p. 1400 (note to *Discourse on Political Economy*, p. 261).

75. *Discourse on Political Economy*, pp. 260-261.

76. *Discourse on Political Economy*, p. 1400.

77. *Letter to d'Alembert*, p. 128; *The Social Contract*, p. 469 (Rousseau's note).

78. *Social Contract*, p. 469, note.

79. *Letter to d'Alembert*, pp. 34-35.

80. *Emile*, p. 258; *La Nouvelle Héloise*, Second Preface, p. 24.

81. *Emile*, p. 262.

82. *Emile*, p. 700.

83. *Letter to d'Alembert*, p. 117.

CHAPTER 9

1. I would like to acknowledge the help and inspiration I have gained in thinking about this issue from the work of Mary L. Shanley, of Vassar College, Carole Pateman, of the University of Sydney, and Teresa Brennan of Macquarie University. Conversations with Dr. Shanley have helped me to clarify my ideas on the subject of women and the liberal tradition. See Shanley, "Individual, Family and State: The Equal Rights Amendment and Beyond," "Marriage Contract in Seventeenth-Century Political Thought"; and Pateman and Brennan, " 'Mere Auxiliaries to the Commonwealth': Women and the Origins of Liberalism."

2. *Leviathan*, XIII, pp. 101-102; also *De Corpore Politico*, I, 1, and *De Cive*, I, 3.

3. *Leviathan*, xx, p. 168; also *De Cive*, ix, 3.

4. *De Cive*, ix, 3.

5. *Leviathan*, xx, pp. 168-169.

6. *Leviathan*, p. 172; also *De Cive*, ix, 10.

7. *A Dialogue Between a Philosopher and a Student of the Common Laws of England*, p. 159.

8. On Hobbes' use of the family as the basic unit of his politics, see Gordon Schochet, "Thomas Hobbes on the Family and the State of Nature," and *Patriarchalism in Political Thought*; Richard Allen Chapman, "Leviathan Writ Small: Thomas Hobbes on the Family."

9. *Two Treatises of Government*, ii, 52-53, pp. 345-346.

10. *Two Treatises*, ii, 65, p. 353.

11. *Two Treatises*, i, 47, p. 210; ii, 82, p. 364.

12. "Government," p. 9.

13. "Government," p. 28.

14. "Government," p. 21.

15. In her recent book, *On Liberty and Liberalism*, Gertrude Himmelfarb argues that Mill's feminist writings are not an application of his more general principles, but rather that the arguments of *On Liberty* are largely explainable in terms of his preoccupation with the subject of women and their need for liberation. Since my concern is not with *On Liberty* and the motivations behind it, this is not the place to argue against Himmelfarb's account of its origins. It seems to me, however, that she is treading a very fine line in saying *both* that "The essays on women were not . . . the application of *On Liberty* to a particular problem," and also that "*On Liberty* was the case of women writ large" (p. 181).

16. *The Subjection of Women*, pp. 427.

17. See, for example, Michael St. John Packe, *The Life of John Stuart Mill*, pp. 90, 294-295; F. A. Hayek, *John Stuart Mill and Harriet Taylor*, pp. 208, 248; Himmelfarb, *On Liberty and Liberalism*, pp. 170, 204-205; *The Subjection of Women*, p. 451.

18. Letter to John Nichol, August 18, 1869, *The Later Letters*, *Collected Works*, Vol. 17, p. 1634.

19. The two essays on the subject of marriage and divorce which Mill and Harriet Taylor wrote for each other in 1832 are reprinted in Hayek, *John Stuart Mill and Harriet Taylor*, and also in Alice Rossi's edition of their *Essays on Sex Equality*, where

the pamphlet *The Enfranchisement of Women*, which was probably, though not certainly, written by Harriet Taylor, is also to be found.

20. Jeremy Bentham, *Plan of Parliamentary Reform*, pp. 463-464, and *Constitutional Code*, pp. 107-109. See Miriam Williford, "Bentham on the Rights of Women."

21. *Autobiography*, p. 107.

22. *Autobiography*, p. 104.

23. See Packe, *The Life of John Stuart Mill*, p. 90.

24. "Periodical Literature 'Edinburgh Review,'" *Westminster Review*, Vol. 1, No. 2, April, 1824.

25. *Principles of Political Economy*, *Collected Works*, Vol. 2, p. 209.

26. See R. K. P. Pankhurst, *The Saint-Simonians, Mill and Carlyle*; pp. 3-4, 108-109.

27. *Autobiography*, pp. 167-168; see also letters to Harriet Taylor, February 19, 1849, and January 18, 1855, *Later Letters*, *Collected Works*, Vol. 14, pp. 9-10, and 298.

28. Francis Mineka, *The Dissidence of Dissent*, p. 296.

29. *The Earlier Letters*, *Collected Works*, Vol. 12, passim, e.g., pp. 160, 229.

30. Until the 1960s, twentieth-century biographers of Mill, such as Ruth Borchard, Hayek and Packe, had tended to accept Mill's estimate of the great extent of Harriet Taylor's intellectual influence on him. This is especially true of Packe, who talks as if Taylor all but wrote all of Mill's major works except the *Logic* (*The Life of John Stuart Mill*, p. 317). In more recent years, however, there has been considerable reaction against this view, from Jack Stillinger, who edited the earlier draft of Mill's *Autobiography*; H. O. Pappe, in *John Stuart Mill and the Harriet Taylor Myth*; and John M. Robson, in *The Improvement of Mankind*. None of these writers disputes that Harriet Taylor was a very important part of Mill's life, and that she certainly provided him with emotional well-being and intellectual companionship without which he may well have been far less productive. What they disagree about with the earlier critics, and with Mill himself, is that the principal ideas of his works were hers, not his. Most recently, Himmelfarb argues that Harriet Taylor was immensely influential, particularly during their married life, but in a way which Himmelfarb considers led Mill

astray from his most worthwhile thought. For a more balanced recent view of Taylor's influence, see Virginia Held, "Justice and Harriet Taylor."

31. Letter from J. S. M. to H. T., in Hayek, p. 185. For other examples of Mill's very high praises of her, see, for example, his introduction to *The Enfranchisement of Women*, his *Autobiography*, passim, and the inscription he placed on her tombstone, in Hayek, p. 34.

32. *Autobiography*, p. 244, note; cf. also letter to Paulina Wright Davis, December 11, 1869, *Later Letters, Collected Works*, Vol. 17, p. 1670-1671.

33. *Autobiography*, p. 266. I have, however, assumed below that those more radical views expressed in *The Enfranchisement of Women*, which Mill did not repeat in *The Subjection of Women*, were Harriet Taylor's alone.

34. *On Liberty*, p. 16; *The Subjection of Women*, p. 521.

35. *The Subjection of Women*, p. 487.

36. *On Liberty*, p. 16.

37. "Bentham," in *Utilitarianism*, p. 97.

38. *On Liberty*, p. 73.

39. The famous argument about the quality of pleasures is found at the beginning of Chapter 2 of the essay *Utilitarianism*, pp. 258-262. Taken simply as it is presented there, without the unspoken premise that Mill took his own highly intellectual nature as his model of human nature no less than Bentham used his, the argument is quite unsatisfactory. Mill certainly fails to convince us that Socrates really knew what it was like to be a happy pig, any more than Mill himself did.

40. *Utilitarianism*, p. 265.

41. *Utilitarianism*, pp. 289-290.

42. *Principles of Political Economy, Collected Works*, Vol. 3, p. 765; see also Vol. 2, p. 373, and *Later Letters, Collected Works*, Vol. 17, pp. 1535, 1801.

43. *The Subjection of Women*, p. 542.

44. *On Liberty*, p. 15.

45. *The Subjection of Women*, p. 542.

46. *The Subjection of Women*, p. 547.

47. "Early Essay on Marriage and Divorce," *Essays on Sex Equality*, p. 72.

48. *On Liberty*, p. 87.

49. *The Subjection of Women*, p. 525.

50. *The Subjection of Women*, p. 536; see also p. 540.
51. *Utilitarianism*, p. 320.
52. *Utilitarianism*, p. 320.
53. *The Subjection of Women*, p. 434.
54. *The Subjection of Women*, p. 522.
55. *The Subjection of Women*, p. 440.
56. *The Subjection of Women*, p. 441.
57. Letter to Alexander Bain, July 14, 1869, *Later Letters, Collected Works*, Vol. 17, p. 1622.
58. *Essays on Sex Equality*, p. 73.
59. In a letter to George Croome Robertson, August 18, 1869, Mill says "it is not certain that the differences spoken of are not partly at least natural ones." *Later Letters, Collected Works*, Vol. 17, p. 1635.
60. *The Subjection of Women*, p. 450.
61. *The Subjection of Women*, pp. 505-506, 451.
62. *The Subjection of Women*, p. 451.
63. *The Subjection of Women*, p. 451.
64. *The Subjection of Women*, p. 495.
65. *The Subjection of Women*, pp. 518-519.
66. *The Subjection of Women*, p. 519.
67. *Westminster Review*, Vol. 1, No. 2, April, 1824, p. 526.
68. Letter to Thomas Carlyle, October 5, 1833, *Earlier Letters, Collected Works*, Vol. 12, p. 184.
69. *The Subjection of Women*, pp. 452-453.
70. *Earlier Letters, Collected Works*, Vol. 13, pp. 590-611, and Auguste Comte, *Lettres d'Auguste Comte à John Stuart Mill*, pp. 175-212.
71. *Lettres*, p. 175 (my translation).
72. *Lettres*, p. 199.
73. He reports having read several volumes of the biologist, Gall, during the correspondence. Comte assumes the superior attitude that the only explanation for the divergent opinions of two such great thinkers on such a fundamental subject is that Mill is going through a passing phase, from which he will soon, no doubt, recover. *Lettres*, p. 184.
74. Mill adds, for the benefit of those who are impressed by such statistics, that he knows of a man who has weighed many human brains, the heaviest of which was that of a woman. *The Subjection of Women*, p. 503.
75. *The Subjection of Women*, p. 452.

76. *Logic*, pp. 451-463.

77. *The Subjection of Women*, p. 453.

78. *The Subjection of Women*, p. 489.

79. *The Subjection of Women*, p. 493.

80. *The Subjection of Women*, pp. 536, 544.

81. Letter to T. E. Cliffe Leslie, October 5, 1869, *Later Letters, Collected Works*, Vol. 17, p. 1643.

82. Letter to Cliffe Leslie, p. 1643.

83. "Speech of John Stuart Mill, M.P., on the Admission of Women to the Electoral Franchise," p. 12. See also *Representative Government*, pp. 292-293.

84. *The Subjection of Women*, p. 477.

85. *The Subjection of Women*, p. 479.

86. This is clear from the way he argues (*The Subjection of Women*, p. 483) that the husband should earn the family's income (since most working class women then as now had no choice whether to work outside the home or not), as well as from the fact that the general preoccupations of his feminist writings are mainly the concerns of middle-class women, rather than issues such as wages, which he was well aware were far lower for women than men (*Principles of Political Economy*, pp. 394-396).

87. Letter to Emile de Laveleye, September 9, 1869, *Later Letters, Collected Works*, Vol. 17, p. 1638.

88. *The Subjection of Women*, p. 479.

89. *The Subjection of Women*, p. 484.

90. Letter to Isabella Beecher Hooker, September 14, 1869, *Later Letters, Collected Works*, Vol. 17, p. 1640.

91. Letter to Princess Marie Stcherbatov and Associates, December 18, 1868, *Later Letters, Collected Works*, Vol. 17, p. 1528.

92. *The Subjection of Women*, pp. 473-474, 483.

93. *Essays on Sex Equality*, pp. 73-77 (emphasis added).

94. *The Subjection of Women*, p. 482.

95. *Essays on Sex Equality*, p. 105, text and note.

96. *The Subjection of Women*, pp. 502, 514-515. He says: "The superintendence of a household . . . requires incessant vigilance, an eye which no detail escapes, and presents questions for consideration and solution, foreseen and unforeseen, at every hour of the day, from which the person responsible for them can hardly ever shake herself free."

97. *Later Letters, Collected Works*, Vol. 14, p. 12.

98. *Essays on Sex Equality*, p. 107.

NOTES TO 10. WOMEN AND FUNCTIONALISM

CHAPTER 10

1. I have been unable to find the original source of this quotation. It is quoted by A. O. Lovejoy, in *The Great Chain of Being*, Cambridge, Mass., 1936, p. 24, but without reference to its source. Even a search of the *Penguin Dictionary of Modern Quotations* proved fruitless, since it lists the quotation as "attributed" to Whitehead. Perhaps he said it in a lecture.

2. Ernest Jones, *The Life and Work of Sigmund Freud*, New York, 1961, Vol. ii, p. 421.

3. See Naomi Weisstein, "Psychology Constructs the Female." I am grateful to Weisstein for directing me to the examples that follow.

4. "The Commitment required of a woman entering a scientific profession in present day American society," *Woman and the Scientific Professions*, The MIT Symposium on American Women in Science and Engineering, ed. J. Mattfeld and C. Van Aken, Cambridge, Mass., 1965, p. 15.

5. *The Fear of Being a Woman*, New York, 1964, p. 714.

6. "Inner and Outer Space: Reflections on Womanhood."

7. "Inner and Outer Space," 596.

8. "Inner and Outer Space," 604.

9. "Inner and Outer Space," 605.

10. "Inner and Outer Space," 588-593.

11. "Inner and Outer Space," 598-599.

12. "Inner and Outer Space," 586.

13. "Inner and Outer Space," 598 (emphasis added).

14. "Inner and Outer Space," 593.

15. *Family, Socialization and Interaction Process*, p. 22.

16. See, for example, Ann Oakley, *Woman's Work*, pp. 178-185; Juliet Mitchell, *Woman's Estate*, pp. 116-117.

17. *Family, Socialization*, pp. 12-15; "Age and Sex in the Social Structure of the United States," 605, 608-609.

18. "Age and Sex," 605.

19. "Age and Sex," 609.

20. *Family, Socialization*, p. 129.

21. "Age and Sex," 613.

22. "Age and Sex," 610.

23. *Family, Socialization*, p. 15, and note 13.

24. *Woman's Work*, pp. 181-185.

25. *Family, Socialization*, p. 23.

26. *Family, Socialization*, pp. 43, 63.
27. *Family, Socialization*, pp. 35, 80, 94, 98, 387.
28. *Family, Socialization*, p. 51, Fig. 4.

CHAPTER 11

1. In 1872, only four years after ratification of the Fourteenth Amendment, the Supreme Court stated that it was very unlikely that any type of discrimination other than racial would be held to come within the purview of the Equal Protection Clause. Ruth B. Ginsburg, *Constitutional Aspects of Sex-Based Discrimination*, p. 10. Their prediction was, of course, subsequently proved wrong.

2. *Constitutional Aspects*, p. 3.

3. *Bunim v. Bunim*, 298, N.Y. 391, quoting *Maynard v. Hill*, 125 U.S. 190, 205.

4. 75 Ariz. 308, 309, quoted in Leo Kanowitz, *Women and the Law: The Unfinished Revolution*, p. 50.

5. Quoted in M. Gruberg, *Women in American Politics*, Oshkosh, Wisc., 1968, p. 4.

6. Book I, Chap. 15, pp. 468-470, 2nd American ed., Boston, 1799.

7. *Commentaries*, p. 471.

8. See below, for example, at note 14.

9. *Forbush v. Wallace*, U.S. District Court, M.D. Alabama, N.D., 1971, 341 F. Supp. 241, quoted in Kanowitz, *Sex Roles in Law and Society*, pp. 517-520.

10. *In re* Lockwood, 154 U.S. 116 (emphasis added).

11. *Commonwealth v. Welosky*, 276 Mass. 398, *cert. denied*, 284 U.S. 684 (1932).

12. *Bradwell v. The State*, 83 U.S. (16 Wall.) 130 (1872). The expression "the sex" was a not uncommon, and clearly deprecating, nineteenth-century mode of referring to the female sex.

13. The Creator was cited as an authority as recently as 1970 by the Oregon Court of Appeals. "The Creator took care of classifying men and women differently," the Court argued, "and if the legislature accepts these differences in a matter like this, we are not prepared to say that the classifications made were without good reason." *State v. Bearcub*, Or. App., 465 P.2d 253. In a

similar vein, Senator Sam Ervin regards the Equal Rights Amendment as an attempt to "repeal the handiwork of God." Quoted in Kanowitz, *Sex Roles in Law and Society*, p. 45.

14. 83 U.S. 130, 141.

15. *Tigner v. Texas*, 310 U.S., 141, 147.

16. For brief discussions of this, see for example Brown, et al., "The Equal Rights Amendment,"879-880; DeCrow, *Sexist Justice*, pp. 38-39; Ginsburg, *Constitutional Aspects of Sex-Based Discrimination*, pp. 62-63, citing appellant's brief in *Reed v. Reed*; and Kanowitz, *Sex Roles*, p. 486. The quotations in this paragraph are from key cases discussed in these sources: *Korematsu v. U.S.*, 323 U.S. 214, 216 (1944), *McLaughlin v. Florida*, 379 U.S. 184, 186 (1965), and *Loving v. Virginia*, 388 U.S. 1, 11 (1967). I am grateful to Samuel Krislov for clarifying this issue for me.

17. In *White v. Crook*, 1966, the U.S. District Court said "jury service on the part of the citizens of the United States is considered under our law in this country as one of the basic rights and obligations of citizenship." 251 F. Supp. 401. In *Eisenstadt v. Baird*, a person was held to have a right "to be free from unwarranted governmental intrusion into matters so affecting a person as the decision to bear or beget a child." 405 U.S. 438, 453. In 1915, the U.S. Supreme Court asserted that "the right to work for a living in the common occupations of the community is of the very essence of the personal freedom and opportunity that it was of the purpose of the (14th) Amendment to secure." *Truax v. Raich*, 239 U.S. 33, 41.

18. 208 U.S. 412.

19. *Lochner v. N.Y.* 198 U.S. 45 (1905).

20. *Women and the Law*, p. 153.

21. Quoted in Ginsburg, pp. 12-13, n. 1.

22. The brief was actually to a large extent the work of Josephine Goldmark.

23. 208 U.S., 412, 421.

24. 208 U.S., 412, 421.

25. 208 U.S., 412, 421-422.

26. *Frontiero v. Richardson*, 411 U.S. 677, 684 (1973).

27. *Women and the Law*, p. 154.

28. Murray and Eastwood, "Jane Crow and the Law," 237.

29. *Goesaert v. Cleary*, 335 U.S. 464.

30. 335 U.S. 464, at 466.

31. 335 U.S. 464, at 466.

32. *White v. Crook*, 251 F. Supp. 401 (1966).

33. *Strauder v. West Virginia*, 100 U.S. 303

34. *State v. Hall*, Miss. 187 So. 2d. 861 (1966).

35. *White v. Crook*, 251 F. Supp. 401 (1966).

36. Jury service is no small obligation to take on voluntarily, and the conditions and financial rewards offered have not been such as to encourage voluntary participation by those who are not legally liable. Clearly, if a woman had the responsibility for small children, or had a job where she would not be compensated for the time spent in jury service, she would be unlikely, if exempt, to volunteer for such service. The result has been that the numbers of women in many jury venires have been small in relation to the female proportion of the population. (See Copelon, et al., "Constitutional Perspectives," 5.) Given this, it is interesting to note the extraordinary "double-think" of a New York State judge who, in 1970, in response to a challenge to the state's automatic exemption of women from juries, told the female plaintiff that she was "in the wrong forum" to have her grievances redressed, and that she should address herself to "the Nineteenth Amendment State of Womanhood which prefers cleaning and cooking, rearing of children and television soap operas, bridge and canasta, the beauty parlor and shopping, to becoming embroiled in plaintiff's problems. . . . *DeKosenko v. Brandt*, 313 N.Y. S. 2d. 827, 830 (1970). Four years earlier, this *same judge* had upheld a regulation which ruled as "reasonable" full salary less jury fees for male teachers but not for female teachers, on the grounds that women could avoid jury duty by claiming exemption! *Goldblatt v. Board of Education*, N.Y. S. 2d. 550 (1966). I am indebted to Ruth Ginsburg for this example, *Constitutional Aspects of Sex Discrimination*, p. 32.

37. *Hoyt v. Florida*, 368 U.S. 57 (1961). Compare the Court's reasoning in 1879 on the equal protection rights of a black plaintiff (bearing in mind that in the earlier case it was an absolute exclusion, not a practical one resulting from an affirmative registration provision that was at issue):

> How can it be maintained that compelling a colored man to submit to a trial for his life by a jury drawn from a panel from which the State has expressly excluded every man of his race, because of color alone, however well qualified in other respects, is not a denial to him of equal legal protection? *Strauder v. West Virginia*, 100 U.S. 303, 309.

38. *Hoyt v. Florida*, 368 U.S. 57, 122.

39. *Leighton v. Goodman*, 311 F. Supp. 1181, 1183, S.D.N.Y. (1970).

40. *Taylor v. Louisiana*, 419 U.S. 522, 531 (1975), quoting *Ballard v. U.S.*, 329 U.S. 187, 193 (1946).

41. *Taylor*, at 534.

42. *Taylor*, at 534, note 17.

43. *Taylor*, at 537.

44. Johnston, and Knapp, "Sex Discrimination by Law," 676.

45. Brown, et al., "The Equal Rights Amendment," 881-882.

46. *Reed v. Reed*, 404 U.S. 71 (1971).

47. 465 P. 2d. at 638, quoted in Ginsburg, pp. 61-62.

48. *Reed*, at 76-77.

49. *Sail'er Inn, Inc. v. Kirby*, 5 Cal. 3d. 1 (1971).

50. *Frontiero v. Richardson*, 411 U.S. 677 (1973).

51. *Frontiero*, at 686. Another serious blow was dealt to the traditional judicial view of the female sex in a 1975 Supreme Court majority opinion which states explicitly: "No longer is the female destined solely for the home and the rearing of the family, and only the male for the marketplace and the world of ideas." *Stanton v. Stanton*, 421 U.S. 7, at 14-15 (1975).

52. In recent years, the Supreme Court has been faced with a number of hard cases in which differentiation between the sexes has been tested against the equal protection component of the Due Process Clause of the Fifth Amendment, or against Title VII of the Civil Rights Act of 1964. See, for example, *Kahn v. Shevin*, 416 U.S. 351 (1974), *Schlesinger v. Ballard*, 419 U.S. 498 (1975), *Califano v. Webster*, 430 U.S. 313 (1977), *Los Angeles Department of Water and Power v. Manhart*, 435 U.S. 702 (1978). The Court is divided on these issues, and some of the cases have been decided by very narrow margins. For those justices more sympathetic to the women's cause, the deciding factor has been whether the differentiation in question is based on "archaic and overbroad generalizations about women, or the role-typing that society had long imposed upon women," or, rather, whether it serves "the permissible purpose of redressing society's long-standing disparate treatment of women." There is no doubt about the complexity of making equitable decisions concerning legal or programmatic differentiation between the sexes, in a world in which many, and especially older, women, have had their lives and life expectations shaped by a society which treated

them so unequally. See "The Supreme Court, 1974 Term," *Harvard Law Review*, Vol. 89, No. 1, 96-103, for a critical treatment of the Court's decisions in the earlier cases.

53. *Geduldig v. Aiello*, 417 U.S. 484 (1974).

54. "Pregnancy and the Constitution: The Uniqueness Trap," 1562.

55. *Geduldig*, at 496, Note 20.

56. *General Electric Co. v. Gilbert*, 429 U.S. 125 (1976) (emphasis added). See also *Nashville Gas Company v. Satty*, 434 U.S. 136 (1977), in which the Court again decided, citing *Gilbert*, that the exclusion of pregnancy from an otherwise inclusive disability-benefits plan is "not a gender-based discrimination at all," but ruled that, for seniority purposes, pregnancy leave could not be treated differently from other forms of leave. A majority of the Court thus appears to be treading a fine line here, which is aptly summarized by Justice Stevens in his (regretfully) concurring opinion:

> Although the *Gilbert* Court was unwilling to hold that discrimination against pregnancy—as compared with other physical disabilities—is discrimination on account of sex, it may nevertheless be true that discrimination against pregnant or formerly pregnant employees—as compared with other employees—does constitute sex discrimination (*Nashville*, at 155).

57. *General Electric*, at 162.

58. "Pregnancy and the Constitution," 1563-1564.

59. This mode of reasoning about legal discrimination between the sexes is, of course, not unique to judges. In a clear ratification of such functionalism, Senator Ervin has proposed that the Equal Rights Amendment be worded so as to allow legal distinctions between the sexes which are "based on physiological or functional differences between them." *Women and the "Equal Rights" Amendment*, ed. Catherine Stimpson, Bowker/CIS Congressional Document Series, N.Y. and London, 1972, p. xiii, see also pp. 521-532. Recognizing as we now do how radical and pervasive are the inequalities that can be justified by the "functional" differences between the sexes, as defined and elaborated by male philosophers and a male-dominated judical system, we can see the futility of such an "Equal Rights" Amendment. *Hoyt, Goesaert, Muller*, even *Bradwell*—all the famous cases confirming the legal inequality of women could stand unaffected by it.

NOTES TO 12. CONCLUSIONS

CHAPTER 12

1. See Carole Pateman, *Participation and Democratic Theory*, Cambridge, 1970, pp. 31-35, and Dennis F. Thompson, *John Stuart Mill and Representative Government*, Princeton, 1976, pp. 36-43, for discussion of Mill's ideas about political education through direct participation.

2. *The Liberal Theory of Justice*, Oxford, 1973, p. 166.

3. See, e.g., cases referred to in note 52, of Chap. 11, above.

4. An obvious example of this is found in local zoning ordinances, which frequently limit the number of unrelated, though not the number of related, persons who may live in any housing unit. For a criticism of the general prejudice of our society in favor of monogamy, see John McMurtry, "Monogamy: A Critique."

5. *Hegel's Philosophy of Right*, Pars. 158-181, pp. 110-122. Hegel explicitly says that "the family becomes one person" (Remark to Par. 163, p. 112). He says that "marriage results from the free surrender by both sexes of their personality" (Par. 168, p. 115), but the fact that the man manages the family property, and is its sole representative in the public sphere, suggests that his surrender of his personality is more symbolic than real. For the correspondence of men to animals and of women to plants, see Add. 107 to Par. 166, p. 263.

6. See Gordon Schochet, *Patriarchalism in Political Thought*.

7. *Elites and Society*, Harmondsworth, England, 1964, pp. 121-122.

8. "A Theory of Stable Democracy," Appendix B to *Division and Cohesion in Democracy*, Princeton, 1966, pp. 232-269. I am grateful to Peter Stillman, of Vassar College, for pointing out this example to me.

9. *Division and Cohesion*, pp. 262-263 and 265.

10. *Division and Cohesion*, pp. 160-161.

11. *Division and Cohesion*, p. 237.

12. *Letter to d'Alembert*, p. 98.

13. Statement of Mabel Vernon, Executive Secretary of the National Women's Party, Hearings on H. R. J. Res. 75 before the House Committee on the Judiciary, 68th Congress, 2d Sess. 2, 1925; quoted in Ginsburg, *Constitutional Aspects of Sex-based Discrimination*, pp. 9-10.

14. For a concise statement of evidence on this subject, see Dean Knudsen, "The Declining Status of Women."

15. "Employment in Perspective: Working Women," U.S. Department of Labor, Employment Standards Administration, Women's Bureau, 1978, p. 1; "Women Workers Today," U.S. Department of Labor, Women's Bureau, 1976, p. 1.

16. "Why Women Work," U.S. Department of Labor, Women's Bureau, 1976, p. 1.

17. *Kahn v. Shevin*, 416 U.S. 351 (1974) at 353.

18. "The Earnings Gap Between Women and Men," U.S. Department of Labor, Women's Bureau, 1976, p. 1.

19. "The Earnings Gap," pp. 2-3, 8.

20. See, for example, Eli Zaretsky, "Capitalism, the Family and Personal Life" Parts 1 and 2; Juliet Mitchell, *Woman's Estate*; Margaret Benston, "The Political Economy of Women's Liberation"; Charnie Guettel, *Marxism and Feminism*.

21. The following paragraph relies heavily on evidence and analysis presented in Smith and Miller, "The Importance of Being Marginal."

22. Dean Knudsen, "The Declining Status of Women," p. 190.

23. Alice S. Rossi, "Equality Between the Sexes," p. 111.

24. *Woman's Work*, pp. 234, 236.

25. *The Dialectic of Sex*, Conclusion, *passim*.

26. *Dialectic of Sex*, pp. 212, 221.

27. *Dialectic of Sex*, p. 205.

28. *Dialectic of Sex*, pp. 198, 206, 225-226, 241.

29. For example, Mitchell, *Woman's Estate*, p. 149; Rowbotham, *Woman's Consciousness, Man's World*, pp. 59-60; Rossi, "A Bio-Social Perspective on Parenting."

30. *Woman's Estate*, pp. 99-100 and 106. See also Christine Pierce, "Natural Law Language and Women," for an interesting discussion of the usage of "Nature" to oppress women.

31. *Women: The Longest Revolution; Woman's Estate*, Chaps. 5-8, especially pp. 107, 150.

32. See above, Introduction; also Simone de Beauvoir, *The Second Sex*, Conclusion, especially pp. 449, 463-464; Benjamin R. Barber, *Liberating Feminism*, especially Chap. 3.

33. New York, 1973; New York, 1974.

34. Quoted in De Crow, *Sexist Justice*, p. 60.

APPENDIX TO CHAPTER 2

1. "Equality: *Republic* v," 10.
2. "Interpretive Essay," p. 380.
3. "Interpretive Essay," p. 380.
4. "Interpretive Essay," p. 380. For some recent and sensible objections to Bloom's comic interpretation of Book v, see Dale Hall's "The *Republic* and the 'Limits of Politics,'" *Political Theory*, Vol. 5, No. 3, 1977, 295-298. Nothing that Bloom says in his "Response to Hall" (315-330 of the same issue) substantiates his claim that Plato's proposals in Book v are intended to be ridiculous. By suggesting that Hall has failed to see the clear signs of connection between Book v and Aristophanes' *Ecclesiazusae*, Bloom has missed Hall's point, which is *not* that there is no connection between the two works, but that Plato's proposals can be more plausibly read as a response to Aristophanes than as a parallel satire on female equality (Bloom, 325; Hall, 295-296).
5. *Republic*, 472a; "Interpretive Essay," p. 390.
6. "Interpretive Essay," p. 382. Even within Plato's dialogues, there is ample evidence that the practice of men and boys exercising together naked acted as a stimulus to homosexual eroticism. See, e.g., *Phaedrus*, 255b, *Symposium*, 217e, *Laws*, 636b-e. Other commentators on the ancient world, such as Aristophanes and Cicero, agreed with this impression. See Symonds, *A Problem in Greek Ethics*, pp. 37 and 41. Modern students of Greek sexual practices also agree, e.g., Symonds, pp. 61-62: "The nakedness which Greek custom permitted in gymnastic games and some religious rites no doubt contributed to the erotic force of masculine passion." In his "Response to Hall," Bloom qualifies his statement. What he meant, he says, was that homosexual relations and connected attractions can be consistently forbidden by a legislator, but heterosexual ones cannot (p. 324). Plato, however, argues that in his city it is both necessary and possible to regulate both strictly, though not to outlaw either.
7. "Interpretive Essay," p. 382.
8. *Republic*, 458d-e.
9. *Republic*, 499d.
10. "Interpretive Essay," p. 383; "Equality: *Republic* v," 9.
11. *Republic*, 434b; p. 10.

12. *Republic*, 456b-c. Again, in his "Response to Hall," Bloom claims as evidence for his interpretation of Book v as comic, the fact that "Socrates speaks repeatedly of comedy and laughter with respect to his proposals" (p. 324). What he still fails to take into account is the crucial passage in which Socrates makes it clear that though "empty" people may find his proposals ridiculous, he whose standard of beauty is the good will not laugh (*Republic*, 452d).

Bibliography

I. GENERAL
(primarily works referred to in the Introduction, Chapter 10 and the Conclusion).

Barber, Benjamin R. *Liberating Feminism.* New York, 1975.

Beardsley, Elizabeth Lane. "Referential Genderization." *The Philosophical Forum,* Vol. 5, Nos. 1-2, 1973-1974, 285-293.

de Beauvoir, Simone. *The Second Sex.* Trans. H. M. Parshley. London, 1953 (first published in French, 1949).

Bebel, August. *Woman Under Socialism.* Trans. David de Leon; intro. Lewis Coser. New York, 1971.

Benston, Margaret. "The Political Economy of Women's Liberation." *Monthly Review,* September 1969.

Campanella, Tommaso. *The City of the Sun,* in *Ideal Empires and Republics.* Ed. Charles M. Andrews. London, 1901.

Chodorow, Nancy. "Family Structure and Feminine Personality," in *Woman, Culture and Society.* Eds. Michelle Zimbalist Rosaldo and Louise Lamphere. Stanford, 1974.

Coser, Lewis. *Greedy Institutions.* New York, 1974.

Daly, Mary. *Beyond God the Father.* Boston, 1973.

Elshtain, Jean Bethke. "Moral Woman and Immoral Man," *Politics and Society,* Vol. 4, 1974, 453-473.

Engels, Frederick. *The Origin of the Family, Private Property and the State,* in Karl Marx and Frederick Engels, *Selected Works,* Vol. 3. Moscow, 1970.

Erikson, Erik H. "Inner and Outer Space: Reflections on Womanhood." *Daedalus,* Vol. 93, No. 2, 1964, 582-606.

Figes, Eva. *Patriarchal Attitudes.* Greenwich, Conn., 1970.

Firestone, Shulamith. *The Dialectic of Sex.* New York, 1970.

Fourier, Charles. *The Utopian Vision of Charles Fourier.* Trans. J. Beecher and R. Bienvenu. Boston, 1971.

Guettel, Charnie. *Marxism and Feminism.* Toronto, 1974.

Hegel, G. W. F. *The Philosophy of Right.* Trans. T. M. Knox. Oxford, 1952.

BIBLIOGRAPHY I. GENERAL

Hegel, G. W. F. *The Phenomenology of Mind*. Trans. James Baillie, 2nd ed. London, 1931.

Held, Virginia. "Marx, Sex, and the Transformation of Society." *The Philosophical Forum*, Vol. 5, Nos. 1-2, 1973-1974, 168-184.

Horney, Karen. "The Dread of Woman." *International Journal of Psychoanalysis*, Vol. 13, No. 3, 1932, 348-360.

Knudsen, Dean D. "The Declining Status of Women: Popular Myths and the Failure of Functionalist Thought." *Social Forces*, Vol. 48, No. 2, 1969, 183-193.

MacIntyre, Alasdair. *A Short History of Ethics*. London, 1967.

Manuel, Frank. *The Prophets of Paris*. Cambridge, Mass., 1962.

Marx, Karl. *Early Writings*. Trans. and ed. T. B. Bottomore. London, 1963.

McMurtry, John. "Monogamy: A Critique." *The Monist*, Vol. 56, No. 4, October 1972, 587-599.

Mitchell, Juliet. *Women: The Longest Revolution*. Reprinted in Boston from the *New Left Review*, November-December 1966.

———. *Woman's Estate*. New York, 1973.

———. *Psychoanalysis and Feminism*. New York, 1974.

More, Thomas. *Utopia*. Trans. Paul Turner. London, 1975.

Mothersill, Mary. "Notes on Feminism." *Monist*, Vol. 57, No. 1, 1973, 105-114.

Oakley, Ann. *Woman's Work: The Housewife, Past and Present*. New York, 1974.

O'Faolain, Julia, and Lauro Martines, eds. *Not in God's Image*, New York, 1973.

Parsons, Talcott. "Age and Sex in the Social Structure of the United States." *American Sociological Review*, Vol. 7, No. 5, 1942, 604-616.

Parsons, Talcott, and Robert F. Bales. *Family, Socialization and Interaction Process*. Glencoe, 1955.

Patai, Daphne. "Utopia for Whom?" *Aphra*, Vol. 5, No. 3, 1974, 2-16.

Pierce, Christine. "Natural Law Language and Women." *Woman in Sexist Society*, ed. Vivian Gornick and Barbara K. Moran. New York, 1971.

347

BIBLIOGRAPHY II. PLATO AND ARISTOTLE

Rosenthal, Abigail. "Feminism without Contradictions." *Monist*, Vol. 57, No. 1, January 1973, 28-42.

Rossi, Alice S. "A Biosocial Perspective on Parenting." *Daedalus*, Vol. 106, Spring 1977, 1-31.

———. "Equality between the Sexes: An Immodest Proposal." *Daedalus*, Vol. 93, No. 2, 1964, 607-652.

Rowbotham, Sheila. *Women, Resistance and Revolution*. New York, 1974.

———. *Woman's Consciousness, Man's World*. London, 1973.

Savramis, Demosthenes. *The Satanizing of Woman*. Trans. Martin Ebon. New York, 1974.

Schlozman, Kay. "Women and Unemployment: Assessing the Biggest Myths." *Women: A Feminist Perspective*, 2nd ed. Ed. Jo Freeman. Palo Alto, 1979.

Smith, Joan, and David K. Miller. "The Importance of Being Marginal: Feminization of the Labor Force." Unpublished manuscript, Department of Sociology, Dartmouth College, 1976.

Strauss, Leo, and Joseph Cropsey. *History of Political Philosophy*. 2nd ed. Chicago, 1972.

Weisstein, Naomi. "Psychology Constructs the Female." Warner Modular Publications Reprint 752. Andover, Mass., 1973.

Whitbeck, Caroline. "Theories of Sex Difference." *The Philosophical Forum*, Vol. 5, Nos. 1-2, 1973-1974, 54-80.

Wolin, Sheldon. *Politics and Vision*. London, 1961.

Wollstonecraft, Mary. *A Vindication of the Rights of Woman*. London, 1792.

Zaretsky, Eli. "Capitalism, the Family and Personal Life." Parts 1 and 2. *Socialist Revolution*, Vol. 3, 1973, No. 1, 69-125 and No. 3, 19-70.

II. PLATO AND ARISTOTLE

Adam, J. "On the relation of the fifth book of the *Republic* to Aristophanes' Ecclesiazusae." Appendix 1 to Book v of *The Republic of Plato*. 2nd ed. Cambridge, 1975, Vol. 1.

Adkins, A. W. H. *Merit and Responsibility: A Study in Greek Values*. Oxford, 1960.

BIBLIOGRAPHY II. PLATO AND ARISTOTLE

Adkins, A. W. H. *Moral Values and Political Behaviour in Ancient Greece.* London, 1972.

Allan, D. J. *The Philosophy of Aristotle.* 2nd ed. London, 1970.

Annas, Julia. "Plato's *Republic* and Feminism." *Philosophy*, Vol. 51, No. 3, July 1976, 307-321.

Aristophanes. *The Birds.* Trans. William Arrowsmith. Ann Arbor, 1961.

―――. *Ecclesiazusae.* Trans. Douglass Parker. Ann Arbor, 1967.

―――. *Lysistrata.* Trans. Douglass Parker. Ann Arbor, 1967.

Aristotle. *De Anima.* Trans. Kendon Foster and Silvester Humphries, from the version of William of Moerbecke. London, 1951.

―――. *Eudemian Ethics.* Trans. H. Rackham. Loeb Classical Library, 1935.

―――. *The Generation of Animals.* Trans. A. L. Peck. Loeb Classical Library, 1943.

―――. *History of Animals.* Trans. A. L. Peck. Loeb Classical Library, 1965-1970.

―――. *Metaphysics.* Trans. Richard Hope. New York, 1952.

―――. *Nichomachean Ethics.* Trans. David Ross. London, 1954.

―――. *Poetics.* Trans. W. Hamilton Fyfe. Loeb Classical Library, 1927.

―――. *Politics.* Trans. Ernest Barker, Oxford, 1946.

―――. *The "Art" of Rhetoric.* Trans. John Henry Freese. Loeb Classical Library, 1967.

―――. *Oeconomica* (now considered to be spurious, but written by one of the Aristotelian School). Trans. G. C. Armstrong. Loeb Classical Library, 1933.

Barker, Ernest. *The Political Thought of Plato and Aristotle.* London, 1906.

Cornford, F. M. "Psychology and Social Structure in the *Republic* of Plato." *The Classical Quarterly*, Vol. 6, No. 4, 1912, 246-265.

―――. *Before and After Socrates.* Cambridge, 1968 (first published 1932).

―――. *From Religion to Philosophy*, New York, 1957 (first published 1912).

BIBLIOGRAPHY II. PLATO AND ARISTOTLE

Crombie, I. M. *Plato: The Midwife's Apprentice*. London, 1964.

Demosthenes. *Private Orations*, Vol. 6, trans. A. T. Murray. Loeb Classical Library, 1939.

Diamond, Stanley. "Plato and the Definition of the Primitive," in *Culture in History*, ed. Diamond. New York, 1960, pp. 118-141.

Dickason, Anne. "Anatomy and Destiny: The Role of Biology in Plato's Views of Women." *The Philosophical Forum*, Vol. 5, Nos. 1-2, 1973-1974, 45-52.

Ehrenberg, Victor. *The People of Aristophanes*. 2nd rev. ed. Oxford, 1951.

———. *Society and Civilization in Greece and Rome*. Cambridge, Mass., 1964.

Ferguson, John. *Moral Values in the Ancient World*. London, 1958.

Finley, John H. *Four Stages of Greek Thought*. Stanford, 1966.

Finley, M. I. *The World of Odysseus*. London, 1956.

———. *The Ancient Greeks*, New York, 1963.

Gomme, A. W. *Essays in Greek History and Literature*. Oxford, 1937.

Gouldner, Alvin W. *Enter Plato. Classical Greece and the Origins of Social Theory*. New York, 1965.

Grube, G. M. A. *Plato's Thought*. London, 1935.

Hall, Dale. "The Republic and the 'Limits of Politics.' " *Political Theory*, Vol. 5, No. 3, 1977, 293-313.

Havelock, Eric. *The Liberal Temper in Greek Politics*. London, 1957.

Herodotus. *Histories*. Trans. A. D. Godley. Loeb Classical Library, Vol. 4.

Hesiod. *The Works of Hesiod, Callimachus and Theognis*. Trans. J. Banks. London, 1889.

Homer. *The Iliad*. Trans. E. V. Rieu. London, 1950.

———. *The Odyssey*. Trans. E. V. Rieu. London, 1946.

Ithurriague, Jean. *Les Idées de Platon sur la condition de la femme au regard des traditions antiques*. Paris, 1931.

Levinson, Ronald B. *In Defense of Plato*. Cambridge, Mass., 1953.

Licht, Hans. *Sexual Life in Ancient Greece*. London, 1932.

BIBLIOGRAPHY II. PLATO AND ARISTOTLE

Lloyd, G. E. R. *Aristotle: The Growth and Structure of his Thought.* Cambridge, 1968.

Morrow, Glenn R. *Plato's Cretan City: A Historical Interpretation of the Laws.* Princeton, 1960.

Osborne, Martha Lee. "Plato's Unchanging View of Woman: A Denial that Anatomy Spells Destiny." *The Philosophical Forum,* Vol. 6, No. 4, 1975, 447-452.

Pierce, Christine. "Equality: *Republic* v." *Monist,* Vol. 57, No. 1, January 1973, 1-11.

Plato. *The Republic of Plato.* Trans. with Notes and an "Interpretive Essay," Allan Bloom. New York, 1968.

————. *The Laws.* Trans. R. G. Bury. Loeb Classical Library, 1968.

————. *Plato: The Collected Dialogues.* Eds. Edith Hamilton and Huntington Cairns. New York, 1961. This edition was used for all Plato's works except *The Republic* and *The Laws.*

Plutarch. *Moralia.* Trans. Frank Cole Barrett. Loeb Classical Library, 1931.

Pomeroy, Sarah B. *Goddesses, Whores, Wives, and Slaves: Women in Classical Antiquity.* New York, 1975.

Randall, John Herman, Jr. *Aristotle.* New York, 1960.

Rankin, H. D. *Plato and the Individual.* New York, 1964.

Rawson, Elizabeth. *The Spartan Tradition in European Thought.* Oxford, 1969.

Rice, T. Talbot. *The Scythians.* New York, 1957.

Ross, W. D. *Aristotle.* London, 1923.

Sophocles. *Ajax, Electra, Trachiniae, Philoctetes.* Trans. F. Storr. Loeb Classical Library, 1913.

————. *Antigone.* Trans. R. C. Trevelyan, London, 1924.

Strauss, Leo. *The City and Man.* Chicago, 1964.

Sulimirski, T. *The Sarmatians.* Southampton, 1970.

Symonds, John Addington. *A Problem in Greek Ethics.* Printed for private circulation, London, 1901.

Taylor, A. E. *Plato, the Man and his Work.* London, 1926; 7th ed., 1960.

Theognis. *See* under Hesiod.

BIBLIOGRAPHY III. ROUSSEAU

Thucydides. *The Peloponnesian War*. Trans. Richard Crawley, intro. John H. Finley, Jr. New York, 1951.

Vlastos, Gregory, ed. *Plato: A Collection of Critical Essays*. New York, 1971.

——. *Platonic Studies*. Princeton, 1973.

Xenophon. *Recollections of Socrates* and *Socrates' Defense before the Jury*. Trans. Anne S. Benjamin. New York, 1965.

III. ROUSSEAU

Baud-Bovy, Samuel, et al. *Jean-Jacques Rousseau*. Neuchâtel, 1962.

Burgelin, Pierre. "L'Education de Sophie." *Annales Jean-Jacques Rousseau*, 35. Geneva, 1959-1962, 113-120.

Charvet, John. *The Social Problem in the Philosophy of Rousseau*. Cambridge, 1974.

Diderot, D. *Rameau's Nephew and Other Works*. Trans. Jacques Barzun and Ralph H. Bowen. New York, 1956.

Diderot, D., and J. Le R. d'Alembert, eds. *Encyclopédie ou dictionnaire raisonné des sciences, des arts at des métiers*. Paris, 1756.

Fénelon, François. *Adventures of Telemachus*. Trans. W. Hawkesworth. London, 1841.

——. *The Education of Girls*. Trans. Kate Lupton. Boston, 1891.

Grimsley, Ronald. *Jean-Jacques Rousseau*. Cardiff, 1961.

——. *The Philosophy of Rousseau*. Oxford, 1973.

Helvétius, C. A. *A Treatise on Man, His Intellectual Faculties and His Education*. Trans. W. Hooper. London, 1810.

Holbach, P-H. Baron d'. *Système sociale ou principes naturels de la morale et de la politique*. London, 1773.

Masters, Roger D. *The Political Philosophy of Rousseau*. Princeton, 1968.

Montesquieu, C-L. *Persian Letters*. Trans. Christopher Betts. London, 1973.

——. *The Spirit of the Laws*. Trans. Thomas Nugent. New York, 1949.

Rapaport, Elizabeth. "On the Future of Love: Rousseau and the Radical Feminists." *The Philosophical Forum,* Vol. 5, Nos. 1-2, 1973-1974, 185-205.

Rousseau, Jean-Jacques. *Correspondance générale.* Ed. T. Dufour, Paris, 1924-1934.

————. *Oeuvres complètes.* Hachette, Paris, 1909.

————. *Oeuvres complètes,* Vols. 1-4. Ed. B. Gagnebin and M. Raymond. Pléiade Edition. Paris, 1959-1969.

————. *The First and Second Discourses.* Trans. Roger D. and Judith R. Masters. New York, 1964.

————. *Politics and the Arts. Letter to M. d'Alembert on the Theater.* Trans. Allan Bloom. Ithaca, 1968.

Shklar, Judith N. *Men and Citizens: A Study of Rousseau's Social Theory.* Cambridge, 1969.

Starobinski, Jean. *Jean-Jacques Rousseau: La Transparence et l'obstacle* (2nd ed.), with *Sept essais sur Rousseau.* Paris, 1971.

Wexler, Victor G. " 'Made for Man's Delight': Rousseau as Anti-feminist." *American Historical Review,* Vol. 81, No. 1, 1976, 266-291.

IV. MILL *(AND OTHER LIBERALS)*

Banks, J. A., and O. *Feminism and Family Planning in Victorian England.* Liverpool, 1964.

Bentham, Jeremy. *Plan of Parliamentary Reform in the Form of a Catechism.* Vol. 3 of *Works,* ed. Bowring, 1843.

————. *Constitutional Code,* Vol. 4 of *Works,* ed. Bowring.

Burns, J. H. "John Stuart Mill and Democracy 1829-1861." *Political Studies,* 1957, Vol. 5, Nos. 2 and 3.

Chapman, Richard Allen. "*Leviathan* Writ Small: Thomas Hobbes on the Family." *The American Political Science Review,* Vol. 69, No. 1, 1975, 76-90.

Clark, Lorenne M. G. "Women and John Locke; or, Who Owns the Apples in the Garden of Eden?" *Canadian Journal of Philosophy,* Vol. 7, No. 4, December 1977, 699-724.

Comte, Auguste. *Lettres d'Auguste Comte à John Stuart Mill,* (1841-1846). Paris, 1877.

BIBLIOGRAPHY IV. MILL

Hayek, F. A. *John Stuart Mill and Harriet Taylor: Their Correspondence and Subsequent Marriage.* London and Chicago, 1951.

Held, Virginia. "Justice and Harriet Taylor." *The Nation,* October 25, 1971, 405-406.

Himes, N. E. "The Place of John Stuart Mill and Robert Owen in the History of English Neo-Malthusianism." *Quarterly Review of Economics,* Vol. 42, May 1928.

Himmelfarb, Gertrude. *On Liberty and Liberalism.* New York, 1974.

Hinton, R. W. K. "Husbands, Fathers and Conquerors," *Political Studies,* Vol. 15, No. 3, 1967, 291-300, and Vol. 16, No. 1, 1968, 55-67.

Hobbes, Thomas. *De Corpore Politico,* in *Body, Man and Citizen.* Ed. Richard S. Peters. New York, 1962.

———. *De Cive,* in *Man and Citizen.* Ed. Bernard Gert. New York, 1972.

———. *Leviathan.* Ed. A. D. Lindsay. New York, 1950.

———. *A Dialogue between a Philosopher and a Student of the Common Laws of England.* Ed. Joseph Cropsey. Chicago, 1971.

Locke, John. *Two Treatises of Government.* Ed. Peter Laslett. Cambridge, 1963.

Mill, James. "Government." Written for the 1820 Supplement to the *Encyclopaedia Britannica,* and reprinted as a pamphlet, London, 1821.

Mill, John Stuart. *Autobiography.* London, 1873.

———. *Collected Works of J. S. Mill.* Toronto, 1963-.

———. *Logic,* 9th ed. London, 1875.

———. *On Liberty, Representative Government and The Subjection of Women.* Ed. Millicent Garrett Fawcett. London, 1912.

———. "Periodical Literature 'Edinburgh Review.'" *Westminster Review,* Vol. 1, No. 2, April 1824, 505-541.

———. "Speech of John Stuart Mill, M.P., on the Admission of Women to the Electoral Franchise." Spoken in the House of

Commons, May 20th, 1867, and published as a pamphlet, London, 1873.

———. *Utilitarianism.* Ed. Mary Warnock. London, 1962.

Mill, John Stuart, and Harriet Taylor. *Essays on Sex Equality,* Ed. Alice Rossi. Chicago, 1970.

Mineka, Francis E. *The Dissidence of Dissent: The Monthly Repository, 1806-1838.* Chapel Hill, 1944.

Packe, Michael St. John. *The Life of John Stuart Mill.* London, 1954.

Pankhurst, R. K. P. *The Saint-Simonians, Mill and Carlyle; A Preface to Modern Thought.* London, 1957.

Pappe, H. O. *John Stuart Mill and the Harriet Taylor Myth.* Melbourne, 1960.

Pateman, Carole, and Teresa Brennan. " 'Mere Auxiliaries to the Commonwealth': Women and the Origins of Liberalism." Forthcoming in *Political Studies,* 1979.

Robson, J. M. *The Improvement of Mankind, The Social and Political Thought of John Stuart Mill.* Toronto, 1968.

Schochet, Gordon. *Patriarchalism in Political Thought.* New York, 1975.

———. "Thomas Hobbes on the Family and the State of Nature." *Political Science Quarterly,* Vol. 82, No. 3, 1967, 427-445.

Shanley, Mary L. "Individual, Family and State: The Equal Rights Amendment and Beyond." *Women Organizing.* Ed. Bernice Cummings and Victoria Schuck. N.Y., 1979.

———. "Marriage Contract and Social Contract in Seventeenth Century English Political Thought." *Western Political Quarterly,* Vol. 32, No. 1, 1979, 79-91.

Stephen, James Fitzjames. *Liberty, Equality, Fraternity.* 1873, 2nd ed. London, 1874.

Stephen, Leslie. *The English Utilitarians,* London, 1900. Vol. 3, *John Stuart Mill.*

Stillinger, Jack, ed. *The Early Draft of John Stuart Mill's Autobiography.* Urbana, 1961.

Thompson, William. *Appeal of One Half the Human Race, Women, against the Pretensions of the Other Half, Men, to*

Retain Them in Political, and thence in Civil and Domestic Slavery. London, 1825.

Whittaker, Thomas. *Comte and Mill*. New York, 1908.

Williford, Miriam. "Bentham on the Rights of Women." *Journal of the History of Ideas*, Vol. 36, No. 1, 1975, 167-176.

V. WOMEN AND THE LAW

Bartlett, Katharine T. "Pregnancy and the Constitution: The Uniqueness Trap." *California Law Review*, Vol. 62, No. 5, 1974, 1532-1566.

Brown, Barbara A., Thomas I. Emerson, Gail Falk, and Anne E. Freedman. "The Equal Rights Amendment: A Constitutional Basis for Equal Rights for Women." *Yale Law Journal*, Vol. 80, No. 5, April 1971, 871-985.

Copelon, Rhonda, Elizabeth M. Schneider, and Nancy Stearns. "Constitutional Perspectives on Sex Discrimination in Jury Selection." *Women's Rights Law Reporter*, Vol. 2, No. 4, June 1975, 3-12.

DeCrow, Karen, *Sexist Justice*. New York, 1974.

Ginsburg, Ruth B. *Constitutional Aspects of Sex-Based Discrimination*. St. Paul, 1974.

Johnston, J. D., and C. L. Knapp. "Sex Discrimination by Law: A Study in Judicial Perspective." *New York University Law Review*, Vol. 46, No. 4, 1971, 675-747.

Kanowitz, Leo. *Women and the Law: The Unfinished Revolution*. Albuquerque, 1969.

———. *Sex Roles in Law and Society*, Albuquerque, 1973.

Murray, Pauli, and Mary O. Eastwood. "Jane Crow and the Law: Sex Discrimination and Title VII." *George Washington Law Review*, Vol. 34, No. 2, December, 1965, 232-256.

Peratis, Kathleen, and Elizabeth Rindskopf. "Pregnancy Discrimination as a Sex Discrimination Issue." *Women's Rights Law Reporter*, Vol. 2, 1975, 26-34.

Weitzman, Lenore J. "Legal Regulation of Marriage: Tradition and Change." *California Law Review*, Vol. 62, No. 4, 1974, 1169-1288.

Index

361

Library of Congress Cataloging in Publication Data

Okin, Susan Moller.
    Women in Western political thought.

    Based on the author's thesis.
    Bibliography: p.
    Includes index.
    1. Women.   2. Sex role.   3. Feminism.   4. Plato—
Political science.   5.   Rousseau, Jean Jacques, 1712-
1778—Political science.   6.   Mill, John Stuart, 1806-
1873—Political science.   I.   Title.
HQ1206.O38   301.41′2   79-84004
ISBN 0-691-07613-8
ISBN 0-691-02191-0 pbk.